HOTEL FRONT OFFICE MANAGEMENT

HOTEL FRONT OFFICE MANAGEMENT

M. C. METTI

ANMOL PUBLICATIONS PVT. LTD.
NEW DELHI - 110 002 (INDIA)

ANMOL PUBLICATIONS PVT. LTD.

H.O.: 4374/4B, Ansari Road, Darya Ganj,
New Delhi-110 002 (India)
Ph.: 23278000, 23261597

B.O.: No. 1015, Ist Main Road, BSK IIIrd Stage
IIIrd Phase, IIIrd Block
Bangalore - 560 085 (India)
Visit us at: www.anmolpublications.com

Hotel Front Office Management

ISBN 978-81-261-3238-6

PRINTED IN INDIA

Printed at Mehra Offset Press, Delhi.

Contents

Preface *vii*

1. Introduction 1

2. Hotels and its Specific Service 34

3. Foreign Exchange 73

4. Tracking Transaction at Hotels 173

Index 286

Preface

The book discusses step by step through each part of the guest cycle, from the reservation process to the night audit. The hotel property management systems used by hundreds of hotels are being discussed. The matters feature room virtual hotel that helps users practice and hone their front office skills in a remarkably true-to-life setting.

Hotel Front Office Management uses a human resources approach to cover the unique management and operational challenges in the front offices of today's hotels and lodging facilities. This continues its emphasis on applying theory and management strategies, as well as providing updated material on technology's tole in the modernized front office.

Material is logically presented in the order of operations, beginning with an overview of lodging and then progressing through a tour of the today's front office, a review of the guest cycle, and an analysis of guest services. This includes new sections on hotel risk management, security, and housekeeping management.

Author

Chapter 1

Introduction

FRONT DESK RECEPTIONIST

The Front Desk Receptionist is responsible for assisting and directing tenants/guests/owners, monitoring incoming inquiries and ensuring proper check in procedures are followed. This position also provides customer service support to the guests and owners. This ever smiling happy person has administrative skills and needs limited supervision to take the decision in every parties interest.

Front Desk/Concierge Cast Members work in an environment with a high level of Guest interaction. These roles involve the use of computer based systems, resolving challenging Guest situations and cash handling.

Responsibilities may include checking Guests in and out of resorts, assisting Guests with itinerary planning and ticket sales, tagging and delivering luggage, and providing information to Guests. Cast Members receive Theme Park admission and discounts at select dining, merchandise and recreation locations. Full-time Cast Members may be eligible to receive medical, dental & vision benefits, plus paid vacation & sick days.

The purpose of the Front Desk Lead is to handle the daily operation of the Front Desk activities, reservations, and their coordination with other departments. Responsibilities include training and scheduling of Front Desk personnel as directed by the Front Office Manager. Must be willing and able to work any shift as necessary as dictated by the needs of the Resort to insure adequate coverage at all times. Assist in maintaining proper working relationships between the Front Desk, Housekeeping, Maintenance, and Sales departments. Prepare daily reports as directed by Front Office Manager. Track and maintain housekeeping/maintenance reports on a daily basis. Ensure the satisfaction of all guests by implementing and maintaining proper Guest/Owner relation programmes. Respond to Guest/Owner Issues. Assist in maintaining continued training for Front Desk staff. Assist in coaching, counseling, and developing of Front Desk staff as necessary.

The award-winning Nickelodeon Family Suites Resort has welcomed guests to the Orlando area for the past 4 years. With a management team that has always been on the cutting edge with innovative ideas designed to make family travel more enjoyable, they are poised once again to make their mark on the hotel industry. Partnering with the number one kid's television network, Nickelodeon, the first-ever Nickelodeon themed hotel premiered in Spring 2005. The Nickelodeon Family Suites showcases a 25 million dollar infusion of water park attractions, Nickelodeon themed suites, banquet space, character breakfasts and a show room hosting Nickelodeon entertainment nightly. The hotel is a world class resort destination - a virtual city where "Kids Rule."

At the first-ever Nickelodeon Family Suites, We are seeking positive, energetic employees who desire to be part of an industry leading team, and are prepared to exceed our guest's expectations daily. Our Human Resources Department looks forward to helping you soak up the Nickelodeon Family Suites Values. Become part of our world-class team where we live by the motto: It's a cool place for families, a hot place for kids, where employees make IT happen! The first-ever Nickelodeon Family Suites by Holiday Inn is seeking "A" level talent for our Front Desk Team.

Hotel, motel, and resort desk clerks perform a variety of services for guests of hotels, motels, and other lodging establishments. Regardless of the type of accommodation, most desk clerks have similar responsibilities. Primarily, they register arriving guests, assign rooms, and check guests out at the end of their stay. They also keep records of room assignments and other registration information on computers. When guests check out, they prepare and explain the charges, as well as process payments.

Front desk clerks are always in the public eye and, through their attitude and behaviour, greatly influence the public's impressions of the establishment. When answering questions about services, checkout times, the local community, or other matters of public interest, clerks must be courteous and helpful. Should guests report problems with their rooms, clerks contact members of the housekeeping or maintenance staff to correct them.

In some smaller hotels and motels, clerks may have a variety of additional responsibilities usually performed by specialized employees in larger establishments. In these places, the desk clerk is often responsible for all front office operations, information, and services. These clerks, for example, may perform the work of a bookkeeper, advance reservation agent, cashier, laundry attendant, and telephone switchboard operator.

WORKING CONDITIONS

Working conditions vary for different types of information clerks, but most clerks work in areas that are clean, well lit, and relatively quiet. This is especially true for information clerks who greet customers and visitors and usually work in highly visible areas that are furnished to make a good impression. Reservation agents and interviewing clerks who spend much of their day talking on the telephone, however, commonly work away from the public, often in large centralized reservation or phone centres. Because a number of agents or clerks may share the same work space, it may be crowded and noisy. Interviewing clerks may conduct surveys on the street, in shopping malls, or go door to door.

Although most information clerks work a standard 40-hour week, about 3 out of 10 work part time. Some high school and college students work part time as information clerks, after school or during vacations. Some jobs—such as those in the transportation industry, hospitals, and hotels, in particular—may require working evenings, late night shifts, weekends, and holidays. This is also the case for a growing number of new accounts clerks who work for large banks with call centres that are staffed around the clock. Interviewing clerks conducting surveys or other research may mainly work evenings or weekends. In general, employees with the least seniority tend to be assigned the less desirable shifts.

The work performed by information clerks may be repetitious and stressful. For example, many receptionists spend all day answering telephones while performing additional clerical or secretarial tasks. Reservation agents and travel clerks work under stringent time constraints or have quotas on the number of calls answered or reservations made. Additional stress is caused by technology that enables management to electronically monitor use of computer systems, tape record telephone calls, or limit the time spent on each call.

The work of hotel, motel, and resort desk clerks and transportation ticket agents also can be stressful when trying to serve the needs of difficult or angry customers. When flights are canceled, reservations mishandled, or guests are dissatisfied, these clerks must bear the brunt of the customers' anger. Hotel desk clerks and ticket agents may be on their feet most of the time, and ticket agents may have to lift heavy baggage. In addition, prolonged exposure to a video display terminal may lead to eye strain for the many information clerks who work with computers.

Employment

Hotel, motel, and resort desk clerks held about 159,000 jobs in 1998. This occupation is well suited to flexible work schedules, as over 1 in 4 desk clerks works part time. Because hotels and motels need to be staffed 24 hours a day, evening and weekend work is common.

Although hiring requirements for information clerk jobs vary from industry to industry, a high school diploma or its equivalent is the most common educational requirement. Increasingly, familiarity or experience with computers and good interpersonal skills are often equally important to employers. For new account clerk and airline reservation and ticket agent jobs, some college education may be preferred.

Many information clerks deal directly with the public, so a professional appearance and pleasant personality are important. A clear speaking voice and fluency in the English language also are essential because these employees frequently use the telephone or public address systems. Good spelling and computer literacy are often needed, particularly because most work involves considerable computer use. It also is increasingly helpful for those wishing to enter the lodging or travel industries to speak a foreign language fluently.

With the exception of airline reservation and transportation ticket agents, orientation and training for information clerks usually takes place on the job. For example, orientation for hotel and motel desk clerks usually includes an explanation of the job duties and information about the establishment, such as room locations and available services. New employees learn job tasks through on-the-job training under the guidance of a supervisor or an experienced clerk. They often need additional training in how to use the computerized reservation, room assignment, and billing systems and equipment. Most information clerks continue to receive instruction on new procedures and company policies after their initial training ends.

Receptionists usually receive on-the-job training which may include procedures for greeting visitors, operating telephone and computer systems, and distributing mail, fax, and parcel deliveries. Some employers look for applicants who already possess certain skills, such as prior computer and word processing experience, or previous formal education.

Most airline reservation and ticket agents learn their skills through formal company training programmes. In a classroom setting, they learn company and industry policies, computer systems, and ticketing procedures. They also learn to use the airline's computer system to obtain information on schedules, seat availability, and fares; to reserve space for passengers; and to plan passenger itineraries. They must also become familiar with airport and airline code designations, regulations, and safety procedures, and may be tested on this knowledge. After completing classroom instruction, new agents work on the job with supervisors or experienced agents for a period of time. During this period, supervisors may monitor telephone conversations to improve the quality of customer service. Agents are expected to provide good service while limiting the time spent on each call without being discourteous to customers. In contrast to the airlines, automobile clubs, bus lines, and railroads tend to train their ticket agents or travel clerks on the job through short in-house classes that last several days.

Most banks prefer to hire college graduates for new account clerk positions. Nevertheless, many new accounts clerks without college degrees start out as bank tellers and are promoted by demonstrating excellent communication skills and motivation to learn new skills. If a new accounts clerk has not been a teller before, he or she will often receive such training and work for several months as a teller. In both cases, new accounts clerks undergo formal training regarding the bank's procedures, products, and services.

Advancement for information clerks usually comes about either by transfer to a position with more responsibilities or by promotion to a supervisory position. Most companies fill office and administrative support supervisory and managerial positions by promoting individuals within their organization, so information clerks who acquire additional skills, experience, and training improve their advancement opportunities. Receptionists, interviewers, and new accounts clerks with word processing or other clerical skills may advance to a better paying job as a secretary or administrative assistant. Within the airline industry, a ticket agent may advance to lead worker on the shift.

Additional training is helpful in preparing information clerks for promotion. In the lodging industry, clerks can improve their chances for advancement by taking home or group study courses in lodging management, such as those sponsored by the Educational Institute of the American Hotel and Motel Association. In some industries—such as lodging, banking, or the airlines—workers commonly are promoted through the ranks. Positions such as airline reservation agent or hotel and motel desk clerk offer good opportunities for qualified workers to get started in the business. In a number of industries, a college degree may be required for advancement to management ranks.

Employment of hotel, motel, and resort desk clerks is expected to grow about as fast as the average for all occupations through 2008, as more hotels, motels, and other lodging establishments are built and occupancy rates rise. Job opportunities for hotel and motel desk clerks will result from an unusually high turnover rate. These openings occur each year as thousands of workers transfer to other occupations that offer better pay and advancement opportunities or simply leave the work force altogether. Opportunities for part-time work should continue to be plentiful, as nearly all front desks are staffed 24 hours a day, 7 days a week.

Employment of hotel and motel desk clerks should be favourably affected by an increase in business and leisure travel. Shifts in travel preference away from long vacations and toward long weekends and other, more frequent, shorter trips also should increase demand as this trend increases the total number of nights spent in hotels. The expansion of smaller, budget hotels relative to larger, luxury establishments reflects a change in the composition of the hotel and motel industry. As employment shifts from luxury hotels to more "no-frills" operations, the proportion of hotel desk clerks should increase in relation to staff such as waiters and waitresses and recreation workers.

However, the growing effort to cut labour costs while moving towards more efficient service is expected to slow the growth of desk clerk employment. The role of the front desk is changing as some of the more traditional duties are automated. New technologies automating check-in and check-out procedures now allow guests to bypass the front desk in many larger establishments, reducing staffing needs. The expansion of other technologies, such as interactive television and computer systems to dispense information, should further impact employment in the future as such services become more widespread.

Employment of desk clerks is sensitive to cyclical swings in the economy. During recessions, vacation and business travel declines and hotels and motels need fewer clerks. Similarly, desk clerk employment is affected by seasonal fluctuations in travel during high and low tourist seasons.

Earnings vary widely by occupation and experience. Annual earnings ranged from less than $11,750 for the lowest paid 10 percent of hotel clerks to over $39,540 for the top 10 percent of reservation agents in 1998. Salaries of reservation and transportation ticket agents and travel clerks tend to be significantly higher than for other information clerks, while hotel, motel, and resort desk clerks tend to earn quite a bit less, as the following tabulation of median annual earnings shows.

Reservation and transportation ticket agents and travel clerks	$22,120
New accounts clerks	21,340
Receptionists	18,620
Interviewing clerks	18,540
Hotel, motel, and resort desk clerks	15,160

Earnings of hotel and motel desk clerks also vary considerably depending on the location, size, and type of establishment in which they work. For example, clerks at large luxury hotels and those located in metropolitan and resort areas generally pay clerks more than less exclusive or "budget" establishments and those located in less populated areas.

In early 1999, the Federal Government typically paid salaries ranging from $16,400 to $18,100 a year to beginning receptionists with a high school diploma or 6 months of experience. The average annual salary for all receptionists employed by the Federal Government was about $22,700 in 1999.

In addition to their hourly wage, full-time information clerks who work evenings, nights, weekends, or holidays may receive shift differential pay. Some employers offer educational assistance to their employees. Reservation and transportation ticket agents and travel clerks receive free or reduced rate travel on their company's carriers for themselves and their immediate family and, in some companies, for friends.

ACCEPTING VISA CARDS AT HOTELS

If you have signed a merchant agreement to accept Visa cards, you should accept all Visa cards, irrespective of which bank issued them. Banks right around the world offer their customers a range of different Visa cards. This includes Classic cards, Gold cards, Infinite cards, Visa Electron cards, Visa Business cards and Visa Purchasing – as well as cards issued in conjunction with other major corporations. These cards may look different, but they all:

- Have the same basic card elements and security features
- Guarantee payment to you when Visa acceptance procedures are correctly followed

How to Identify a Visa Card

There are many different kinds of Visa cards. All share the same essential card elements and security features. The unembossed Visa card is the new Visa product which has the card number and information printed on the front of the card, making the surface of the card smooth instead of being raised. The unembossed Visa card does not share some of the card elements as the normal Visa card, and these have been included below. Visa Electron cards also have slightly different features, can only be accepted at an electronic terminal and always require authorization. See the following section for more details

1. *Visa flag symbol* – always on the front, right hand side, but can be above or below the hologram.
2. *Microprinting* – should be visible around the Visa flag symbol.
3. *Dove hologram* – always on the front right hand side, and the dove appears to fly when the card is tilted back and forth. The Visa Infinite card, issued by some banks to their very best customers, has a different hologram design.
4. *Four-digit number* – printed above or below the account number. This should always begin with a '4', and should match the first four digits of the account number. If it does not, or if it is missing, the card may be counterfeit.
5. *Account number* – must be even, clear and straight, with all numbers the same size and shape. May be embossed or unembossed.
6. *Embossed letter V* – will be present on embossed Visa cards. On some cards, it may be shown as CV, BV, or PV. For unembossed Visa cards, this feature will not be present.
7. *Cardholder name* – letters must be even and straight. Whenever you are processing a transaction, this should be compared with the cardholder's signature. For unembossed Visa cards and for some prepaid Visa cards, a cardholder name may not be present.
8. *Dates* – whenever you are processing a transaction, you should check the dates are valid. If you are presented with a card where the dates are not valid, you must obtain authorization.
9. *Signature Panel* – look for the signature on the signature panel. You should see the repeated word "Visa" printed diagonally in blue and gold.

10. *CVV2* – there should be a unique three-digit code printed after the account number on the signature panel.
11. *Chip* – many Visa cards now have a chip. If you still have a magnetic stripe terminal, these can be accepted in the normal way. If you have a chip-capable terminal, the card should be inserted into the chip reader for the duration of the transaction.

Visa Electron Card

1. *Visa Electron symbol* – always on the front, right hand side at either the top or bottom of the card.

   These cards may have a Dove hologram. Occasionally they may also have the Visa flag symbol and well as Visa Electron symbol.
2. *Last four digits* – a full account number will not always be printed on the card. Check that the last four digits on the card correspond to the last four digits shown on your terminal.
3. *Electronic use only* – printed on the front of the card to remind you that Visa Electron cards cannot be used with manual systems. This may appear in other languages.
4. *Signature panel* – may appear on the front or back of the card. You should see the repeated word "Electron" printed diagonally in blue, red and yellow.

The Visa reservation service helps you to guarantee room reservations and avoids losses from 'No Show' guests. However, whenever you are using the service, it is important that you correctly follow these simple steps. Failure to do so may result in unnecessary customer queries and complaints.

Guaranteeing a Reservation

While speaking with the guest...

1. Ask the guest for:
   - The Visa card account number

- The card expiration date
- The cardholder's name as it appears on the card
- The billing address and phone number.

2. Tell the guest:
   - The room rate (plus tax)
   - The hotel's address
   - The confirmation code for the guaranteed reservation

   Be sure to keep a record of the code for future reference.
3. Be sure to explain:
   - Guaranteed rooms are held until check out time on the day following the scheduled arrival
   - The deadline for cancelling reservations is 6:00pm on the scheduled arrival date
   - If the room is not claimed or cancelled in time, the cardholder will be billed for one night's stay (plus tax).

   Note: If your deadline is earlier than 6.00pm on the scheduled arrival date, tell the guest the date and time of your deadline, and send a follow up mailing with the cancellation policy.
4. Following up...

   If your guest requests a written confirmation, be sure to include:
   - The Visa card account number
   - The card expiration date
   - The cardholder's name as it appears on the card
   - The room rate with tax, and any other appropriate details about the accommodation
   - The hotel's address
   - The confirmation code
   - The guest's rights and responsibilities under the Visa Reservation Service

- The date and time that the cancellation privileges expire.

Handling Cancellations

While speaking with the guest...

1. Provide a cancellation code.
2. Advise the guest to keep a record of the code for future reference.

Following up...

3. Write 'cancelled' on the reservation form and record the cancellation code provided to the guest.
4. If requested, provide a written cancellation with:
   - The Visa card account number
   - The card expiration date
   - The cardholder's name as it appears on the card
   - The cancellation code.

Handling 'no show' Transactions

If a guest fails to cancel a reservation or claim the room, you may submit a Visa sales draft for one night's accommodation, plus any applicable tax. Simply write 'No Show' on the signature panel of the sales draft and complete all sections of the sales draft normally. Please note that you must still obtain an authorization if the amount exceeds the floor limit.

Handling Overbookings

If the guaranteed accommodation is not available when the guest arrives, you must at least provide the following at your hotel's expense:

- Comparable accommodation at a hotel of at least equal quality for one night
- Transportation to that establishment
- Forwarding of all messages and calls to the establishment
- A three-minute telephone cali

The Visa Advance Deposit Service

Visa cards may be used when your hotel requires an advance deposit to guarantee a reservation. This service also avoids the delay and confusion of handling personal or foreign cheques. However, whenever you are using the service, it is important that you correctly follow these simple steps.

Failure to do so may result in unnecessary customer queries and complaints.

While speaking with a guest...

1. Ask the guest for:
   - The Visa card account number
   - The expiration date
   - The cardholder's name as it appears on the card
   - The cardholder's billing address and telephone number
   - The expected arrival date and length of stay.
2. Tell the guest:
   - The room rate (including tax)
   - The amount of the advance deposit that will be billed on their Visa card. This must not exceed the cost of 14 nights accommodation
   - That the deposit will be deducted from the final bill
   - That you will hold the accommodation for the period covered by the advance deposit
   - The hotel's address
   - The confirmation code of the reservation
   - To keep a record of the confirmation code for their future reference.
3. Be sure to explain:
   - Your hotel's cancellation requirements
   - That all or part of the deposit may be forfeited if cancellation requirements are not met
   - The date and time the cancellation privileges expire

- That a written copy of the cancellation policy will be mailed to the guest Following up.

4. When filling out the Advance Deposit sales draft, be sure to include:
   - The Visa card account number, expiration date, and the cardholder's name
   - The cardholder's billing address and telephone number
   - The hotel identification
   - The words 'Advance Deposit' in the signature panel of the sales draft
   - The scheduled arrival date
   - The reservation confirmation code
   - The transaction date
   - The authorization code, if the transaction is above the floor limit
   - The date and time the cancellation privileges expire
   - The amount of the advance deposit.
5. Mail a written reservation confirmation, along with a copy of the sales draft, within three business days.

   The confirmation should include:
   - The hotel's cancellation policy
   - The guest's rights and responsibilities under the Advance Deposit Service
   - The hotel's refund policy, which must allow for a complete refund of the guest's deposit if a reservation is cancelled before the specified deadline.

Handling Advance Deposit Cancellations

While speaking with the guest...

1. Provide a cancellation code.
2. Advise the guest to keep a record of the code for their future reference.

Following...

3. Write the word "cancelled" on the reservation form, along with the cancellation code provided to the guest.
4. Determine the refund amount and prepare a credit voucher. The voucher should include:
   - The Visa card account number, expiration date, and the cardholder's name
   - The cardholder's billing address
   - The hotel identification
   - The cancellation code
   - The words "Advance Deposit" on the signature panel of the sales draft
   - The transaction date
   - The amount of the advance deposit
5. Mail the cardholder a copy of the credit vouchers within three business days.
6. Include the credit voucher with your daily deposits.

Handling Overbookings

If the guaranteed accommodation is not available when the guest arrives, you must at least provide the following at your hotel's expense:

- Comparable accommodation at a hotel of at least equal quality for one night
- transportation to that establishment
- Forwarding of all messages and calls to the establishment
- Two three-minute telephone calls

In addition, you must complete a credit voucher for the total deposit amount and mail a copy to the guest.

Authorize the Visa Transaction

It is important for you to obtain authorization whenever possible, particularly in the following instances:

- If the total transaction amount is above your hotel's floor limit
- If the card is not signed
- If the transaction involves suspicious or unusual circumstances
- If the card is a Visa Electron card

Note: the Visa Electron card works like any other Visa card. Procedures at the point of sale do not change except that it must always be authorized through a POS terminal. The authorization will stay valid for the length of the guest's stay. For stays longer than two weeks, we recommend that you close out the guest folio and bill the guests every two weeks.

Estimated Authorizations

The estimated authorization procedure allows you to estimate the final transaction amount and receive the protection of an authorization before the guest checks out. However, whenever you are using the service, it is important that you correctly follow these simple steps. Failure to do so may result in unnecessary customer queries and complaints.

When the guest checks in...

1. Estimate the guest's total charges based on:
   - The expected length of stay
   - The room rate including tax
   - Any estimated miscellaneous charges
2. Compare the estimate with your floor limit
3. Proceed according to the following procedures

   If the estimated amount is:

   Do this:

   Below the floor limit Check the current Visa Card Recovery Bulletin to ensure it has not been reported lost, stolen or fraud. Above the floor limit

1. Obtain authorization for the estimated amount do not over-estimate the amount authorized, as this will result in customer complaints

2. Record in the guest folio/sales draft the date, amount authorized and approval code. Authorization reversal

If the authorized amount is higher than the value of the guest's final bill, it is important that you process an authorization reversal for the difference between the authorized amount and the value of the cardholder's final bill.

Revising Estimated Authorizations

You may want to monitor charges to the guest's account to determine whether you need to revise your estimate. If the revised estimate exceeds the floor limit and:

Do this:

- No previous authorization was obtained
- Authorize the total amount
- Previous authorization was obtained
- Obtain authorization approval for the additional incremental amount(s) separately
- For all revised estimates
- Record on the guest folio/sales draft the date, amount authorized and approval code

When the Guest Checks out

When the guest is ready, you should determine the final bill and proceed according to the following procedures.

If the estimated amount is:

Do this:

- Below the floor limit
- No need for authorization Above the floor limit and no previous authorization was obtained
- Authorize the total amount

Above the floor limit and previous authorizations have been obtained, you are protected for the sum of the authorized amounts plus 15% of that sum. To determine whether an additional authorization is required:

- Add up the sum of all authorized amounts
- To that sum add 15%

- Compare this figure to the final transaction amount
- Authorize the total amount

Then do one of these two things:

- If the final transaction amount is less than the sum of all authorized amounts plus 15%
- If the final transaction amount is greater than the sum of all authorized amounts plus 15%.
- No need for authorization

Obtain an additional authorization for the difference between the final transaction amount and the sum of the authorizations already received.

The Visa Priority Check out Service

The Visa Priority Check Out Service is a quick and convenient procedure for you and your guests – allowing them and you to avoid delays at peak check-out times. However, whenever you are using the service, it is important that you correctly follow these simple steps. Failure to do so may result in unnecessary customer queries and complaints.

Check out Procedures

During the guest's stay...

1. Describe the convenience of the Visa Priority Check Out Service. Then, if the guest requests

   Priority Check Out:

   - Ensure that you have recorded the Visa card account number, expiration date, and cardholder name on a Visa sales draft
   - Give the guest a Visa Priority Check Out agreement
   - Inform the guest of your policy regarding any charges discovered after check out
   - Ask the guest to return the completed signed agreement any time before check out.

Following up...

2. When the guest returns the agreement, verify that:
   - It is signed

- The mailing address is included so that you can send a copy of the final bill after the guest's departure
- The cardholder account number on the check out agreement matches the account number of the sales draft.

3. After the guest's stay:
   - Complete the sales draft by entering the total charges incurred during the stay, including any restaurant, telephone or miscellaneous charges
   - Consult your authorization procedures to determine whether authorization is required at this time, and if so, obtain an authorization.
4. If requested, mail to the guest within three business days after check out:
   - A completed sales draft indicating the final amount with the words "Priority Check Out" on the signature panel, or a printout of the Visa billing
   - The itemized hotel bill
   - Another copy of the Visa Priority Check Out agreement.
5. Retain a copy of the itemized bill and completed check out agreement for at least six months.

Add Charges to a Visa card after Check Out

This procedure allows you to bill Visa cardholders for any additional charges which are discovered after they have checked out – such as room service, telephone or mini bar charges.

However, whenever you are billing guests for additional charges, it is important that you correctly follow these simple steps.

When the Guest Checks In

- Explain your policy regarding amended or additional charges.

After the Guest Checks Out

You may deposit a separate sales draft for delayed charges, with the words "Signature on File" on the signature panel of the sales draft. Note: You should only do so if the guest has agreed to be responsible for such charges. You may not submit a separate or amended sales draft for loss, theft or damage to the room. Mail the guest a copy of the sales draft with a detailed explanation of the additional charges. Failure to do so will almost certainly result in customer queries and possible complaints.

The cash disbursement service lets your hotel offer Visa Gold/Premier cardholders free access to extra cash whenever they need it. To offer this service to your guests, use a Cash Disbursement sales draft and take the following steps:

- When they check in, the guest must confirm that they will use their Visa card to pay for the hotel stay
- The guest may receive a maximum cash disbursement of US$250 (or the equivalent amount in local currency) during their stay at the hotel
- Before disbursement, ask the cardholder for identification (such as driver's licence or passport) that includes an identification number
- Imprint the Visa card
- Verify the expiration date.

Terms and Conditions

Brief guide to the terms and conditions of stay at a Hotel, and the terms and conditions for the usage of this internet site. Please allow 12 hours notice prior to your expected arrival to process the booking.

Confirmation of a booking by the client is deemed acceptance of these terms.

1. *Prices:* All published rates include VAT or local service charges at the current rate. Accommodation rates are per room per night with meal plans as indicated.

The Hotel reserves the right to alter prices for any reason up to the date of booking or up to 12 weeks prior to arrival, whichever is the later. After such dates, prices may only be altered to reflect a change in the rate of VAT or local service charge and taxes or for any other reason outside of the control of the Hotel, in which case the changes will be notified to the Client. In the latter event, the Client may cancel the booking without cost.

2. *Availability:* All rooms and rates offered by the Hotel are subject to availability and the discretion of the Hotel manager. Limited numbers of suitable rooms may be allocated to individual rates, packages or promotions and, when these allocations are taken up, remaining available rooms may be offered to the Client at a higher price.

3. *Bookings:* Bookings must be guaranteed for the first night's accommodation by a major credit or debit card, by payment of a deposit or by agreement in writing with a company, travel agent or hotel booking agency. At the discretion of the Hotel, full pre-payment may be required. At least 3 working days are required to process credit and debit card payments and 5 working days to process cheque payments.

4. *Arrival and departure:* Bedrooms are usually available from 2pm local time on the day of arrival. Check out is by 12 noon local time.

There may be occasions, at times of high demand, when clients can check in and use the entire hotel facilities, but the bedroom is still being prepared.

5. *Car parking:* Most Hotels have their own car park, which is usually free to residents. Some Hotels, however, have limited on-site parking and Clients are advised to check with the Hotel whether there is a charge for off-site parking. The Hotel does not accept responsibility for damage to, or for theft from, or for theft of vehicles parked on Hotel premises.

6. *Cancellations, amendments and non-arrivals:* When the booking is confirmed, a reservation number and access code

will be supplied. This must be retained for access to the booking in the event of the need for cancellation and/or amendment. There is no charge, and any deposit paid will be returned, if a guaranteed reservation is cancelled at any time up to 2pm local time on the day of arrival.

In the event of non-arrival or cancellation after 2pm local time and where the booking has been guaranteed, a charge equivalent to one night's accommodation at the package rate at which the reservation was made will be levied. Normal terms of payment apply to these charges. For this purpose the Hotel reserves the right to set-off the amount payable for such cancellation against the Client's credit card without prior notice or approval of the Client, where applicable.

If the Hotel cancels before 2pm local time on the scheduled day of arrival, the Hotel's liability to the Client will be no greater than the amount paid by the client in respect of any booking. If the Hotel cancels after 2pm local time on the day of arrival, the Hotel's liability will be limited to the charge for one night's accommodation. Where possible the Hotel may but is not obliged nor will it be liable to find alternative accommodation for the Client in the event that the Hotel is unable to accommodate the Client. A cancellation number will be provided at the time of cancellation and this should be retained for future reference.

Payment

Settlement of the bill in full, less any advance payments must be made prior to departure from the Hotel. Upon arrival the Hotel reserves the right to request preauthorisation of the Client's credit or debit card or where payment is to be by cash, request the Client to place cash up to an amount of 1.5 times the room rate multiplied by the number of nights booked. All major credit and debit cards are accepted. Company cheques are not accepted without prior clearance.

Please contact the Hotel prior to arrival. Accounts may only be forwarded for payment on completion by the Client and formal acceptance by the Hotel of an application for credit facilities, which may be withdrawn at any time. Credit facilities are not offered to private individuals. All sums are due for payment on presentation of the invoice. In the event of any query relating to the invoice, the Client must notify the Hotel within 7 days of the invoice date and the Client's obligation to pay all outstanding balances immediately will not be affected.

Personal Information and payment details may be used by the system to determine automatically the appropriate way to fulfil your order. In order to process a booking, your Personal Information and payment details may be passed to third party service providers and, where we are lawfully requested to do so, regulatory authorities. Such third party service providers will have access to the Personal Information needed to perform the relevant service. They may not, however, use your Personal Information for any other purposes and are required to process your Personal Information in accordance with the Data Protection Act 1998.

Hospitality is an exciting and multifaceted industry that offers a variety of career opportunities to those who have earned a hotel / restaurant management degree. Careers with hotel, restaurant, airline, cruise line, gaming, and wine and spirit companies are readily available to such graduates. In addition, careers with service firms that support hospitality companies in the areas of accounting, consulting, real estate development, architecture, interior design, real estate brokerage, hotel valuation, investment banking, mortgage brokerage, insurance, advertising, and technology are also available to those with hospitality degrees.

Although dynamic and interesting, the business of hospitality presents many challenges. For example, hospitality businesses operate on low profit margins with fluctuating sales volumes. The ability to forecast revenues and control expenses is critical to achieving budgeted profits and a favourable return on investment for the owners of the company. Also, because hospitality businesses are labour intensive, scheduling employee hours so they are consistent with forecasted revenues and monitoring payroll cost daily are just two major management challenges.

While a hospitality business typically requires a relatively low level of operating inventories, it requires a relatively high level of capital for its real estate component. This component often includes buildings, operating systems, guest room furniture, and restaurant equipment. Securing financing to acquire these assets is a continuing challenge for management.

Finally, hospitality businesses rely heavily on the discretionary income of their customers. During a weak economy, when household discretionary income is low, the hospitality industry usually suffers. High-end establishments, such as resorts and fine dining restaurants, normally feel the effects of a weak economy first, but eventually, the entire industry feels the financial pain. However, as soon as the economy takes a turn for the better, consumers return, discretionary spending increases, and the industry prospers. Accurately predicting these economic fluctuations, and knowing when to buy and sell hospitality assets, can be financially lucrative for the astute hospitality investor. The financial tools utilized by modern-day management to address these challenges and opportunities are the focus of this book. Understanding of these financial tools and applying them to the challenges and opportunities they will soon face when they take jobs in the industry will serve hospitality graduates well throughout their business careers.

Children aged 15 years and under must be accompanied by a responsible adult to ensure that the children's behaviour is appropriate for other guests within the Hotel. Subject to the availability of suitable accommodation, children aged 15 years and under stay free when sharing a room with two adults, on the basis of one child per adult. Children sharing with one adult or in their own room pay 50% of the adult rate.

At the discretion of the Hotel, children may be excluded from certain events or promotions where deemed unsuitable or inappropriate.

Where Hotels have health and leisure facilities, children aged 15 years and under must be accompanied by an adult at all times and they are not permitted to use gymnasium equipment or the sunbed/tanning equipment. Under 5's are excluded from the sauna, spa pools and solaria areas and must be accompanied in the swimming pool by an adult at all times. Clients must read and follow the conditions of use displayed at such facilities.

In the interest and safety of children, some health and leisure clubs may be subject to specific time allocations for use of the facilities by children. Clients are advised to check with the Hotel beforehand. The Client is responsible for controlling the pet and will be liable for any damage, soilage or injury however caused by the pet.

The Hotel reserves the right to judge acceptable levels of noise or behaviour of Clients, guests or representatives, who must take all steps for corrective action as requested by the Hotel. In the event of failure to comply with management requests, the Hotel may terminate the booking or stop any event immediately without being liable for any refund or compensation.

It is the policy of the hotel not to discriminate on the grounds of race, colour, nationality, creed, sex, marital status, age, ethnic origin or disability. Clients, their employees, guests and all sub-contractors engaged by or on behalf of the Client are expected to adhere to this policy and the Hotel may, without incurring any liability to the Client, remove from the Hotel any person or persons offending against this policy.

FRONT-OFFICE/BACK OFFICE RELOCATION FRENZY

Restructuring, reengineering, downsizing, rightsizing, merger mania, unbundling, outsourcing - all of these expressions are 1990s corporate jargon for workplace changes that are sweeping the nation. At the local level, these changes are remapping the regions of growth and decline.

Like the movement of U.S. manufacturing companies overseas during the past 20 years, today's corporate wanderlust is driven by a search for lower operating costs. But unlike the flight of manufacturing, many of today,s corporate moves remain on home soil. Today's relocation manager is looking for lower costs but also requires an English speaking, well-educated workforce, advanced technology, excellent telecommunications, stable utility service, and extensive air transport to make a move successful.

State and local incentives to attract footloose companies are part and parcel of the relocation equation. The bidding war has pitted state against state, municipality against municipality, in a game of chicken that no local government alone can afford to give up.

Relocation frenzy, makes local tax bases more volatile. The receiving community, is likely to expand infrastructure, increase borrowing, and make some tax changes to accommodate the newcomer. The losing community is faced with higher unemployment, excess infrastructure capacity fixed costs to finance that infrastructure, and lower revenues. Whichever side of the market we are on, these chánges will affect our work, our portfolio, and our decision making. By, taking a walk through the land of relocation, we can get a look at the trends that are out there.

The Front Office

The journey, begins with a comparison of the relocation of Fortune 100 headquarters in 1985 and 1995. Among this group, National Municipal Research found a few moves, mostly from New York City to other locations and mostly, among oil and gas companies. Exxon moved from New York City to Irving, Texas; Mobil moved from New York to Fairfax, Virginia; and Texaco from New York to White Plains, New York.

According to the Oil and Gas Journal, restructuring ill the oil industry, is far from over. The Quaker State Corporation recently. moved its headquarters from Oil City, Pennsylvania, to the Dallas area. Quaker State had been a loyal resident of Pennsylvania since 1931.

Other companies moved their headquarters from urban centres to suburban locations. Sears, for example, moved from downtown Chicago to a huge facility in distant Hoffman Estates, Illinois. JC Penney moved its headquarters from Dallas to the northern suburb of Plano, Texas. And United Parcel Service has moved twice in recent history: from New York City to Greenwich, Connecticut, and later to Atlanta. Companies also are moving their headquarters to smaller metropolitan areas, as did Thrifty, Payless, Inc., which moved from Los Angeles to Wilsonville, Oregon, near Portland.

The New York metropolitan region is home to the highest percentage (13.4) of large corporate headquarters, followed by Chicago, Los Angeles, Philadelphia, Boston, San Francisco, Dallas, Fort Worth, Houston, Detroit, Minneapolis, Cleveland, and Atlanta, according to a report in Economic Development Review by Growth Strategies Organization (GSO), Inc. In 1993, Los Angeles, Philadelphia, Boston, and Houston enhanced their shares of corporate headquarters at the expense of New York, Chicago, and Detroit. GSO also found a "modest shift of headquarters from the largest metropolitan areas to MSAS with populations in the 1 to 3 million range." These communities seem to offer the best compromise between lifestyle quality and availability of needed services. Hub airports were cited as one locational advantage for moving to a smaller MSA.

On the whole, large corporate headquarters tend to be loyal to the communities they grew up in. WalMart has stayed in Bentonville, Arkansas, and Coca-Cola in Atlanta. Dennis Donovan, senior manager of the Wadley-Donovan Group, Ltd., has explained why there are so few headquarters moves. "Corporate CEOs" he said, "are looking for specialized locations for their headquarters, and only a few places fit the bill. The location must be part of the global community with extensive international connections. Air service must be excellent and nearby, and which services as banking, courier services, and other support functions help anchor a large corporate headquarters. The image of the location also is important."

Headquarters relocation most commonly occurs within a metropolitan area or when there is a merger, downsizing, or decentralization of functions. More common today, according to Donovan, is the decentralization trend because it has become easier to locate certain back-office functions in remote locations. Donovan cited Metropolitan Life, which broke up its divisions and moved into six or seven locations.

The Back Office

Such back-office functions as accounting, check processing, payroll, data processing, and information management are being spliced and diced and moved around the geographic chess board. Advances in technology and telecommunications also are creating new clusters of back-office functions.

Vast storehouses of information about corporate assets - inventory control, accounting, sales, production, and market conditions - have expanded the potential for corporate data and information centres. Systems for organizing and analyzing this information have become standardized to the point at which companies can outsource, or contract with other companies for a service. M. Ross Boyle wrote in Economic Development Review that "until recently, these centres were always found within or near the corporate office building. Some companies now are concluding that this proximity to the corporate decisionmakers is unnecessary and may not be cost-effective. They can be located in communities with outstanding telecommunications and mail service, plus at least adequate air service."

Boyle continued: "The justification for shifting these facilities to a location some distance from the corporate headquarters lies in the lower operating costs and greater productivity, that can sometimes be achieved by, such a move." The "help desk" function that grew up with the computer industry is one example of a back-office function that is finding new applications for companies that are willing to implement the technology.

For example, Taco Bell uses a system wide help desk that is available to answer questions about hardware, software, procurement, and asset management for its corporate operations, as well as for its 4,00 restaurants. The help desk is credited with cutting costs so low that the chain is able to continue to offer its 59-cent taco and free drink refills without compromising profitability.

Colleen McCormick, research as sociate at the Gartner Group, specializes in covering 22, large help-desk outsourcers. These companies handle calls from around the world for large international corporations. McCormick cited the South, Midwest, and California as areas for help centres. Texas, she noted, has a lot of call centres. Some hot back-office locations have become so overcrowded that the job market is tight or nonexistent. Mark Klender of Deloitte & Touche told the Wall Street Journal last year that Sacramento is one such market. Phoenix, Omaha, suburban San Francisco, Salt Lake City, Tucson, Des Moines, and Seattle are other frequently mentioned back-office locations.

In Florida, Tampa, Orlando, and Jacksonville, as well as newcomers Pensacola and Tallahassee, are strong back-office markets. In February, the Walt Disney Corporation announced that it is looking at Tampa for 500 back-office jobs. According to the Orlando Business Journal, insurance company USF&G chose Tampa for 500 back-office jobs, and American Express Travel Service will be adding 100 jobs there.

In investigating the criteria used to choose new back-office locations, one repeatedly hears "education, education, education." Employees who work computers or toil on a "telephone assembly line,, need to be articulate and to think on their feet in order to provide service to the customers at the other end. Winning locations tend to be those with good schools, colleges, and universities or specialized training programmes. For example, Fitch Investors Service recently moved its corporate and municipal database operations to Powell, Wyoming. Aside from the fact that Chairman Russell Frazer lives a drive away, Fitch had struck a deal with Powell's

Northwest College, part of the state University, system. The two organizations will design courses so that students can work at the facility.

Donovan underscored the importance to a successful back-office move of a good supplv of well-educated, entry-level labour with solid basic skills and moderate wage levels. Air service is important, although it need not be as extensive as for corporate headquarters. The prestige of the address is less important than other factors. "The nation's urban centres missed the boat in the early 1990s" commented Donovan. That was a time when high office vacancies had shrunk the cost of office space in many localities to levels comparable to those in suburban and exurban locations. However, "nobody stepped up to the plate to address three key ingredients: parking facilities, increasing available floor sizes, and, most important, improving the skills attainment of the workforce." As a restilt, the urban centres lost their advantage to savvier locations.

The Incentives War

The price tag for company moves has increased over the past five to six years, according to Bill Schweke of the Corporation for Enterprise Development. Today, it has become easier to move goods and services around, which has led to companies, playing off one jurisdiction against another. Schweke has attributed the increase in competition to "economic insecurity" on the part of local officials. "Politicians don't want to be caught napping by not offering the same incentives as their neighbours," he said. Bidding wars have become more pressworthy, and the politics of competition in the sweepstakes for corporate moves are more visible than ever before. "Today," he added, "every. company that is locationally mobile expects to be given some kind of tax break to make a move."

When Columbia Healthcare Corporation merged with Nashville based Hospital Corporation of America, it decided to move the new company headquarters to Louisville, Kentucky. Following repeated complaints about Kentucky's provider tax and Tennessee's repeal of its hospital services tax (Tennessee has no provider tax), the company chose in 1994 to move its headquarters to Nashville. Modern Healthcare commented that Tennessee dropped its antitrust investigation into the company one day, after the company announced its move. The attorney general's office cited the "transaction's pro-competitive effects."

There is a growing trend toward rolling back some of the incentive competition. Factions on both the left and right ends of the political spectrum support limits on tax incentives. Criticisms range from the wastefulness of "corporate welfare" to the desire to keep government entirely of the way of enterprise. Some states have made it harder for local governments within them to use tax incentives to lure companies around the state. Ohio passed SB19 in 1994 to clarify the use of its urban enterprise zones. Ohio's enterprise zones may carry distressed designation," which gives them certain privileges. According to Bob Stempfer, manager of the tax incentives office of the Ohio Department of Development, there are 319 enterprise zones in the state and about 40 with the "distressed" designation.

At issue in Ohio were a number of communities that essentially were raiding each other's companies using tax incentives. A year ago, Cleveland's Mayor White attempted to block the move of a toolmaking company that was leaving for suburban Solon (he failed). According to Stempfer, the law generally prohibits movements from a distressed enterprise zone (Cleveland) to a nondistressed enterprise zone (Solon), but waivers may be granted with the director's approval if certain conditions are met.

The lack of control that states have over each other has led some observers to suggest federal constraints on the bidding war. Schweke has commented that today's bidding battles are analogous to those of, an earlier era in this country when the adversarial competition among states served to harm the economy giving rise to the Constitution's interstate commerce clause. Melvin Burstein and Art Rolnick have written a number of reports for the Minneapolis Federal Reserve that have criticize tax incentives as harmful to the overall economy. Burstein and Rolnick have been especially critical of intrastate bidding, in which local communities lure businesses away from each other, often with the help of state dollars. It will not be surprising if the bidding war receives attention in Washington when interstate commerce issues are addressed.

Landing a new corporate headquarters or back-office operation can be the ticket to a community's economic success. Locational changes have created new wealth in communities where little affluence existed before. Losers are faced with tax-base shock and the task of meeting public needs with fewer resources. For the foreseeable future, corporate wanderlust is likely to keep underwriters, analysts, portfolio managers, and public officials on their toes.

Natalie R. Cohen is president of National Municipal Research, New York, New York.

This article is adapted with permission from the Fiscal Stress Mollitor, published by, National Municipal Research, which is a specialized research and consulting firm providing strategic information and analysis of trends and policies that affect local government.

Chapter 2

Hotels and its Specific Service

LIMITED-SERVICE HOTELS

The mere mention of the word *hotel* conjures up exciting images: a busy lobby filled with international dignitaries, celebrities, community leaders, attendees of conventions and large receptions, businesspersons, and family vacationers. The excitement you feel in a hotel lobby is something you will have forever in your career. Savor it and enjoy it. It is the beginning of understanding the concept of providing hospitality to guests. As you begin to grasp the principles of a well-operated hotel, you will discover the important role the front office plays in keeping this excitement intact.

The front office is the nerve centre of a hotel property. Communications and accounting are two of the most important functions of a front desk operation. Effective communications—with guests, employees, and other departments of the hotel—are paramount in projecting a hospitable image. Answering guest inquiries about hotel services and other guests, marketing and sales department requests for information on guest room availability, and housekeeping department inquiries concerning guest reservations are but a few of the routine tasks performed almost constantly by a hotel front desk in its role as communications hub. Accounting procedures involving charges to registered and nonregistered hotel guest accounts are also important in the hospitality field. Itemized charges are necessary to show a breakdown of charges if a guest questions a bill. Services for which fees are charged are available 24 hours a day in a hotel property. Moreover, because guests may want to settle their accounts at any time of the day, accounts must be current and accurate at all times. Keeping this data organized is a top priority of good front office management.

FOUNDERS OF THE HOTEL INDUSTRY

A history of the founders of the hotel industry provides an opportunity to reflect on our heritage. Learning about the founding giants such as Statler, Hilton, Marriott, Wilson, and Schultz, to name a few, allows a student of the industry to discover the interesting lineage of hoteliers. Studying the efforts of the innovators who carved out the modern hotel industry may help future professionals with their own career planning. To begin to understand the history of the modern hotel industry, let's look at its early entrepreneurs, who were motivated by wealth and fame on a grand scale. Ellsworth M. Statler (1863–1928) developed the chain of hotels that were known as Statlers, beginning with a hotel in Buffalo, New York, built for the 1901 Pan-American Exposition. Eventually there were Statler hotels in Boston, Cleveland, Detroit, New York City, St. Louis, and other locations. In 1954, he sold the Statler chain to Conrad Hilton. Statler devised a scheme to open an incredible two-story, rectangular wood structure that would contain 2,084 rooms and accommodate 5,000 guests. It was to be a temporary structure, covered with a thin layer of plaster to make it appear substantial, although simple to tear down after the fair closed.

Conrad Hilton (1887–1979) became a successful hotelier after World War I, when he purchased several properties in Texas during its oil boom. In 1919, he bought the Mobley Hotel in Cisco, Texas. In 1925, he built the Hilton Hotel in Dallas, Texas. His acquisitions during and after World War II included the 3,000-room Stevens Hotel (now the Chicago Hilton) and the Palmer House in Chicago and the Plaza and

Waldorf=Astoria in New York City. In 1946, he formed the Hilton Hotels Corporation, and in 1948, he formed the Hilton International Company, which came to number more than 125 hotels. With the purchase of the Statler chain in 1954, Hilton created the first major chain of modern American hotels—that is, a group of hotels that follow standard operating procedures in marketing, reservations, quality of service, food and beverage operations, housekeeping, and accounting. Hilton Hotels now includes Hilton Garden Inns, Doubletree, Embassy Suites, Hampton Inns, Harrison Conference Centres, Homewood Suites by Hilton, Red Lion Hotels and Inns, and Conrad International.

Cesar Ritz was a hotelier at the Grand National Hotel in Lucerne, Switzerland. Because of his management abilities, "the hotel became one of the most popular in Europe and Cesar Ritz became one of the most respected hoteliers in Europe."

In 1893, William Waldorf Astor launched the 13-story Waldorf Hotel at Fifth Avenue near Thirty-fourth Street in New York City. The Waldorf was the embodiment of Astor's vision of a New York hostelry that would appeal to his wealthy friends by combining the opulence of a European mansion with the warmth and homey qualities of a private residence. Four years later, the Waldorf was joined by the 17-story Astoria Hotel, erected on an adjacent site by William Waldorf Astor's cousin, John Jacob Astor IV. The cousins built a corridor that connected the two hotels, which became known by a single hyphenated name, the Waldorf-Astoria. In 1929, after decades of hosting distinguished visitors from around the world, the Waldorf-Astoria closed its doors to make room for the Empire State Building. The 2,200-room, 42-floor Waldorf=Astoria Hotel was rebuilt on its current site at

Park and Lexington avenues between Forty-ninth and Fiftieth streets. Upon the hotel's opening, President Herbert Hoover delivered a message of congratulations. President Hoover later became a permanent resident of the Waldorf Towers, the luxurious "hotel within a hotel" that occupies the twenty-eighth through the forty-second floors. Conrad N.

Hilton purchased the hotel in 1949 and then the land it stands on in 1977. In 1988, the hotel underwent a $150 million restoration. It was designated a New York City landmark in January 1993.

Kemmons Wilson started the Holiday Inn chain in the early 1950s, opening the first in Memphis, Tennessee. He wanted to build a chain of hotels for the traveling family and later expanded his marketing plan to include business travelers. His accomplishments in real estate development coupled with his hotel management skills proved a highly successful combination.

Wilson blazed a formidable path, innovating with amenities and high-rise architecture, including a successful round building concept featuring surprisingly functional pie-shaped rooms. Wilson also introduced the in-house Holidex central reservation system, which set the industry standard for both the volume of business it produced and the important byproduct data it generated (allowing it, for example, to determine feasibility for new locations with cunning accuracy). Wilson died in February 2003 at the age of 90. His legacy to the lodging industry will be serving the traveling public with comfortable, safe accommodations while making a profit for investors.

J. W. Marriott (1900–1985) founded his hotel empire in 1957 with the Twin Bridges Marriott Motor Hotel in Virginia, near Washington, D.C. Marriott Hotels and Resorts had grown to include Courtyard by Marriott and American Resorts Group at the time of J. W. Marriott's death in 1985, at which time J. W. Marriott Jr. acquired the Howard Johnson Company; he sold the hotels to Prime Motor Inns but retained 350 restaurants and 68 turnpike units. In 1987, Marriott completed expansion of its Worldwide Reservation Centre in Omaha, Nebraska, making it the largest single-site reservations operation in U.S. hotel history. Also in 1987, Marriott acquired the Residence Inn Company, an all-suite hotel chain targeted at extended-stay travelers. With the introduction of limited-service hotels—hotels built with guest room accommodations and limited food service and meeting space—Marriott entered the economy lodging segment, opening the first Fairfield Inn in Atlanta, Georgia, in 1987.

Ernest Henderson and Robert Moore started the Sheraton chain in 1937, when they acquired their first hotel, the Stonehaven, in Springfield, Massachusetts. Within two years, they purchased three hotels in Boston and soon expanded their holdings to include properties from Maine to Florida. At the end of its first decade, Sheraton was the first hotel chain to be listed on the New York Stock Exchange. In 1968, Sheraton was acquired by ITT Corporation as a wholly owned subsidiary, and ambitious development plans were put into place to create a truly global network of properties. In the 1980s, under the leadership of John Kapioltas, Sheraton's chairman, president, and chief executive officer, the company received international recognition as an industry innovator in offering modern hotel accommodations. The Sheraton chain is currently owned by Starwood Hotels & Resorts Worldwide.

In the early 1980s, Ray Schultz founded the Hampton Inn hotels, a company in the Holiday Inn Corporation. These hotels were tagged as limited-service, meeting the needs of cost-conscious business travelers and pleasure travelers alike. Schultz's pioneering efforts in developing a product and service for these market segments have proved a substantial contribution to the history of the hotel industry. At a 1998 celebration of the expansion of the Hampton Inn hotel corporation to more than 800 properties, Schultz said: We started the Hampton Inn chain in 1884 to provide guests with a quality room and special amenities like a free continental breakfast and free local phone calls, all at an exceptional value. The opening of this hotel today tells us that we understood our guests' needs and that price/value is still a viable concept nearly 15 years later. Hampton Inn has been, and is committed to remaining, the standard against which all midpriced, limited-service hotel brands are measured.

The history of the hotel industry is filled with concepts that shaped the products and services offered. The atrium concept design, limited-service hotels, and technology were notable innovations. Management concepts such as marketing and total quality management (TQM) offered managers a new way to do business in hotels. The major U.S. economic reorganization in the late 1980s shaped the way hotels could be profitable. Also, in the 1990s, a new financial approach—real estate investment trusts (REITs)—changed the financial structuring and operation of hotels. The terrorist events of September 11, 2001, continue to affect how hotels market their products and services and deliver hospitality.

The hotel industry has seen many notable developments over the past years. The atrium concept, an architectural design in which guest rooms overlook the lobby from the first floor to the roof, was first used in the 1960s by Hyatt Hotels. The dramatic approach to hotel style [was] exemplified by the Hyatt Regency in Atlanta. Designed by architect John Portman, with a striking and impressive atrium soaring up its 21 stories, the hotel literally changed the course of upscale hotel design. As a result hotels became more than a place to rest one's head. They became hubs for excitement, fun, relaxation and entertainment. This 1,260-room hotel "is now one of the nation's premier convention and trade show facilities with 180,000 square feet of ballroom, exhibit, meeting and hospitality space."

The movement of hotel construction from the downtown, centre-city area to the suburbs in the 1950s coincided with the development of the U.S. highway system. The limitedservice concept—hotels built with guest room accommodations and limited food service and meeting space—became prominent in the early 1980s, when many of the major chains adopted this way to serve business travelers and travelers on a limited budget. Hampton Inn revolutionized the hotel industry with the creation of the first national brand targeted to the new limited-service hotel segment. The hotels featured spacious, comfortable rooms but eliminated or reduced other elements common to hotels at that time, such as restaurants, lounges, and meeting and lobby space, passing the resulting cost savings on to guests in the form of lower rates. The company pioneered a number of ideas, including the mounting of the first site by a hotel brand on the Internet. In 1989, Hampton Inn became the first national brand to offer guests an unconditional 100 percent satisfaction guarantee, which today is the cornerstone of all Promus brands and a testament to the company's commitment to quality.

TECHNOLOGICAL ADVANCES

Technology has played a major role in developing the products and services offered to guests. Reservations systems, property management systems, and in-room guest checkout are only the most obvious advances in technology. Impressive firsts in the adaptation of technology to the hotel industry. Note how many of the developments we call technology are recent adaptations.

Recent additions to the list include applications of wireless technology that allow front office staff to alert others on VIP check-ins, housekeeping staff to report guest room cleaning and release, marketing staff to maintain guest profiles, and bell staff to process baggage handling. Guests have also found technology in the 2000s to increase their ability to work and play at the same time; they can check email and print documents as needed from so-called hot spots, or designated wireless transmission and reception areas in the hotel.

Marketing Emphasis

An emphasis on niche marketing to guests was the theme in the 1970s. This technique surveyed potential guest markets and built systems around the needs of identified segments. The larger hotel-management and franchise companies also were discovering the advantages of forging strong reservations and marketing systems. For a guest, this meant that by calling a single phone number, he or she could be assured of a reservation and feel confident of the quality of accommodations expected. The marketing emphasis continues in the 2000s through the routine use of the Internet to place guest reservations. A research study of PhoCusWright data indicated "Internet reservations consisted of about 13 percent of all U.S. hotel reservations in 2003."

- 1846 Central heating
- 1859 Elevator
- 1881 Electric lights
- 1907 In-room telephone
- 1927 In-room radio
- 1940 Air-conditioning
- 1950 Electric elevator
- 1958 Free television
- 1964 Holiday Inn reservation system with centralized computer
- 1965 Message lights on telephone
- Initial front office computer systems introduced followed by room status capability
- 1970s Electric cash register
- POS (point of sale) systems and keyless locks
- Colour television standard
- 1973 Free in-room movies (Sheraton)
- 1980s Property management systems
- In-room guest checkout
- 1983 In-room personal computers
- Call accounting
- 1990s On Command Video (on-demand movies)

LodgeNet Entertainment (interactive video games) Interactive guest room shopping, interactive visitor's guide, fax delivery on TV, interactive guide to hotel's facilities and activities, reservations from the guest room for other hotels within the same organization, and interactive weather reports Internet reservations Introduction of legislation that monitored hotel ownership through real estate investment trusts (REITs) 2000s Wireless Technology – Wireless Technology VIP Check-

In, Housekeeping Guestroom Glean and Release Status, Marketing Guest Profile, Bell Staff Baggage Handling; Guest "hot spot" centres in hotels for wireless transmission and reception of emails and documents.

Total Quality Management

Total quality management (TQM), a technique that helps managers look at processes used to create products and services with a critical eye on improving those processes, is practiced in hotels today. This emphasis on analyzing the delivery of services and products, with decision making at the front lines, in the 1990s and continues today under terms such as quality assurance and service quality.

Major Reorganization

The economic period of 1987–1988 saw a major reorganization of the hotel industry. 1986 Congress unraveled what it had stitched together in 1981. The revised Tax Act made it clear that passive losses on real estate were no longer deductible. Hotels that were previously economically viable suddenly were not. At this time, there were plenty of Japanese who seemed intent on buying up, at astronomical prices, any piece of U.S. property with a hotel or golf course on it. As a result, the value of American hotel properties continued to increase. Between 1990 and 1995, the recession began and ended, and the full impact of the 1986 law and overbuilding were experienced. Some investors who had built properties in the early 1980s found their properties sales or replacement value had fallen to 50 percent or less of original cost. Some owners simply abandoned their properties to their mortgage holders—which in many cases turned out to be Uncle Sam, because of the simultaneous S&L debacle.

HOTEL INVESTMENT

Real estate investment trusts (REITs) provide an investment opportunity for hoteliers. In the Spring 2000 Virginia Hospitality and Leisure Executive Report, P. Anthony Brown of Arthur Andersen wrote the following about the U.S. Tax Relief Extension Act of 1999. This information will be useful as you plan your career. The most significant provision, however, is creation of a new type of corporation—a "Taxable REIT Subsidiary"—which will allow REITs to create new incremental income streams. With new growth opportunities, shareholders should be rewarded with higher stock prices since companies with increased growth rates typically trade in the market at higher earnings multiples. Under the terms of the 1999 legislation, Taxable REIT Subsidiaries can provide non-customary services to tenants through their subsidiaries. This legislation should enable REITs to provide better customer service, create stronger customer loyalty and sell new, non-customary services to tenants. In addition these new subsidiaries can lease lodging facilities from REITs. However, the lodging facilities must be managed by an independent contractor that is actively engaged in the trade or business of operating lodging facilities for any person other than the REIT.

With these changes, hotel REITs will be able to reorganize their structure in order to retain more of the income generated by their hotels. For example, FelCor Lodging Trust Inc., a hotel REIT based in Irving, Texas, currently leases its hotels to two tenants: 1) a company owned by its executives and directors; and 2) Bristol Hotels and Resorts, a publicly traded company. With the new legislation, FelCor will be able to form a new Taxable REIT Subsidiary and transfer the leases of its hotels to this new subsidiary. Accordingly, the net income of the existing lessee would be transferred to the new Taxable REIT Subsidiary. However, a management company (not owned by FelCor) must manage the hotels and must be actively engaged in the trade or business of operating lodging facilities for any person other than the REIT.

The terrorist events of September 11, 2001, will have a lasting effect on how a hotel markets its products and services and delivers hospitality. The immediate impact of the terrorist attacks was a decrease in the number of people willing to fly and, thus, a decrease in demand for hotel rooms. Hotels (as well as restaurateurs, tourist attractions, government agencies, and the like) and the federal, regional, and state tourism associations continue to cooperate to address the issue of fear as it relates to travel and tourism. Hoteliers reviewed their marketing plans and determined how to attract the post-9/11 corporate traveller. The huge corporate guest market can no longer be taken for granted. Corporate executives, travel planners, and traffic managers now must be greeted personally by hotel staff and asked when business might be expected. New methods of attracting markets such as local and regional residents are being developed. These efforts include special packages emphasizing local history and culture, businesses, sporting events, and natural attractions and are combined with the products and services of an individual hotel. Is this an easy challenge? Indeed no, yet it is one that hoteliers had to grasp with eagerness and enthusiasm in order to succeed.

R. Mark Woodworth reports that this effort is indeed a formidable task in light of the data revealed in Trends in the Hotel Industry—USA, published by PKF Consulting and the Hospitality Research Group (HRG). The 2003 edition reported that "the operating profit for the average U.S. hotel dropped 9.6 percent in 2002, this after a 19.4 percent decline in profits in 2001."

Rick Swig of RSBA & Associates notes that although hotel revenues increased by 2 percent from 2003 to 2004, "other issues such as supply of hotel rooms of 4.4% since June 2001 versus average number of rooms sold increasing only by 3.3%." He urges, "Hotel operators should focus on pricing power for the next 24 months until occupancy returns to pre-2001 levels and compression begins to build. National consortium and high volume travel contracts are being finalized for 2005. Hotels will have to be successful in achieving significant rate hikes through these conduits, since the past two years of negotiations have yielded little or no rate increase as operating expense inflated." Further insight into the challenge facing hoteliers is expressed by Tom Belden of The Philadelphia Inquirer, who relates that 94 percent of the 112 corporations surveyed by the Business Travel Coalition of Radnor, Pennsylvania, cut their travel spending over a three-year period. He reports that one participant increased its use of web-based meeting software by 50 percent in one particular year.

The delivery of hospitality in hotels has also come under review. For example, hoteliers are reviewing security plans to include the front-line employee who must take immediate action based on observations at the front desk, in the dining room and recreational areas, and on guest and public floors. The front-line employee who sees uncommon activities has to know the importance of reporting concerns to supervisors. Special training in what to look for in guest interactions in public areas and on guest floors assists the front-line person in becoming proactive.

Hoteliers must also be concerned with how to support hospitality as part of responsible community citizenship. Hotel general managers should develop emergency plans that allow immediately offering public space to medical personnel and disaster victims. Short term concerns such as feeding disaster victims and emergency personnel and long-term commitments such as housing displaced members of the community are among the many issues faced by the hotel industry.

Liability implications for the owner, management contractor, or lessee with respect to repair of facilities have arisen in addition to concerns for the safety of guests resulting from terrorism. Andrew MacGeoch, reporting in Hotel, notes: The obligation of an owner to repair the hotel under a management agreement usually depends on the extent of the damage. In general, if the costs of repair do not exceed a certain threshold specified in the management agreement [which is usually a certain percentage of the replacement costs of the hotel], the owner will be obliged to repair the hotel to its condition prior to the destruction. However, if the costs of repair exceed the specified threshold, the owner will have the right to choose not to undertake the repair and to terminate the management agreement.

MacGeoch continues with a note on liability toward guests by acts of terrorism. Generally, neither the operator nor the owner would be held liable for any injury or death caused by terrorist activities, unless the owner or operator has failed to exercise reasonable care for the safety and security of their guests. Therefore, to make sure that the reasonable-care standard is met, it is necessary and advisable for owners and operators to take reasonable and necessary steps to protect the safety of guests, including implementing appropriate security policies and measures and providing crisis management training to all employees. These issues of marketing, delivering hospitality, and the ramifications of possible terrorism are ongoing concerns that hoteliers must continue to discuss. They must focus on goals and subsequent planning for implementation of a safe environment for guests and employees.

A working knowledge of the classifications used in the hotel industry is important to understanding its organization. The various types of properties, their market orientation and location, sales indicators, occupancy, and revenues as they relate to levels of service and various types of business affiliations are all means of classifying hotel properties.

Classification of hotel facilities is not based on rigid criteria. The definitions can change depending on market forces, legal criteria, location, function, and, in some cases, personal preference, but the definitions that follow are generally accepted and are the ones intended for these classifications throughout this text.

A hotel usually offers guests a full range of accommodations and services, which may include reservations, suites, public dining and banquet facilities, lounge and entertainment areas, room service, cable television, personal computers, business services, meeting rooms, specialty shops, personal services, valet, laundry, hair care, swimming pool and other recreational activities, gaming/ casino operations, ground transportation to and from an airport, and concierge services. The size of the property can range from 20 to more than 2,000 rooms. Hotels are found in centre-city, suburban, and airport locations. Guest stays can be overnight or long-term, as much as several weeks in length. Properties sometimes specialize in catering to particular markets, such as conventions or gambling. Casino hotels usually take a secondary role to the casino operation, where the emphasis is on profitable gaming operations. Marriott's hotels operated as JW Marriott Hotels & Resorts and Renaissance Hotels, as well as Hyatt Hotels & Resorts brands operated as Hyatt Regency, Grand Hyatt, and Park Hyatt Hotels, are examples in this category.

Motels offer guests a limited range of services, which may include reservations, vending machines, swimming pools, and cable television. The size of these properties averages from 10 to 50 units. Motels are usually in suburban highway and airport locations. Guests typically stay overnight or for a few days. Motels may be located near a freestanding restaurant.

The all-suites concept was developed in the 1980s as a separate marketing concept. These hotels offer guests a wide range of services that may include reservations, living room and separate bedroom, kitchenette, optional public dining room and room service, cable television, videocassette players and recorders, specialty shops, personal services, valet and laundry, swimming pool, and ground transportation to and from an airport. The size of the operation can range from 50 to more than 100 units. This type of property is usually found in centre-city, suburban, and airport locations. The length of guest stay can be overnight, several days, or long term. Although this type of hotel may seem new, many downtown, centre-city hotels have offered accommodations with in-room kitchenette and sitting room since the early 1900s. Now with mass marketing—advertising products and services through mass communications such as television, radio, and the Internet— this type of hotel is considered "new." Examples of the all-suite concept include Hilton's Embassy Suites and InterContinental's Candlewood Suites.

Limited-service hotels appeared in the mid-1980s. Hampton Inn and Marriott were among the first organizations to offer limited-service properties. The concept of limited service was developed for a specific segment of the market: business and cost-conscious travelers. The range of accommodations and services may include reservations, minimal public dining and meeting facilities, cable television, personal computers, personal services (valet and laundry), and ground transportation to and from an airport. The size of the property can range from 100 to more than 200 rooms. Limited-service hotels are found in centre-city, suburban, and airport locations. They are usually located near restaurants for guest convenience. Guest stays can be overnight or long term. These properties sometimes specialize in catering to the business traveller and offer special business technology centres. Limited-service hotel properties include Holiday InnExpress, operated by InterContinetal Hotels Group; Comfort Inn, by Choice Hotels International; and Marriott's Fairfield Inn.

One of only 17 hotels in North America to receive both the Mobil Five Star and AAA Five Diamond ratings, The Jefferson Hotel offers guests the highest level of products and services available, with a strong commitment to warm, genuine, and gracious service. Mr. Longo obtained B.S. degrees in business administration and communication from Saint John's University in New York. While in college, he worked at the front desk at The Saint Regis Hotel in New York City and began his professional career at the Sheraton-Carlton Hotel in Washington, D.C., as the rooms division manager. He then became general manager of The River Inn hotel in Washington, D.C., and then the regional director of operations for the Potomac Hotel Group. Prior to becoming general manager of The Jefferson Hotel, Mr. Longo was regional director of operations for the Field Hotel Association in Valley Forge, Pennsylvania.

The sales and marketing effort for this independently owned property requires aggressive sales and public relations strategies. Focus is placed not only on the guest rooms but also on the 26,000 square feet of function space and the two restaurants, one an AAA Five Diamond Award winner. Mr. Longo encourages students who are pursuing a hospitality management career to remember that, as innkeepers, the hotel is like your home, where all of your guests are made to feel welcome. This means providing all guests with the basics of hospitality: a comfortable room, exceptional food, and a friendly staff to serve them. He adds that hospitality is a diverse business, offering a unique work experience each day.

Extended-Stay Hotels

Extended-stay properties were designed to offer guests a home-away-from-home atmosphere over long stays precipitated by business, leisure, or personal necessity. For example, a person may have to attend to a business project for several days or weeks; another may want to visit with relatives whose home does not have adequate accommodations for visitors; a third may be accompanying a relative or friend receiving an extended health treatment at a medical centre and require overnight accommodations. The patient himself may appreciate the homelike atmosphere of the extended-stay hotel in which to recover between treatments.

Leon Stafford of The *Atlanta Journal-Constitution* writes, "The big, fancy hotels... have struggled to get 60 percent of their rooms filled since 2001. Meanwhile, extended stays... have remained at least 70 percent filled." He adds an interesting concept for your career development consideration: "About three extended-stay lodges were built for every traditional hotel constructed between 2001 and 2004." At Hilton's Homewood Suites, the following room amenities are included: king-size bed or two double beds in the bedroom and foldout sofa in the living room; two remote controlled colour televisions; fully equipped kitchen with a microwave, refrigerator with ice maker, coffeemaker, twin-burner stove, and kitchen utensils; a spacious, well-lit dining area; and ceiling fans and iron and ironing board. Additional hotel services include a business centre, an exercise room, and a pool. This hotel concept also structures its room rates to attract the long-term guest. Charles Gellad is the general manager of the Homewood Suites in Alexandria, Virginia. He began his career at the Hampton Inn in Alexandria as a front desk clerk and progressed to guest services manager there.

Then he took a position as sales manager at the Hampton Inn in Fairfax, Virginia, and then as director of sales at the Hampton Inn in Alexandria. He was on board as director of sales prior to the opening of the Homewood Suites in Alexandria. Mr. Gellad said his market for guests includes people who are going to be in town for an extended period because of government contracts, special projects, training, or relocation in the military or in the private sector. Relocation is a common characteristic with this market. Mr. Gellad's extended-stay hotel offers breakfast in the morning and a manager's reception (light foods and beverages); a fitness centre and an indoor whirlpool; a coin-operated laundry; an executive centre equipped with a fax machine, personal computer, copying machine, and other office amenities; a convenience store called the Suite Shop; free parking; and free local, credit-card, and collect calls.

Mr. Gellad's entry-level experience provided him with many opportunities to learn how to deal with different personalities. He says that when you become a supervisor, your employees want to be treated as individuals, but you must be fair in interpreting the polices to everyone. He also extends his hope that you will develop a balance between work and a personal life. This business can be very time-consuming, but you must take time to develop a life outside the hotel.

Market orientation in the hotel industry is categorized into two segments: (1) residential hotels, which provide guest accommodations for the long term; and (2) commercial hotels, which provide short-term accommodations for traveling guests. Residential properties include hotels, all-suites, limited-service, and extended-stay properties. Services may include (but are not limited to) public dining, recreational facilities, social activities, and personal services. These hotels are usually located in centre-city and suburban areas where other activities (shopping, arts and entertainment, business services, public transportation) are available to round out the living experience. Barry Griffith, general manager of the Holiday Inn Express Hotel & Suites in Reading, Pennsylvania, feels that guest service is the centre of the hospitality business and that this is achieved by finding employees to deliver that service. He states, "We as managers have to be motivators and coaches to ensure that front line employees deliver that service. We must also lead by example."

The customer mix at the Holiday Inn Express Hotel & Suites changes depending on the time of the week. On weekdays, the mix is 80 percent business and 20 percent leisure; on the weekend it is 80 percent leisure and 20 percent business. Mr. Griffith noted that an old, established hospital in the area is relocating near his hotel. He expects this to reconfigure his customer mix: During the week it will be 70 percent business and 30 percent leisure, while on the weekend it will be 90 percent leisure and 10 percent business. What do all these customers want? Guests in both segments want a warm welcome and a clean room. However, the business segment wants quick, efficient service and high-speed Internet service for their computers. The leisure segment wants directions to local attractions and value (free phone calls, breakfast, and manager's reception on selected days).

The Holiday Inn Express is a franchise of Inter-Continental Hotels Group. This franchise offers reservation service, a priority club for free upgrade on rooms, *USA Today,* points on merchandise and free room-nights or air travel, high-speed Internet service, shuttle service, free continental breakfast, and a manager's reception on Mondays, Tuesdays, and Wednesdays featuring cocktails and hors d'oeuvres. Mr.

Griffith graduated from Penn State Berks with an associate degree in housing and food service. His professional experience includes serving as assistant general manager at the Sheraton Reading Hotel and Sheraton Lancaster Resort. He was also in management with the Bennigan's Restaurants chain.

Commercial properties service the short-term transient guest. Services include (but are not limited to) computerized reservation systems, public dining, banquet service, lounge and entertainment areas, personal services, and shuttle transportation to airports. These hotels may be located almost anywhere. It is essential to note the gray areas where these two categories overlap. A commercial lodging establishment may have a certain percentage of permanent residents. Likewise, a residential hotel may have nightly rentals available. Owners and general managers must exhibit a great deal of flexibility in meeting the needs of the available markets.

Sales indicators, including hotel occupancy and average daily rate, are another way of describing hotels. This information is necessary for business investors to estimate the profitability of a hotel. Four factors measure a hotel's degree of financial success: occupancy percentage, average daily rate, yield percentage, and revenue per available room (RevPAR). Occupancy percentage is the number of rooms sold divided by the number of rooms available. Average daily rate (ADR) is the total room revenue divided by the number of rooms sold. Yield percentage, the effectiveness of a hotel at selling its rooms at the highest rate available to the most profitable guest, reveals a facility's success in selling its room inventory on a daily basis. RevPAR is used to indicate the ability of each guest room to produce a profit. Once the daily sales opportunity has presented itself, it cannot be repeated (excluding the opportunity to sell a room at a half-day rate).

Occupancy

Occupancy percentages measure the effectiveness of the marketing and sales department as well as the external and internal marketing efforts of the front office. Occupancy percentage is also used by investors to determine the potential gross income, or the amount of sales a hotel might obtain at a given level of occupancy, average daily rate, and anticipated yield. However, it is important not to assume that occupancy is standard each night. Variations occur daily and seasonally.

Average Daily Rate

The average daily rate (sometimes referred to as average room rate) is also used in projecting room revenues—the amount of room sales received—for a hotel. However, this figure also affects guests' expectations of their hotel experience. Guests expect higher room rates to correlate with higher levels of service; the hotel with a rate of $175 per night is expected to offer more services than a hotel in the same geographic area with a rate of $85 per night. These expectations have been extensively capitalized on by major hotel chains, which develop different properties to meet the expectations of various segments of the hotel market.

Yield Percentage

Yield percentage measures a hotel manager's efforts in achieving maximum occupancy at the highest room rate possible. This term is discussed. It is sufficient to note here that this concept is relatively new in the hotel industry. Prior to the 1990s, hotel managers relied on occupancy and average daily rate as indicators of meeting financial goals. Yield percentage forces managers to think in more active terms.

Revenue per Available Room

RevPAR is determined by dividing room revenue received for a specific day by the number of rooms available in the hotel for that day. The formulas for determining RevPAR are as follows: For example, RevPAR for a hotel that has $10,000 in room revenue for the night of September 15 with 200 rooms available equals $50 ($10,000 ÷ 200 = $50). This same hotel on September 15 with 200 rooms, room revenue of $10,000, 125 rooms sold at an average daily rate of $80 ($10,000 ÷ 125 = $80), and with hotel occupancy of 62.5 percent (125 rooms sold ÷ 200 rooms available × 100 = 62.5 percent), produces the same RevPAR (0.625 × $80 = $50). RevPAR is used in hotels to determine the amount of dollars each hotel room produces for the overall financial success of the hotel. The profit from the sale of a hotel room is much greater than that from a similar food and beverage sale. However, the food and beverage aspect of the hotel industry is essential in attracting some categories of guests who want conference services. "Revenue Management," discusses the importance of considering the potential income from room and food and beverage sales. Consider the following article, "January RevPAR Grows Nearly Ten Percent at Suburban Lodge Company-Owned Hotels," which was published online. It shows how RevPAR is dependent on hotel occupancy. This article also addresses the importance of using RevPAR to present a fuller financial picture based on factors that affect room sales, such as economic conditions, weather patterns, and business travel, and ownership. NEW YORK, September 16, 2004: PricewaterhouseCoopers forecasts revenue per available room (RevPAR) to increase by 6.3 percent in 2004, the largest increase in 20 years.

The 3.7 forecast increase in average daily rate in 2004 will contribute almost 60 percent of the total forecast RevPAR gain for the year. Many factors support the favourable outlook for ADR: 1. upward revisions to inflation forecasts; 2. acceleration of business travel and the consequent increase in higher-rate lodging demand; 3. consolidation of ownership, and therefore, more properties under pricing discipline; 4. dramatic increase in control being exercised by hotel companies and owners over rate integrity and inventory, leading to less discounting on third-party distribution channels; and 5. aftermath of hurricanes in Florida, generating room demand from people involved in damage assessment, insurance, and reconstruction in otherwise low-occupancy months, with especially positive effects on room rates. The lodging expansion that is underway will bring lodging demand to 2.71 million daily occupied rooms in 2004, or 2.1 percent above the previous peak level recorded in the 2000. With supply expanding by only 1.3

percent in 2004 amid 3.7 percent demand growth, occupancy will advance to 60.6 percent, an increase of 1.5 occupancy points from 2003.

"We were criticized for being too negative in 2002 and 2003, but our forecasts were almost exactly the actual results, and for 2004 and 2005 we have been criticized for being too positive. But this regularly scheduled quarterly update is for even more positive growth in rate; our demand forecast for 2004 is unchanged," said Dr. Bjorn Hanson, Global Practice Leader of PricewaterhouseCoopers Hospitality & Leisure Practice. Real GDP is forecast by Macroeconomic Advisers to grow by 4.4 percent in 2004, followed by 3.9 percent growth in 2005 and 3.6 percent growth in 2006. Consumer prices are expected to advance by 2.7 percent in 2004, followed by 2.2 percent annual increases in both 2005 and 2006. These new forecasts represent slightly slower real GDP growth and an acceleration in inflationary pressures, compared to the macroeconomic forecasts underlying our June 2004 forecasts. Demand growth is expected to moderate in the next two years to the long-term annual growth rate of approximately 2.8 percent. Occupancies will improve to 62.1 percent by 2006, as supply growth remains moderate at 1.5 percent in 2005 and 1.7 percent in 2006. After achieving 3.7 percent growth in 2004, ADR will increase by 3.5 percent in 2005 and 3.4 percent in 2006, making ADR increases the primary driver of the robust forecast RevPAR growth of 5.0 percent in 2005 and 4.5 percent in 2006.

The four commonly used market segments—identifiable groups of customers with similar needs for products and services—are full service, all-suites, limited service, and extended stay. There is a great deal of overlap among these divisions, and much confusion, some of which occurs because leaders in the hotel industry do not agree on terminology. Some industry leaders avoid the "budget" tag because of its connotations of cheapness and poor quality. Others welcome the label because it appeals to travelers looking for basic accommodations at inexpensive rates. Nevertheless, the following definitions provide some idea of what is offered at each level of service.

Full service is a level that provides a wide range of conveniences for the guest. These services include, but are not limited to, reservations, on-premises dining, banquet and meeting facilities, and recreational facilities. Examples of full-service hotels include Marriott Hotels and Resorts, Renaissance Hotels, and Holiday Inns.

As discussed earlier, the all-suites category indicates a level of service appropriate for a guest who desires an at-home atmosphere. Services include separate sleeping and living areas or working areas, kitchenette facilities, wet bars, and other amenities at the midprice level. This concept appeals to the business traveller as well as to families. Marriott's SpringHill Suites and Embassy Suites Hotels are examples of all-suite hotels. It is interesting to note that this concept is also employed in older centre-city commercial hotels, in which rooms adjoining the bedroom and bath have been remodeled as living rooms and kitchenettes to create suites. Limited service emphasizes basic room accommodations, guest amenities, and minimal public areas.

A continental breakfast and/or an evening cocktail is often included in the price of the room. The guest has the opportunity to trade the public meeting room for free in-room movies, the dining room for free local phone calls. Hampton Inns and Holiday Inn Express Limited are examples of limited-service hotels. Extended stay is a level of service that offers a home-away-from-home atmosphere for business executives, visitors, and families who are planning to visit an area for an extended period. A fully equipped kitchenette allows international guests to prepare comforting foods in a new environment. The spacious bedrooms and living areas provide work and recreational areas. Light breakfast and evening meals included. Examples of this level of service include Hilton's Homewood Suites hotels, InterContinental's Staybridge Suites, and Choice Hotels International's MainStay Suites.

Business affiliations, which indicate either chain or independent ownership of hotels, also categorize the hotel industry. These classifications are the most easily recognizable by consumers with regard to such features as brand name, structural appearance, and ambience. Long-lasting marketing effects develop a brand loyalty and acceptance that are most important to the long-term profitability for a hotel.

Chain Affiliation

When asked to name several chain operations (a group of hotels that follow standard operating procedures such as marketing, reservations, quality of service, food and beverage operations, housekeeping, and accounting), most people would probably mention Holiday Inn, Marriott, Sheraton, Days Inn, Hyatt, Hilton, or Econo Lodge. Students should stay up to date regarding developments in the industry, such as acquisitions, restructuring, and other changes in these organizations. This information, important to know when making career decisions, can be obtained from trade journals such as Hotels, whose annual July issue includes a listing of hotel chains, addresses, and number of rooms; the Wall Street Journal; and other newspapers, magazines, and websites.

Chain affiliations, which include hotels that purchase operational and marketing services from a corporation, are further divided into franchisee, referral, company-owned properties, and management contract companies. Franchise corporations offer support to the franchisee, who is the owner of the land and building, in the form of reservation systems, advertising, operations management, and management development. In return for these services, the franchisee pays fees for items such as initial startup, rental of signs and other equipment, use of the corporation's reservation referral system, and national advertising.

Anyone wishing to enter the hotel business by investing personal funds wants to be sure of realizing a profit. Perhaps due to lack of experience in operating a hotel or motel, a lack of business acumen, a poor credit rating, or limited knowledge of real estate development, this type of entrepreneur may need to seek the guidance of others. He or she can receive direction from a corporation, such as Days Inn, Sheraton, or Hilton, concerning land, building, and management development.

Referral Property

Sometimes a hotel organization chooses to become a referral property—that is, to operate as an independent in association with a certain chain. Because the property is already physically developed, the entrepreneur may want assistance only with management, marketing and advertising, or reservation referral. Likewise, the fees are based on services required. The chain's quality assurance standards must, however, be met by the referral property.

Company-Owned Property

A company-owned property, a hotel that is owned and operated by a chain organization, allows the hotel company developer to act as an independent entrepreneur. The hotel company developer operates the hotel property in competition with all other properties in the area. It uses its own expertise in site selection, property development, marketing and advertising, and operations management. The hotel company developer recruits talented professions into the organization to manage such properties. It uses the chain's reservation system. The hotel company developer may set a limit on the number of franchises so that a majority of the properties remain company-owned.

Management Contract Property

A management contract property, a hotel operated by a consulting company that provides operational and marketing expertise and a professional staff, is similar to a referral property. Several management contract organizations develop business relationships with existing hotels and operate the hotels as their own. Their business relationship requires financial accountability and profitability. Management contract companies may choose to operate each hotel as a member of a franchise or as an independent.

Brands

Hotel brands are an important part of the lodging industry, especially in consumer marketing. Branding allows a hotel company to create a concept in the mind of a consumer. This mind-concept helps the consumer classify a hotel's offerings. For example, a fictitious brand such as the Hotel Flower Chain may have three distinct offerings in its portfolio of lodgings: the Tulip Extended Stay, the Rose Limited Inn, and the Violet All-Suites. Another fictitious brand such as the Timber Chain may have seven more brands in their chain with similar facilities, such as the Pine All-Suites, the Maple All-Suites, the Sunset Extended-Stay Suites, the Timber Express, the Timber Grand Hotels, the Timber Falls, and the Pine Limited Service. Each of these brands has distinct product and service offerings such as communication via website, reservation service, reservation reward point programme, room accommodations, food service, personal fitness and business equipment, and meeting and convention facilities. Therefore, when guests have certain needs for business or pleasure traveling, they can match them up to a certain brand. The following is a list of major hotel brands. Further information can be accessed on each of the hotel companies on the Internet.

Independent Properties

An independent hotel is one that is not associated with a franchise. It provides a greater sense of warmth and individuality than does a property associated with a chain. Independent hotel characteristics include an owner who functions as a manager, room rates similar to chain properties, rooms decorated in different styles, and inviting dining rooms. These hotels may be residential or commercial, with locations in the centre city, suburbia, along the highway, or near an airport. The number of rooms can range from 50 to 1,000. They may offer full services to the guest, including suites, dining room, room service, banquets, gift shop, beauty shop, athletic facilities, swimming pool, theaters, valet services, concierge, and airport shuttle service. Some older independent hotels have refurbished their suites to capture a share of the all-suites market. With all of these advantages, why aren't all lodging properties independent? The answer lies with the U.S. economy. The development of large chains and of smaller properties often brings tax advantages and improved profits to investors. Millions of dollars in capital are required to develop a 2,000-room full-service property. Business, financial, and managerial expertise is more readily available in a company in which there is a pool of skilled experts. Large corporations can also offset financial losses in certain fiscal years or from certain properties against financial gains of other companies or properties in their diversified portfolios.

The independent entrepreneur operates his or her business without the advantages of consultation and assistance. This person may have worked for a large chain or gained a great deal of operations and development experience in the industry. He or she may also purchase a hotel property to balance an investment portfolio. As for any financial investment, the entrepreneur seeks a professional to manage and operate the establishment. The person chosen for this job must manage all aspects of the business: room, food and beverage, housekeeping, security, maintenance, parking, controller's office, and marketing and sales. All business decisions on expenditures must be coordinated with a profit-and loss statement and a balance sheet. Every sale of a guest room, every guest purchase of food and beverage, occurs because the management of that property has been able to market and manage the property effectively. The challenge of managing an independent property can be overwhelming. It can, however, also offer enormous satisfaction and financial independence.

Future professionals in the hotel industry must be able to analyze who their customers will be and why they will have customers. Marketing classes teach how to determine the buyers of a particular product—who the potential guests of a particular hotel property are. Such courses show how to evaluate demographic data (the size, density, distribution, and vital statistics of a population broken down into, for example, age, sex, martial status, and occupation categories) and psychographic data (emotional and motivational forces that affect a service or product) for potential markets.

The second question—why there will be customers—is an important one. Students will explore this question many times during their career in the lodging industry. A manager must plan for profitable results. This plan must take into account the reasons customers purchase a product—what trends will increase or decrease the need for hotel facilities? Factors include the growth of leisure time, the development of the me/pleasure concept, increases in discretionary income, the trend toward smaller families, changes in business travel, and expansion of the travel experience. Other economics and political trends— such as public liability, insurance costs, overbuilding, the value of the U.S. dollar overseas, gasoline prices, safety from random danger while traveling, and legislation—affect commerce; labour and the airline industry also have an impact on current sales as well as growth in the lodging industry.

Leisure Time

The trend toward increased leisure time—in the form of three-day weekends, paid vacations and personal days, a workweek of 40 hours or less, and early retirement—sets the stage for the growth of the lodging industry. As more people have available leisure time to explore new geographical areas, try new hobbies, sample culinary trends, participate in sporting events, and just relax, the customer base of the hotel industry expands. Workers are spending fewer years in the labour force as the concept of early retirement becomes more popular. As the population segment known as the baby boom ages, the number of retirees is projected to soar. Many of them will take on a second career, but part-time jobs will likely be more common. With the two prime ingredients for using hotel facilities – time and money – readily at hand, these people will be a primary market for the hotel industry.

Me/Pleasure Concept

The idea of deserving recreation away from the job to restore mental acuity and improve attitude has evolved over the years. The work ethic of the eighteenth and nineteenth centuries strongly influenced the way Americans played, as recreation and leisure were considered privileges reserved for the wealthy. Today, most workers enjoy vacations and the feeling of getting away from it all. This trend toward fulfilling personal needs continues in the twenty-first century. The isolated nature of many jobs increases the need for respite. As more and more people find themselves spending more time communicating via computer and other machinery rather than face to face, social needs continue to grow. Workers need the away-from-job experience to balance their social and mental needs with their daily-life demands. Travel helps satisfy these needs, and the hotel industry benefits as a result.

Discretionary Income

Discretionary income, the money remaining from wages after paying for necessities such as food, clothing, and shelter, is the most important of all the trends that support the growth of the hospitality industry. One of the main reasons for the increase in discretionary income of American families is the emergence of the two-income family. An almost double-income family unit has emerged over the years as more married women join or stay in the labour force. The strong growth in this labour segment will undoubtedly continue. As more income becomes available to pay for the necessities of life, discretionary income for leisure time and corresponding goods and services also becomes available.

Discretionary income is not a constant. It is strongly affected by economic factors; an economic downturn with increased unemployment reduces discretionary income, for example. Different economic conditions tend to favour different ways of spending discretionary income; for example, low interest rates, which make the purchase of high-ticket items (such as homes, cars, boats, and aircraft) more desirable, make less discretionary income available for short vacations or quick day trips. Students of the U.S. economy need only review the effects of recessions, the energy crisis of the 1970s, and September 11, 2001, to see how quickly discretionary income formerly directed to the hospitality industry can evaporate.

Family Size/Household Size

The current trend toward smaller families also indicates growth for the hospitality industry. The discretionary income available for a family with two children is greater than that for a family with five children when total incomes are equal. Household size—the number of persons in a home—has decreased over the years. Like the trend toward smaller families, the increased number of small households indicates that more discretionary income is available. The costs associated with a one- or two-person household are less than those for a household of four or more people. Moreover, people who live in smaller households are more likely to dine out, travel, and participate in leisure-time activities.

Business Travel

Corporate business travel should not be taken for granted by hotel managers in today's world of high energy prices and speedy communication. Oil prices significantly affect business travel; as the cost of fuel oil rises, higher prices for air travel and other means of transportation result. A business is not always willing or able to increase its travel budget. When travel costs increase, less travel is undertaken and the necessity for any business travel is reviewed. Executives no longer hop the next plane to clinch a deal if the same task can be accomplished via a phone call, (conference call) in which three or more persons are linked by telephone (or PictureTel, which is the use of telephone lines to send and receive video and audio impressions). Shorter trips (day trips or one-night stays) are another response to the increased cost of travel. Business travel often represents the largest portion of the regular income of a hotel property. This prime market must be constantly reviewed for economic details that affect its viability.

Female Business Travel

Female business travelers represent an increasing segment of the corporate travel market. As previously discussed, their travel is affected by energy prices and speedy communication. This particular market segment requires close attention to fulfilling special needs. Female travelers request particular amenities and demand close attention to safety. Marketing and sales managers must develop products and services to capture this growing market segment.

Travel as Experience

At one time, people traveled primarily out of necessity; business and family visits were the usual reasons for traveling. Today, people travel for many reasons, including education, culture, and personal development. Many people want to learn more about the society in which they live. They have studied American or world history and want to see the places they have read about. Cultural pursuits—art, theater, music, opera, ballet, and museums— can attract a constant flow of people. Sports and nature attract travelers who want to enjoy the great outdoors as well as those who prefer to watch their favourite teams. The push for lifelong learning has provided an incentive for many to take personal development/ enrichment courses, whether to update professional skills or to increase knowledge of a particular hobby. Ecotourists, people who plan vacations to study the culture and environment of a particular area, want to enjoy nature in its unblemished and unsullied form.

An introductory chapter on hotel management would not be complete without attention to career development. People planning a career in the hotel industry need to review the fundamentals of career development, which revolve around five important concepts: educational preparation, practical experience, membership in professional organizations, ports of entry, and growth areas for the industry.

Educational Preparation

The educational base you build now will serve you well over time. The classes you are taking in your major course of study – including management and supervision, cost control, human resources management, quantity food production, hotel management, purchasing, sanitation, layout and design, accounting, and marketing – constitute a strong foundation for your continued development of technical skills. Courses outside your major – such as English, speech communication, computer training, arts, economics, psychology, sociology, nutrition, science, and math – will help develop the skills you need to cope in the professional world. The formal education you receive in your classroom study will be enhanced by extracurricular activities such as clubs, student government, sports, and other areas of special interest. These activities are a microcosm of the environment in which you will apply your technical, liberal arts, and science courses. Clubs associated with your major, in particular, allow you to apply theoretical concepts learned in class to a real-life business environment.

Your educational experience will open the door to your career. You must apply your skills and knowledge after graduation to be an effective, successful employee in the hotel industry. Use your degree as a starting point for an exciting career in hospitality. The educational experience you are now obtaining must be nurtured beyond graduation day. There are many opportunities for in-service education, which are courses that update a professional's educational background for use in current practice; these are offered by professional organizations, sponsors of trade shows, community colleges and universities, technical schools, correspondence schools, trade journals, and other industry groups, providing the professional an opportunity to stay current in industry practices. Just as professionals in other industries take classes to refresh their skills and learn new concepts and procedures, so must professionals in the hotel industry maintain awareness of industry advances. One particularly relevant area is computer training. Professionals who attended school before the early 1980s had little exposure to computers and their ever-changing technology; even recent graduates are not always aware of the most current trends and advances.

The professional has the choice of overlooking this need or enrolling in computer applications courses. The next choice is to determine whether these new procedures and equipment are applicable to a particular establishment. Professional organizations—such as the American Hotel & Lodging Association, the Hotel Sales and Marketing Association International, and the National Restaurant Association—offer professionals continuing education opportunities through correspondence courses and seminars. The American Hotel & Lodging Association offers opportunities for hotel employees to become a Certified Hotel Administrator (CHA) and Certified Rooms Division Executive (CRDE), among other certifications. Trade shows sponsored by these organizations promote the latest concepts in technology, products, and supplies as well as providing mini seminars on how to use current technology in human resources management, food production, marketing, and general management. Community colleges and technical schools offer special-interest courses in management and skills application to keep you and your staff abreast of new areas and to review basic concepts. Attending these courses can provide new insight into operational problems. Each of these professional organizations sponsors a website and provides opportunities to access the abovementioned career information.

Correspondence courses are another way to learn new skills and understand new areas. New technology in distance learning—classes offered via satellite broadcasts, cable, PictureTel, or online computer interaction—is offered by colleges, universities, and professional groups.

Trade journals are also extremely helpful in keeping professionals up to date with new management concepts, technical applications, marketing principles, equipment innovations, and the like. The isolation experienced by managers in out-of-the-way hotel establishments can be alleviated by reading trade journals. Such journals help all managers feel connected to the community of hotel industry professionals, perhaps providing insight into solving technical problems as well as boosting morale. Some trade journals are offered free on the Internet. Education is a lifelong venture; it does not stop with the attainment of a degree from a university or community college. The degree is only the beginning of a commitment to nurturing your career.

Work Experience

The practical experience you obtain from entry-level hotel jobs—whether you are a desk clerk, waiter/waitress, host/hostess, maid/houseman/room attendant, bellhop, or groundskeeper—will be invaluable as you plan and develop your career in the hotel industry. It will give you an opportunity to learn what hotel employees do and how departments interact, and it will expose you to the momentum of a hotel—the time frame of service available for the guest, management applications, and service concept applications, to name just a few.

Your work experience will enable you to evaluate theoretical concepts offered in the classroom. You will have a basis for comparing your work experiences with those of other students. You will also develop your own beliefs and behaviours, which can be applied to other hotel properties throughout your career. At times, you will have to think on your feet in order to resolve a guest complaint, evaluate equipment proposals, reorganize work areas for efficiency, or achieve cost-effective spending. Your work experience provides you with the proper foundation on which to base a successful career.

Professional Memberships

A professional trade organization is a group of people who voluntarily pool their efforts to achieve a set of goals. These goals may have a political nature, such as lobbying legislators or providing certification of achievement. Professional trade organizations in the hospitality industry serve members in many ways. First and foremost, they are a political voice in government. Through use of membership fees, trade organizations are able to lobby local, state, and federal legislators to be sure the entrepreneur's views are recognized. Members can opt not to have their membership fee used to support legislators who they don't politically support on personal issues. These organizations also offer significant opportunities for continuing education by sponsoring seminars and trade shows. They offer group plans for insurance and other programmes that can be cost-efficient to the entrepreneur. Professional trade associations also allow you to interact with others in the industry on both a professional and a social level. Valuable advice and rewarding friendships often result.

Ports of Entry

A review of the organizational structure of a hotel shows many departmental managers in a large organization. Which area is the best for you to enter to develop your career goals? Four of the ports of entry are marketing and sales, front office, food and beverage, and controller. It is impossible to say which the best port of entry is; all are avenues for career development. The hotel industry demands a great deal of its professionals. All employees must have extensive knowledge of all areas of the facility, and they must understand the overall function of all departments. This understanding must be reflected in professional business plans. Employees must also have good communication skills and good interpersonal skills. The industry requires great flexibility in scheduling work responsibilities and personal life. It demands that the professional understand the entrepreneurial role of corporate owners while operating within budgeted resources. Students who enter the lodging industry will find that each area in which they work contributes to a good background for the ultimate position of general manager. When trying to decide where to begin, consider reviewing the job responsibilities of department managers to learn what tasks are required to complete each job and who is involved in doing so.

Try to work in as many areas as you can before taking the leap into a general manager position. The job will be a lot easier, and you will go a long way toward meeting the establishment's goals if you are well prepared. You will make mistakes, no matter how much experience you have had; however, your success rate will be much higher if you have a varied background in many departments.

RESEARCHING GROWTH AREAS IN THE HOSPITALITY INDUSTRY

Areas that offer the most potential for growth should be explored. Because such areas change frequently, it is not possible to list them in a textbook. However, factors that support continued growth and strong business activity are regularly reported in such publications as Trends in the Lodging Industry, by Pannell, Kerr, and Forster. Hospitality industry futures projections publications usually cover such issues as new hotel developments; hotels under consideration; activities of convention and visitors' bureaus; strength of local economies; development of business, recreation, and arts activities; the need for office space; and area hotel occupancy percentages and average room rates. This information is listed for selected cities both within the United States and at international sites. The Internet is increasingly used as a method for researching career opportunities in hospitality management. Search engines will produce multiple listings of hospitality recruiters with key words such as "hotel manager," "front office manager," and "hotel careers." Also, professional hospitality organizations usually offer a job-posting service on their websites.

The Internet provides many opportunities for a new graduate to examine trends that are driving the industry and new technologies that will shape a career in hotel management. This information can assist job applicants in exploring the employment possibilities and prospects in different geographic areas. Your survey of career possibilities should include a review of a potential employer's economic performance on a balance sheet and other features of its profit-and-loss statement. This information is available on computerized business databases. Take the time to research the economic potential of the company you are considering. Your interview preparations should include reviewing the regional economic prospects and the company's economic performance. This preparation could set the stage for an investment that lasts many years, perhaps a lifetime.

The effort you put into preparing for a visit to a career fair is essential for making this a learning and networking opportunity for you. Questions you could ask a representative of a limited-service hotel include, "What are the typical management responsibilities of an assistant general manager in your organization? What types of visitors frequent your hotels during the week and on the weekend? What is the typical size of your hotels?" Questions you may want to consider asking a representative of a full-service hotel include, "What size staff is employed in your hotel? Do you have any convention hotels in your portfolio? What services do you typically offer in a hotel in your organization?" These types of questions open lines of communication and help you present yourself as a future professional. Students of hotel management should consider international employment opportunities. Current trade journals allow you to review the many job opportunities for hospitality professionals who have prepared themselves through education and work experience. International employment requires managers to know operations *and* to have a desire to learn and work in another culture. This option can be very exciting and a great addition to your career. Either, front office manager of The Times Extended-Stay Hotel, received a phone call from the home office of The Times Hotel Management Company asking her to participate in a meeting to discuss the new trend in long-term visitors. The home office is thinking of renovating some of the rooms to attract the guest who wants to stay for 5 to 15 days. How would Esther prepare for this meeting?

This introduced the future professional to the hotel industry. It began with a historical review, including founders of the hotel industry—Statler, Hilton, Ritz, Astor, Waldorf, Wilson, J. W. Marriott and J. W. Marriott Jr., Henderson and Moore, and Schultz. It also discussed historical developments that have shaped the products and services offered to guests, management trends, and economic factors. It covered the atrium concept, marketing and operational emphasis, geographic relocation, the emergence of limited-service hotels, the major reorganization of 1987–1988, adoption of total quality management, technological advances, the continued effects of 9/11, and wireless technology in the hotel industry.

It provided an overview of the industry in terms of types of hotels; market orientation/ location (residential, commercial, airport, and highway); sales indicators of occupancy, average daily rate, and RevPAR; levels of service (full-service, all-suites, limited-service, and extended-stay); and type of affiliation or nonaffiliation (franchise, referral, company-owned, management contract, and independent ownership). Branding was discussed as an approach to understanding the industry configuration. A review of trends fostering growth in the hotel industry was presented (leisure time, me/pleasure concept, discretionary income, family size, household size, business travel, female business traveller, and travel as an experience). Factors affecting a student's career development choice were discussed, including educational preparation, work experience, professional memberships, ports of entry in a hotel, and researching growth areas in the hospitality industry.

Professor Catherine Vicente has allotted time in the HRI-201 Introduction to Front Office Management course for a field trip this semester. After the first few lectures, she wants to take her class to the hotel establishments in the vicinity of City College. The area is well known for its tourist attractions and is the headquarters of several major U.S. businesses. She appoints a group of students to assist her in setting up tours.

One of the students, Maria, is a resident of the area and suggests they visit the grand old St. Thomas Hotel in the downtown area. She would also like to see a hotel located at the Wide World Airport. Ryan, another student, has worked at a limited-service property in his hometown. He understands another hotel in that chain is located on the outskirts of the city. David, who is applying for a job at a local hotel, wants to get information on all-suites hotels. Linda has heard of a new extended-stay hotel in town and wants to know what makes it different from a limited-service hotel. The group has sifted through all the requests and decided to form five teams to visit these places. Each team will appoint one spokesperson for a panel discussion. The spokesperson will present a five-minute summary of what was learned from the visit. What items do you think each spokesperson will include in his or her summary?

A recent survey in a suburban community projects an influx of new citizens into the area. Several computer industries will be relocating to the area, and they are expected to employ 25,000 persons at all levels of the organizations. Also, one of these computer companies will locate its corporate headquarters here, with an additional 500 executives arriving soon. The local hotel association has contacted Professor Catherine Vicente of the HRI programme at City College for assistance in determining the impact these new residents will have on their hotels with regard to occupancy and use of facilities. If you were Professor Vicente, what actions would you undertake? Justify your responses with regard to hotel operations and development. If you lived in this community, how would these developments affect your career in the hotel industry?

Chapter 3

Foreign Exchange

Authorised dealers may remit foreign exchange upto a reasonable limit, at the request of a traveller towards his hotel accommodation, tour arrangements, etc., in the countries proposed to be visited by him, provided it is out of the foreign exchange purchased by the traveller from an authorised person (including exchange drawn for private travel abroad) in accordance with the Rules, Regulations and Directions in force.

Authorised dealers may effect remittances at the request of agents in India who have tie up arrangements with hotels/ agents, etc., abroad for providing hotel accommodations or making other tour arrangements for travellers from India provided the authorised dealer is satisfied that the remittance is being made out of the foreign exchange purchased by the concerned traveller from an authorised person (including exchange drawn for private travel abroad) in accordance with the Rules, Regulations and Directions in force. Authorised dealer may open foreign currency accounts in the name of agents in India who have tie up arrangements with hotels/ agents, etc., abroad for providing hotel accommodations or making other tour arrangements for travellers from India provided:

- The credits to the account are by way of depositing
- Collections made in foreign exchange from travellers, and

- Refunds received from outside India on account of cancellation of bookings/tour arrangements, etc., and
- the debits in foreign exchange are for making payments towards hotel accommodation, tour arrangements, etc., outside India, in accordance with (ii) above.

An Act to consolidate and amend the law relating to foreign exchange with the objective of facilitating external trade and payments and for promoting the orderly development and maintenance of foreign exchange market in India.

BE it enacted by Parliament in the Fiftieth Year of the Republic of India as follows:—

SHORT TITLE, EXTENT, APPLICATION AND COMMENCEMENT

1. This Act may be called the Foreign Exchange Management Act, 1999.
2. It extends to the whole of India.
3. It shall also apply to all branches, offices and agencies outside India owned or controlled by a person resident in India and also to any contravention thereunder committed outside India by any person to whom this Act applies.
4. It shall come into force on such date as the Central Government may, by notification in the Official Gazette, appoint:

Provided that different dates may be appointed for different provisions of this Act and any reference in any such provision to the commencement of this Act shall be construed as a reference to the coming into force of that provision.

In this Act, unless the context otherwise requires—

a. "Adjudicating Authority" means an officer authorised under sub-section (1) of section 16;
b. "Appellate Tribunal" means the Appellate Tribunal for Foreign Exchange established under section 18;

c. "authorised person" means an authorised dealer, money changer, off-shore banking unit or any other person for the time being authorised under sub-section (1) of section 10 to deal in foreign exchange or foreign securities;

d. "Bench" means a Bench of the Appellate Tribunal;

e. "capital account transaction" means a transaction which alters the assets or liabilities, including contingent liabilities, outside India of persons resident in India or assets or liabilities in India of persons resident outside India, and includes transactions referred to in sub-section (3) of section 6;

f. "Chairperson" means the Chairperson of the Appellate Tribunal;

g. "chartered accountant" shall have the meaning assigned to it in clause (b) of sub-section (1) of section 2 of the Chartered Accountants Act, 1949 (38 of 1949);

h. "currency" includes all currency notes, postal notes, postal orders, money orders, cheques, drafts, travellers cheques, letters of credit, bills of exchange and promissory notes, credit cards or such other similar instruments, as may be notified by the Reserve Bank;

i. "currency notes" means and includes cash in the form of coins and bank notes;

j. "current account transaction" means a transaction other than a capital account transaction and without prejudice to the generality of the foregoing such transaction includes:—

(i) Payments due in connection with foreign trade, other current business, services, and short-term banking and credit facilities in the ordinary course of business,

(ii) Payments due as interest on loans and as net income from investments,

(iii) Remittances for living expenses of parents, spouse and children residing abroad, and

(iv) Expenses in connection with foreign travel, education and medical care of parents, spouse and children;

(k) "Director of Enforcement" means the Director of Enforcement appointed under sub-section (1) of section 36;

(l) "Export", with its grammatical variations and cognate expressions, means—

(i) The taking out of India to a place outside India any goods,

(ii) Provision of services from India to any person outside India;

(m) "Foreign currency" means any currency other than Indian currency;

(n) "Foreign exchange" means foreign currency and includes—

(i) Deposits, credits and balances payable in any foreign currency,

(ii) Drafts, travellers cheques, letters of credit or bills of exchange, expressed or drawn in Indian currency but payable in any foreign currency,

(iii) Drafts, travellers cheques, letters of credit or bills of exchange drawn by banks, institutions or persons outside India, but payable in Indian currency;

(o) "Foreign security" means any security, in the form of shares, stocks, bonds, debentures or any other instrument denominated or expressed in foreign currency and includes securities expressed in foreign currency, but where redemption or any form of return such as interest or dividends is payable in Indian currency;

(p) "Import", with its grammatical variations and cognate expressions, means bringing into India any goods or services;

(q) "Indian currency" means currency which is expressed or drawn in Indian rupees but does not include special bank notes and special one rupee notes issued under section 28A of the Reserve Bank of India Act, 1934 (2 of 1934);

(r) "Legal practitioner" shall have the meaning assigned to it in clause (i) of sub-section (1) of section 2 of the Advocates Act, 1961 (25 of 1961);

(s) "Member" means a Member of the Appellate Tribunal and includes the Chairperson thereof;

(t) "Notify" means to notify in the Official Gazette and the expression "notification" shall be construed accordingly;

(u) "Person" includes—

(i) An individual,

(ii) A Hindu undivided family,

(iii) A company,

(iv) A firm,

(v) An association of persons or a body of individuals, whether incorporated or not,

(vi) Every artificial juridical person, not falling within any of the preceding sub-clauses, and

(vii) Any agency, office or branch owned or controlled by such person;

(v) "Person resident in India" means—

(i) A person residing in India for more than one hundred and eighty-two days during the course of the preceding financial year but does not include—

A. A person who has gone out of India or who stays outside India, in either case—

a. For or on taking up employment outside India, or

b. For carrying on outside India a business or vocation outside India, or

c. For any other purpose, in such circumstances as would indicate his intention to stay outside India for an uncertain period;

B. A person who has come to or stays in India, in either case, otherwise than—

a. For or on taking up employment in India, or

b. For carrying on in India a business or vocation in India, or

c. For any other purpose, in such circumstances as would indicate his intention to stay in India for an uncertain period;

(ii) Any person or body corporate registered or incorporated in India,

(iii) An office, branch or agency in India owned or controlled by a person resident outside India,

(iv) An office, branch or agency outside India owned or controlled by a person resident in India;

(w) "Person resident outside India" means a person who is not resident in India;

(x) "Prescribed" means prescribed by rules made under this Act;

(y) "Repatriate to India" means bringing into India the realised foreign exchange and—

(i) The selling of such foreign exchange to an authorised person in India in exchange for rupees, or

(ii) The holding of realised amount in an account with an authorised person in India to the extent notified by the Reserve Bank, and includes use of the realised amount for discharge of a debt or liability denominated in foreign exchange and the expression "repatriation" shall be construed accordingly;

(z) "Reserve Bank" means the Reserve Bank of India constituted under sub-section (1) of section 3 of the Reserve Bank of India Act, 1934 (2 of 1934);

(za)"Security" means shares, stocks, bonds and debentures, Government securities as defined in the Public Debt Act, 1944 (18 of 1944), savings certificates to which the Government Savings Certificates Act, 1959 (46 of 1959) applies, deposit receipts in respect of deposits of securities and units of the Unit Trust of India established under sub-section (1) of section 3 of the Unit Trust of India Act, 1963 (52 of 1963) or of any mutual fund and includes certificates of title to securities, but does not include bills of exchange or promissory notes other than Government promissory notes or any other instruments which may be notified by the Reserve Bank as security for the purposes of this Act; (zb) "service" means service of any description which is made available to potential users and includes the provision of facilities in connection with banking, financing, insurance, medical assistance, legal assistance, chit fund, real estate, transport, processing, supply of electrical or other energy, boarding or lodging or both, entertainment, amusement or the purveying of news or other information, but does not include the rendering of any service free of charge or under a contract of personal service; (zc) "Special Director (Appeals)" means an officer appointed under section 18; (zd) "specify" means to specify by regulations made under this Act and the expression "specified" shall be construed accordingly; (ze) "transfer" includes sale, purchase, exchange, mortgage, pledge, gift, loan or any other form of transfer of right, title, possession or lien.

Regulation and Management of Foreign Exchange

Save as otherwise provided in this Act, rules or regulations made thereunder, or with the general or special permission of the Reserve Bank, no person shall—

(a) Deal in or transfer any foreign exchange or foreign security to any person not being an authorised person;

(b) Make any payment to or for the credit of any person resident outside India in any manner;

(c) Receive otherwise through an authorised person, any payment by order or on behalf of any person resident outside India in any manner;

Explanation—For the purpose of this clause, where any person in, or resident in, India receives any payment by order or on behalf of any person resident outside India through any other person (including an authorised person) without a corresponding inward remittance from any place outside India, then, such person shall be deemed to have received such payment otherwise than through an authorised person;

(d) Enter into any financial transaction in India as consideration for or in association with acquisition or creation or transfer of a right to acquire, any asset outside India by any person.

Explanation—For the purpose of this clause, "financial transaction" means making any payment to, or for the credit of any person, or receiving any payment for, by order or on behalf of any person, or drawing, issuing or negotiating any bill of exchange or promissory note, or transferring any security or acknowledging any debt.

Holding of Foreign Exchange

Save as otherwise provided in this Act, no person resident in India shall acquire, hold, own, possess or transfer any foreign exchange, foreign security or any immovable property situated outside India.

Current Account Transactions

Any person may sell or draw foreign exchange to or from an authorised person if such sale or drawal is a current account transaction:

Provided that the Central Government may, in public interest and in consultation with the Reserve Bank, impose such reasonable restrictions for current account transactions as may be prescribed.

Capital Account Transactions

1. Subject to the provisions of sub-section (2), any person may sell or draw foreign exchange to or from an authorised person for a capital account transaction.
2. The Reserve Bank may, in consultation with the Central Government, specify—
   (a) Any class or classes of capital account transactions which are permissible;
   (b) The limit up to which foreign exchange shall be admissible for such transactions:
   Provided that the Reserve Bank shall not impose any restriction on the drawal of foreign exchange for payments due on account of amortization of loans or for depreciation of direct investments in the ordinary course of business.
3. Without prejudice to the generality of the provisions of sub-section (2), the Reserve Bank may, by regulations, prohibit, restrict or regulate the following—
   (a) Transfer or issue of any foreign security by a person resident in India;
   (b) Transfer or issue of any security by a person resident outside India;
   (c) Transfer or issue of any security or foreign security by any branch, office or agency in India of a person resident outside India;
   (d) Any borrowing or lending in foreign exchange in whatever form or by whatever name called;
   (e) Any borrowing or lending in rupees in whatever form or by whatever name called between a person resident in India and a person resident outside India;

(f) Deposits between persons resident in India and persons resident outside India;

(g) Export, import or holding of currency or currency notes;

(h) Transfer of immovable property outside India, other than a lease not exceeding five years, by a person resident in India;

(i) Acquisition or transfer of immovable property in India, other than a lease not exceeding five years, by a person resident outside India;

(j) Giving of a guarantee or surety in respect of any debt, obligation or other liability incurred—

(i) By a person resident in India and owed to a person resident outside India; or

(ii) By a person resident outside India.

4. A person resident in India may hold, own, transfer or invest in foreign currency, foreign security or any immovable property situated outside India if such currency, security or property was acquired, held or owned by such person when he was resident outside India or inherited from a person who was resident outside India.

5. A person resident outside India may hold, own, transfer or invest in Indian currency, security or any immovable property situated in India if such currency, security or property was acquired, held or owned by such person when he was resident in India or inherited from a person who was resident in India.

6. Without prejudice to the provisions of this section, the Reserve Bank may, by regulation, prohibit, restrict, or regulate establishment in India of a branch, office or other place of business by a person resident outside India, for carrying on any activity relating to such branch, office or other place of business.

Export of Goods and Services

1. Every exporter of goods shall—

(a) Furnish to the Reserve Bank or to such other authority a declaration in such form and in such manner as may be specified, containing true and correct material particulars, including the amount representing the full export value or, if the full export value of the goods is not ascertainable at the time of export, the value which the exporter, having regard to the prevailing market conditions, expects to receive on the sale of the goods in a market outside India;

(b) Furnish to the Reserve Bank such other information as may be required by the Reserve Bank for the purpose of ensuring the realisation of the export proceeds by such exporter.

2. The Reserve Bank may, for the purpose of ensuring that the full export value of the goods or such reduced value of the goods as the Reserve Bank determines, having regard to the prevailing market conditions, is received without any delay, direct any exporter to comply with such requirements as it deems fit.
3. Every exporter of services shall furnish to the Reserve Bank or to such other authorities a declaration in such form and in such manner as may be specified, containing the true and correct material particulars in relation to payment for such services.

Realisation and Repatriation of Foreign Exchange

8. Save as otherwise provided in this Act, where any amount of foreign exchange is due or has accrued to any person resident in India, such person shall take all reasonable steps to realise and repatriate to India such foreign exchange within such period and in such manner as may be specified by the Reserve Bank.

Exemption from Realisation and Repatriation in Certain Cases

The provisions of sections 4 and 8 shall not apply to the following, namely:—

(a) Possession of foreign currency or foreign coins by any person up to such limit as the Reserve Bank may specify;

(b) Foreign currency account held or operated by such person or class of persons and the limit up to which the Reserve Bank may specify;

(c) Foreign exchange acquired or received before the 8th day of July, 1947 or any income arising or accruing thereon which is held outside India by any person in pursuance of a general or special permission granted by the Reserve Bank;

(d) Foreign exchange held by a person resident in India up to such limit as the Reserve Bank may specify, if such foreign exchange was acquired by way of gift or inheritance from a person referred to in clause *(c)*, including any income arising therefrom;

(e) Foreign exchange acquired from employment, business, trade, vocation, services, honorarium, gifts, inheritance or any other legitimate means up to such limit as the Reserve Bank may specify; and

(f) Such other receipts in foreign exchange as the Reserve Bank may specify.

Authorised Person

1. The Reserve Bank may, on an application made to it in this behalf, authorise any person to be known as authorised person to deal in foreign exchange or in foreign securities, as an authorised dealer, money changer or off-shore banking unit or in any other manner as it deems fit.
2. An authorisation under this section shall be in writing and shall be subject to the conditions laid down therein.
3. An authorisation granted under sub-section (1) may be revoked by the Reserve Bank at any time if the Reserve Bank is satisfied that—

(a) It is in public interest so to do; or

(b) The authorised person has failed to comply with the condition subject to which the authorisation was granted or has contravened any of the provisions of the Act or any rule, regulation, notification, direction or order made thereunder:

Provided that no such authorisation shall be revoked on any ground referred to in clause (b) unless the authorised person has been given a reasonable opportunity of making a representation in the matter.

4. An authorised person shall, in all his dealings in foreign exchange or foreign security, comply with such general or special directions or orders as the Reserve Bank may, from time to time, think fit to give, and, except with the previous permission of the Reserve Bank, an authorised person shall not engage in any transaction involving any foreign exchange or foreign security which is not in conformity with the terms of his authorisation under this section.

5. An authorised person shall, before undertaking any transaction in foreign exchange on behalf of any person, require that person to make such declaration and to give such information as will reasonably satisfy him that the transaction will not involve, and is not designed for the purpose of any contravention or evasion of the provisions of this Act or of any rule, regulation, notification, direction or order made thereunder, and where the said person refuses to comply with any such requirement or makes only unsatisfactory compliance therewith, the authorised person shall refuse in writing to undertake the transaction and shall, if he has reason to believe that any such contravention or evasion as aforesaid is contemplated by the person, report the matter to the Reserve Bank.

6. Any person, other than an authorised person, who has acquired or purchased foreign exchange for any

purpose mentioned in the declaration made by him to authorised person under sub-section (5) does not use it for such purpose or does not surrender it to authorised person within the specified period or uses the foreign exchange so acquired or purchased for any other purpose for which purchase or acquisition of foreign exchange is not permissible under the provisions of the Act or the rules or regulations or direction or order made thereunder shall be deemed to have committed contravention of the provisions of the Act for the purpose of this section.

Reserve Bank's Powers to Issue Directions to Authorised Person

1. The Reserve Bank may, for the purpose of securing compliance with the provisions of this Act and of any rules, regulations, notifications or directions made thereunder, give to the authorised persons any direction in regard to making of payment or the doing or desist from doing any act relating to foreign exchange or foreign security.
2. The Reserve Bank may, for the purpose of ensuring the compliance with the provisions of this Act or of any rule, regulation, notification, direction or order made thereunder, direct any authorised person to furnish such information, in such manner, as it deems fit.
3. Where any authorised person contravenes any direction given by the Reserve Bank under this Act or fails to file any return as directed by the Reserve Bank, the Reserve Bank may, after giving reasonable opportunity of being heard, impose on the authorised person a penalty which may extend to ten thousand rupees and in the case of continuing contravention with an additional penalty which may extend to two thousand rupees for every day during which such contravention continues.

Power of Reserve Bank to Inspect Authorised Person

1. The Reserve Bank may, at any time, cause an inspection to be made, by any officer of the Reserve Bank specially authorised in writing by the Reserve Bank in this behalf, of the business of any authorised person as may appear to it to be necessary or expedient for the purpose of—
   (a) Verifying the correctness of any statement, information or particulars furnished to the Reserve Bank;
   (b) Obtaining any information or particulars which such authorised person has failed to furnish on being called upon to do so;
   (c) Securing compliance with the provisions of this Act or of any rules, regulations, directions or orders made thereunder.
2. It shall be the duty of every authorised person, and where such person is a company or a firm, every director, partner or other officer of such company or firm, as the case may be, to produce to any officer making an inspection under sub-section (1), such books, accounts and other documents in his custody or power and to furnish any statement or information relating to the affairs of such person, company or firm as the said officer may require within such time and in such manner as the said officer may direct.

Contravention and Penalties

1. If any person contravenes any provision of this Act, or contravenes any rule, regulation, notification, direction or order issued in exercise of the powers under this Act, or contravenes any condition subject to which an authorisation is issued by the Reserve Bank, he shall, upon adjudication, be liable to a penalty up to thrice the sum involved in such contravention where such amount is quantifiable, or up to two lakh rupees where the amount is not quantifiable, and where such contravention is a

continuing one, further penalty which may extend to five thousand rupees for every day after the first day during which the contravention continues.

2. Any Adjudicating Authority adjudging any contravention under sub-section (1), may, if he thinks fit in addition to any penalty which he may impose for such contravention direct that any currency, security or any other money or property in respect of which the contravention has taken place shall be confiscated to the Central Government and further direct that the foreign exchange holdings, if any of the persons committing the contraventions or any part thereof, shall be brought back into India or shall be retained outside India in accordance with the directions made in this behalf.

   Explanation—For the purposes of this sub-section, "property" in respect of which contravention has taken place, shall include—

   (a) Deposits in a bank, where the said property is converted into such deposits;

   (b) Indian currency, where the said property is converted into that currency; and

   (c) Any other property which has resulted out of the conversion of that property.

Enforcement of the orders of Adjudicating Authority.

1. Subject to the provisions of sub-section (2) of section 19, if any person fails to make full payment of the penalty imposed on him under section 13 within a period of ninety days from the date on which the notice for payment of such penalty is served on him, he shall be liable to civil imprisonment under this section.

2. No order for the arrest and detention in civil prison of a defaulter shall be made unless the Adjudicating Authority has issued and served a notice upon the defaulter calling upon him to appear before him on the date specified in the notice and to show cause

why he should not be committed to the civil prison, and unless the Adjudicating Authority, for reasons in writing, is satisfied—

(a) That the defaulter, with the object or effect of obstructing the recovery of penalty, has after the issue of notice by the Adjudicating Authority, dishonestly transferred concealed, or removed any part of his property, or

(b) That the defaulter has, or has had since the issuing of notice by the Adjudicating Authority, the means to pay the arrears or some substantial part thereof and refuses or neglects or has refused or neglected to pay the same.

3. Notwithstanding anything contained in sub-section (1), a warrant for the arrest of the defaulter may be issued by the Adjudicating Authority if the Adjudicating Authority is satisfied, by affidavit or otherwise, that with the object or effect of delaying the execution of the certificate the defaulter is likely to abscond or leave the local limits of the jurisdiction of the Adjudicating Authority.

4. Where appearance is not made pursuant to a notice issued and served under sub-section (1), the Adjudicating Authority may issue a warrant for the arrest of the defaulter.

5. A warrant of arrest issued by the Adjudicating Authority under sub-section (3) or sub-section

6. May also be executed by any other Adjudicating Authority within whose jurisdiction the defaulter may for the time being be found.

7. Every person arrested in pursuance of a warrant of arrest under this section shall be brought before the Adjudicating Authority issuing the warrant as soon as practicable and in any event within twenty-four hours of his arrest (exclusive of the time required for the journey):

Provided that, if the defaulter pays the amount entered in the warrant of arrest as due and the costs of the arrest to the officer arresting him, such officer shall at once release him.

Explanation—For the purposes of this sub-section, where the defaulter is a Hindu undivided family, the *karta* thereof shall be deemed to be the defaulter.

8. When a defaulter appears before the Adjudicating Authority pursuant to a notice to show cause or is brought before the Adjudicating Authority under this section, the Adjudicating Authority shall give the defaulter an opportunity showing cause why he should not be committed to the civil prison.
9. Pending the conclusion of the inquiry, the Adjudicating Authority may, in his discretion, order the defaulter to be detained in the custody of such officer as the Adjudicating Authority may think fit or release him on his furnishing the security to the satisfaction of the Adjudicating Authority for his appearance as and when required.
10. Upon the conclusion of the inquiry, the Adjudicating Authority may make an order for the detention of the defaulter in the civil prison and shall in that event cause him to be arrested if he is not already under arrest:

    Provided that in order to give a defaulter an opportunity of satisfying the arrears, the Adjudicating Authority may, before making the order of detention, leave the defaulter in the custody of the officer arresting him or of any other officer for a specified period not exceeding fifteen days, or release him on his furnishing security to the satisfaction of the Adjudicating Authority for his appearance at the expiration of the specified period if the arrears are not satisfied.
11. When the Adjudicating Authority does not make an order of detention under sub-section (9), he shall, if the defaulter is under arrest, direct his release.

12. Every person detained in the civil prison in execution of the certificate may be so detained,–
    a. Where the certificate is for a demand of an amount exceeding rupees one crore, up to three years, and
    b. In any other case, up to six months:

    Provided that he shall be released from such detention on the amount mentioned in the warrant for his detention being paid to the officer-in-charge of the civil prison.
13. A defaulter released from detention under this section shall not, merely by reason of his release, be discharged from his liability for the arrears, but he shall not be liable to be arrested under the certificate in execution of which he was detained in the civil prison.
14. A detention order may be executed at any place in India in the manner provided for the execution of warrant of arrest under the Code of Criminal Procedure, 1973 (2 of 1974).

Power to Compound Contravention

1. Any contravention under section 13 may, on an application made by theperson committing such contravention, be compounded within one hundred and eighty days from the date of receipt of application by the Director of Enforcement or such other officers of the Directorate of Enforcement and Officers of the Reserve Bank as may be authorised in this behalf by the Central Government in such manner as may be prescribed.
2. Where a contravention has been compounded under sub-section (1), no proceeding or further proceeding, as the case may be, shall be initiated or continued, as the case may be, against the person committing such contravention under that section, in respect of the contravention so compounded.

Appointment of Adjudicating Authority

1. For the purpose of adjudication under section 13, the Central Government may, by an order published in the Official Gazette, appoint as many officers of the Central Government as it may think fit, as the Adjudicating Authorities for holding an inquiry in the manner prescribed after giving the person alleged to have committed contravention under section 13, against whom a complaint has been made under sub-section
2. (hereinafter in this section referred to as the said person) a reasonable opportunity of being heard for the purpose of imposing any penalty:

   Provided that where the Adjudicating Authority is of opinion that the said person is likely to abscond or is likely to evade in any manner, the payment of penalty, if levied, it may direct the said person to furnish a bond or guarantee for such amount and subject to such conditions as it may deem fit.
3. The Central Government shall, while appointing the Adjudicating Authorities under sub-section (1), also specify in the order published in the Official Gazette, their respective jurisdictions.
4. No Adjudicating Authority shall hold an enquiry under sub-section (1) except upon a complaint in writing made by any officer authorised by a general or special order by the Central Government.
5. The said person may appear either in person or take the assistance of a legal practitioner or a chartered accountant of his choice for presenting his case before the Adjudicating Authority.
6. Every Adjudicating Authority shall have the same powers of a civil court which are conferred on the Appellate Tribunal under sub-section (2) of section 28 and—

(a) All proceedings before it shall be deemed to be judicial proceedings within the meaning of sections 193 and 228 of the Indian Penal Code (45 of 1860);

(b) Shall be deemed to be a civil court for the purposes of sections 345 and 346 of the Code of Criminal Procedure, 1973 (2 of 1974).

7. Every Adjudicating Authority shall deal with the complaint under sub-section (2) as expeditiously as possible and endeavour shall be made to dispose of the complaint finally within one year from the date of receipt of the complaint:

Provided that where the complaint cannot be disposed off within the said period, the Adjudicating Authority shall record periodically the reasons in writing for not disposing off the complaint within the said period.

Appeal to Special Director (Appeals)

1. The Central Government shall, by notification, appoint one or more Special Directors (Appeals) to hear appeals against the orders of the Adjudicating Authorities under this section and shall also specify in the said notification the matter and places in relation to which the Special Director (Appeals) may exercise jurisdiction.
2. Any person aggrieved by an order made by the Adjudicating Authority, being an Assistant Director of Enforcement or a Deputy Director of Enforcement, may prefer an appeal to the Special Director (Appeals).
3. Every appeal under sub-section (1) shall be filed within forty-five days from the date on which the copy of the order made by the Adjudicating Authority is received by the aggrieved person and it shall be in such form, verified in such manner and be accompanied by such fee as may be prescribed:

   Provided that the Special Director (Appeals) may entertain an appeal after the expiry of the said period of forty-five days, if he is satisfied that there was sufficient cause for not filing it within that period.

4. On receipt of an appeal under sub-section (1), the Special Director (Appeals) may after giving the parties to the appeal an opportunity of being heard, pass such order thereon as he thinks fit confirming, modifying or setting aside the order appealed against.
5. The Special Director (Appeals) shall send a copy of every order made by him to the parties to appeal and to the concerned Adjudicating Authority.
6. The Special Director (Appeals) shall have the same powers of a civil court which are conferred on the Appellate Tribunal under sub-section (2) of section 28 and–
   (a) All proceedings before him shall be deemed to be judicial proceedings within the meaning of sections 193 and 228 of the Indian Penal Code (45 of 1860);
   (b) Shall be deemed to be a civil court for the purposes of sections 345 and 346 of the Code of Criminal Procedure, 1973 (2 of 1974).

Establishment of Appellate Tribunal

The Central Government shall, by notification, establish an Appellate Tribunal to be known as the Appellate Tribunal for Foreign Exchange to hear appeals against the orders of the Adjudicating Authorities and the Special Director (Appeals) under this Act.

Appeal to Appellate Tribunal

1. Save as provided in sub-section (2), the Central Government or any person aggrieved by an order made by an Adjudicating Authority, other than those referred to sub-section (1) of section 17, or the Special Director (Appeals), may prefer an appeal to the Appellate Tribunal:

   Provided that any person appealing against the order of the Adjudicating Authority or the Special Director

(Appeals) levying any penalty, shall while filing the appeal, deposit the amount of such penalty with such authority as may be notified by the Central Government:

Provided further that where in any particular case, the Appellate Tribunal is of the opinion that the deposit of such penalty would cause undue hardship to such person, the Appellate Tribunal may dispense with such deposit subject to such conditions as it may deem fit to impose so as to safeguard the realisation of penalty.

2. Every appeal under sub-section (1) shall be filed within a period of forty-five days from the date on which a copy of the order made by the Adjudicating Authority or the Special Director (Appeals) is received by the aggrieved person or by the Central Government and it shall be in such form, verified in such manner and be accompanied by such fee as may be prescribed:

   Provided that the Appellate Tribunal may entertain an appeal after the expiry of the said period of forty-five days if it is satisfied that there was sufficient cause for not filing it within that period.

3. On receipt of an appeal under sub-section (1), the Appellate Tribunal may, after giving the parties to the appeal an opportunity of being heard, pass such orders thereon as it thinks fit, confirming, modifying or setting aside the order appealed against.

4. The Appellate Tribunal shall send a copy of every order made by it to the parties to the appeal and to the concerned Adjudicating Authority or the Special Director (Appeals), as the case may be.

5. The appeal filed before the Appellate Tribunal under sub-section (1) shall be dealt with by it as expeditiously as possible and endeavour shall be made by it to dispose of the appeal finally within one hundred and eighty days from the date of receipt of the appeal:

Provided that where any appeal could not be disposed of within the said period of one hundred and eighty days, the Appellate Tribunal shall record its reasons in writing for not disposing of the appeal within the said period.

6. The Appellate Tribunal may, for the purpose of examining the legality, propriety or correctness of any order made by the Adjudicating Authority under section 16 in relation to any proceeding, on its own motion or otherwise, call for the records of such proceedings and make such order in the case as it thinks fit.

Composition of Appellate Tribunal

1. The Appellate Tribunal shall consist of a Chairperson and such number of Members as the Central Government may deem fit.
2. Subject to the provisions of this Act,—
   (a) The jurisdiction of the Appellate Tribunal may be exercised by Benches thereof;
   (b) A Bench may be constituted by the Chairperson with one or more Members as the Chairperson may deem fit;
   (c) The Benches of the Appellate Tribunal shall ordinarily sit at New Delhi and at such other places as the Central Government may, in consultation with the Chairperson, notify;
   (d) The Central Government shall notify the areas in relation to which each Bench of the Appellate Tribunal may exercise jurisdiction.
3. Notwithstanding anything contained in sub-section (2), the Chairperson may transfer a Member from one Bench to another Bench.
4. If at any stage of the hearing of any case or matter it appears to the Chairperson or a Member that the case or matter is of such a nature that it ought to be heard by a Bench consisting of two Members, the case or

matter may be transferred by the Chairperson or, as the case may be, referred to him for transfer, to such Bench as the Chairperson may deem fit.

Qualifications for Appointment

1. A person shall not be qualified for appointment as the Chairperson or a Member unless he—
   (a) In the case of Chairperson, is or has been, or is qualified to be, a Judge of a High Court; and
   (b) In the case of a Member, is or has been, or is qualified to be, a District Judge.
2. A person shall not be qualified for appointment as a Special Director (Appeals) unless he—
   (a) Has been a member of the Indian Legal Service and has held a post in Grade I of that Service; or
   (b) Has been a member of the Indian Revenue Service and has held a post equivalent to a Joint Secretary to the Government of India.

Term of Office

The Chairperson and every other Member shall hold office as such for a term of five years from the date on which he enters upon his office:

Provided that no Chairperson or other Member shall hold office as such after he has attained,—

(a) In the case of the Chairperson, the age of sixty-five years;

(b) In the case of any other Member, the age of sixty-two years.

Terms and Conditions of Service

The salary and allowances payable to and the other terms and conditions of service of the Chairperson, other Members and the Special Director (Appeals) shall be such as may be prescribed:

Provided that neither the salary and allowances nor the other terms and conditions of service of the Chairperson or a Member shall be varied to his disadvantage after appointment.

Vacancies

If, for reason other than temporary absence, any vacancy occurs in the office of the Chairperson or a Member, the Central Government shall appoint another person in accordance with the provisions of this Act to fill the vacancy and the proceedings may be continued before the Appellate Tribunal from the stage at which the vacancy is filled.

Resignation and Removal

1. The Chairperson or a Member may, by notice in writing under his hand addressed to the Central Government, resign his office:

   Provided that the Chairperson or a Member shall, unless he is permitted by the Central Government to relinquish his office sooner, continue to hold office until the expiry of three months from the date of receipt of such notice or until a person duly appointed as his successor enters upon his office or until the expiry of term of office, whichever is the earliest.

2. The Chairperson or a Member shall not be removed from his office except by an order by the Central Government on the ground of proved misbehaviour or incapacity after an inquiry made by such person as the President may appoint for this purpose in which the Chairperson or a Member concerned has been informed of the charges against him and given a reasonable opportunity of being heard in respect of such charges.

Member to act as Chairperson in Certain Circumstances

1. In the event of the occurrence of any vacancy in the office of the Chairperson by reason of his death, resignation or otherwise, the senior-most Member

shall act as the Chairperson until the date on which a new Chairperson, appointed in accordance with the provisions of this Act to fill such vacancy, enters upon his office.

2. When the Chairperson is unable to discharge his functions owing to absence, illness or any other cause, the senior most Member shall discharge the functions of the Chairperson until the date on which the Chairperson resumes his duties.

Staff of Appellate Tribunal and Special Director (Appeals)

1. The Central Government shall provide the Appellate Tribunal and the Special Director (Appeals) with such officers and employees as it may deem fit.
2. The officers and employees of the Appellate Tribunal and office of the Special Director (Appeals) shall discharge their functions under the general superintendence of the Chairperson and the Special Director (Appeals), as the case may be.
3. The salaries and allowances and other conditions of service of the officers and employees of the Appellate Tribunal and office of the Special Director (Appeals) shall be such as may be prescribed.

Procedure and powers of Appellate Tribunal and Special Director

1. The Appellate Tribunal and the Special Director (Appeals) shall not be bound by the procedure laid down by the Code of Civil Procedure, 1908 (5 of 1908) but shall be guided by the principles of natural justice and, subject to the other provisions of this Act, the Appellate Tribunal and the Special Director (Appeals) shall have powers to regulate its own procedure.
2. The Appellate Tribunal and the Special Director (Appeals) shall have, for the purposes of discharging its functions under this Act, the same powers as are vested in a civil court under the Code of Civil

Procedure, 1908 (5 of 1908); while trying a suit, in respect of the following matters, namely:—

(a) Summoning and enforcing the attendance of any person and examining him on oath;

(b) Requiring the discovery and production of documents;

(c) Receiving evidence on affidavits;

(d) Subject to the provisions of sections 123 and 124 of the Indian Evidence Act, 1872 (1 of 1872) requisitioning any public record or document or copy of such record or document from any office;

(e) Issuing commissions for the examination of witnesses or documents;

(f) Reviewing its decisions;

(g) Dismissing a representation of default or deciding it *ex parte;*

(h) Setting aside any order of dismissal of any representation for default or any order passed by it *ex parte;* and

(i) Any other matter which may be prescribed by the Central Government.

3. An order made by the Appellate Tribunal or the Special Director (Appeals) under this Act shall be executable by the Appellate Tribunal or the Special Director (Appeals) as a decree of civil court and, for this purpose, the Appellate Tribunal and the Special Director (Appeals) shall have all the powers of a civil court.

4. Notwithstanding anything contained in sub-section (3), the Appellate Tribunal or the Special Director (Appeals) may transmit any order made by it to a civil court having local jurisdiction and such civil court shall execute the order as if it were a decree made by that court.

5. All proceedings before the Appellate Tribunal and the Special Director (Appeals) shall be deemed to be

judicial proceedings within the meaning of sections 193 and 228 of the Indian Penal Code (45 of 1860) and the Appellate Tribunal shall be deemed to be a civil court for the purposes of sections 345 and 346 of the Code of Criminal Procedure, 1973 (2 of 1974)

Distribution of Business Amongst Benches

Where Benches are constituted, the Chairperson may, from time to time, by notification, make provisions as to the distribution of the business of the Appellate Tribunal amongst the Benches and also provide for the matters which may be dealt with by each Bench.

Power of Chairperson to Transfer Cases

On the application of any of the parties and after notice to the parties, and after hearing such of them as he may desire to be heard, or on his own motion without such notice, the Chairperson may transfer any case pending before one Bench, for disposal, to any other Bench.

Decision to be by Majority

If the Members of a Bench consisting of two Members differ in opinion on any point, they shall state the point or points on which they differ, and make a reference to the Chairperson who shall either hear the point or points himself or refer the case for hearing on such point or points by one or more of the other Members of the Appellate Tribunal and such point or points shall be decided according to the opinion of the majority of the Members of the Appellate Tribunal who have heard the case, including those who first heard it.

Right of appellant to take assistance of legal practitioner or chartered accountant and of Government, to appoint presenting officers.

1. A person preferring an appeal to the Appellate Tribunal or the Special Director (Appeals) under this Act may either appear in person or take the assistance of a legal practitioner or a chartered accountant of his choice to present his case before the Appellate

Tribunal or the Special Director (Appeals), as the case may be.

2. The Central Government may authorise one or more legal practitioners or chartered accountants or any of its officers to act as presenting officers and every person so authorised may present the case with respect to any appeal before the Appellate Tribunal or the Special Director (Appeals), as the case may be.

Members, etc. to be Public Servants

The Chairperson, Members and other officers and employees of the Appellate Tribunal, the Special Director (Appeals) and the Adjudicating Authority shall be deemed to be public servants within the meaning of section 21 of the Indian Penal Code (45 of 1860).

Civil court not to have Jurisdiction

No civil court shall have jurisdiction to entertain any suit or proceeding in respect of any matter which an Adjudicating Authority or the Appellate Tribunal or the Special Director (Appeals) is empowered by or under this Act to determine and no injunction shall be granted by any court or other authority in respect of any action taken or to be taken in pursuance of any power conferred by or under this Act.

Appeal to High Court

Any person aggrieved by any decision or order of the Appellate Tribunal may file an appeal to the High Court within sixty days from the date of communication of the decision or order of the Appellate Tribunal on any question of law arising out of such order:

Provided that the High Court may, if it is satisfied that the appellant was prevented by sufficient cause from filing the appeal within the said period, allow it to be filed within a further period not exceeding sixty days.

Explanation—In this section "High Court" means—

(a) The High Court within the jurisdiction of which the aggrieved party ordinarily resides or carries on business or personally works for gain; and

(b) Where the Central Government is the aggrieved party, the High Court within the jurisdiction of which the respondent, or in a case where there are more than one respondent, any of the respondents, ordinarily resides or carries on business or personally works for gain.

Directorate Of Enforcement

1. The Central Government shall establish a Directorate of Enforcement with a Director and such other officers or class of officers as it thinks fit, who shall be called officers of Enforcement, for the purposes of this Act.
2. Without prejudice to provisions of sub-section (1), the Central Government may authorise the Director of Enforcement or an Additional Director of Enforcement or a Special Director of Enforcement or a Deputy Director of Enforcement to appoint officers of Enforcement below the rank of an Assistant Director of Enforcement.
3. Subject to such conditions and limitations as the Central Government may impose, an officer of Enforcement may exercise the powers and discharge the duties conferred or imposed on him under this Act.

Power of Search, Seizure, etc

1. The Director of Enforcement and other officers of Enforcement, not below the rank of an Assistant Director, shall take up for investigation the contravention referred to in section 13.
2. Without prejudice to the provisions of sub-section (1), the Central Government may also, by notification,

authorise any officer or class of officers in the Central Government, State Government or the Reserve Bank, not below the rank of an Under Secretary to the Government of India to investigate any contravention referred to in section 13.

3. The officers referred to in sub-section (1) shall exercise the like powers which are conferred on income-tax authorities under the Income-tax Act, 1961 (43 of 1961) and shall exercise such powers, subject to such limitations laid down under that Act.

Empowering other Officers

1. The Central Government may, by order and subject to such conditions and limitations as it thinks fit to impose, authorise any officer of customs or any central excise officer or any police officer or any other officer of the Central Government or a State Government to exercise such of the powers and discharge such of the duties of the Director of Enforcement or any other officer of Enforcement under this Act as may be stated in the order.
2. The officers referred to in sub-section (1) shall exercise the like powers which are conferred on the income-tax authorities under the Income-tax Act, 1961 (43 of 1961), subject to such conditions and limitations as the Central Government may impose.

Presumption as to Documents in Certain Cases

Where any document—

(i) Is produced or furnished by any person or has been seized from the custody or control of any person, in either case, under this Act or under any other law; or

(ii) Has been received from any place outside India (duly authenticated by such authority or person and in such manner as may be prescribed) in the course of investigation of any contravention under this Act alleged to have been committed by any person, and such document is tendered in any proceeding under this Act in evidence against him, or against him and any other person who is proceeded against jointly with him, the court or the Adjudicating Authority, as the case may be, shall—

(a) Presume, unless the contrary is proved, that the signature and every other part of such document which purports to be in the handwriting of any particular person or which the court may reasonably assume to have been signed by, or to be in the handwriting of, any particular person, is in that person's handwriting, and in the case of a document executed or attested, that it was executed or attested by the person by whom it purports to have been so executed or attested;

(b) Admit the document in evidence notwithstanding that it is not duly stamped, if such document is otherwise admissible in evidence;

(c) In a case falling under clause *(i)*, also presume, unless the contrary is proved, the truth of the contents of such document.

Suspension of Operation of this Act

1. If the Central Government is satisfied that circumstances have arisen rendering it necessary that any permission granted or restriction imposed by this Act should cease to be granted or imposed, or if it considers necessary or expedient so to do in public interest, the Central Government may, by notification, suspend or relax to such extent either indefinitely or for such period as may be notified, the operation of all or any of the provisions of this Act.
2. Where the operation of any provision of this Act has under sub-section (1) been suspended or relaxed indefinitely, such suspension or relaxation may, at

any time while this Act remains in force, be removed by the Central Government by notification.

3. Every notification issued under this section shall be laid, as soon as may be after it is issued, before each House of Parliament, while it is in session, for a total period of thirty days which may be comprised in one session or in two or more successive sessions, and if, before the expiry of the session immediately following the session or the successive sessions aforesaid, both Houses agree in making any modification in the notification or both Houses agree that the notification should not be issued, the notification shall thereafter have effect only in such modified form or be of no effect, as the case may be; so, however, that any such modification or annulment shall be without prejudice to the validity of anything previously done under that notification.

Power of Central Government to Give Directions

For the purposes of this Act, the Central Government may, from time to time, give to the Reserve Bank such general or special directions as it thinks fit, and the Reserve Bank shall, in the discharge of its functions under this Act, comply with any such directions.

Contravention by Companies

1. Where a person committing a contravention of any of the provisions of this Act or of any rule, direction or order made thereunder is a company, every person who, at the time the contravention was committed, was in charge of, and was responsible to, the company for the conduct of the business of the company as well as the company, shall be deemed to be guilty of the contravention and shall be liable to be proceeded against and punished accordingly:

   Provided that nothing contained in this sub-section shall render any such person liable to punishment if he proves that the contravention took place without his knowledge or that he exercised due diligence to prevent such contravention.

2. Notwithstanding anything contained in sub-section (1), where a contravention of any of the provisions of this Act or of any rule, direction or order made thereunder has been committed by a company and it is proved that the contravention has taken place with the consent or connivance of, or is attributable to any neglect on the part of, any director, manager, secretary or other officer of the company, such director, manager, secretary or other officer shall also be deemed to be guilty of the contravention and shall be liable to be proceeded against and punished accordingly.

   Explanation—For the purposes of this section—

   (i) "Company" means any body corporate and includes a firm or other association of individuals; and

   (ii) "Director", in relation to a firm, means a partner in the firm.

Death or Insolvency in Certain Cases

Any right, obligation, liability, proceeding or appeal arising in relation to the provisions of section 13 shall not abate by reason of death or insolvency of the person liable under that section and upon such death or insolvency such rights and obligations shall devolve on the legal representative of such person or the official receiver or the official assignee, as the case may be:

Provided that a legal representative of the deceased shall be liable only to the extent of the inheritance or estate of the deceased.

Bar of Legal Proceedings

No suit, prosecution or other legal proceeding shall lie against the Central Government or the Reserve Bank or any officer of that Government or of the Reserve Bank or any other person exercising any power or discharging any functions or performing any duties under this Act, for anything in good faith done or intended to be done under this Act or any rule, regulation, notification, direction or order made thereunder.

Removal of Difficulties

1. If any difficulty arises in giving effect to the provisions of this Act, the Central Government may, by order, do anything not inconsistent with the provisions of this Act for the purpose of removing the difficulty:

   Provided that no such order shall be made under this section after the expiry of two years from the commencement of this Act.
2. Every order made under this section shall be laid, as soon as may be after it is made, before each House of Parliament.

Power to Make Rules

1. The Central Government may, by notification, make rules to carry out the provisions of this Act.
2. Without prejudice to the generality of the foregoing power, such rules may provide for,—
   (a) The imposition of reasonable restrictions on current account transactions under section 5;
   (b) The manner in which the contravention may be compounded under sub-section (1) of section 15;
   (c) The manner of holding an inquiry by the Adjudicating Authority under sub-section (1) of section 16;
   (d) The form of appeal and fee for filing such appeal under sections 17 and 19;
   (e) The salary and allowances payable to and the other terms and conditions of service of the Chairperson and other Members of the Appellate Tribunal and the Special Director (Appeals) under section 23;
   (f) The salaries and allowances and other conditions of service of the officers and employees of the

Appellate Tribunal and the office of the Special Director (Appeals) under sub-section (3) of section 27;

(g) the additional matters in respect of which the Appellate Tribunal and the Special Director (Appeals) may exercise the powers of civil court under clause *(i)* of sub-section (2) of section 28;

(h) the authority or person and the manner in which any document may be authenticated under clause *(ii)* of section 39; and

(i) any other matter which is required to be, or may be, prescribed.

Power to Make Regulations

1. The Reserve Bank may, by notification, make regulations to carry out the provisions of this Act and the rules made thereunder.
2. Without prejudice to the generality of the foregoing power, such regulations may provide for,—

(a) The permissible classes of capital account transactions, the limits of admissibility of foreign exchange for such transactions, and the prohibition, restriction or regulation of certain capital account transactions under section 6;

(b) The manner and the form in which the declaration is to be furnished under clause *(a)* of sub-section (1) of section 7;

(c) The period within which and the manner of repatriation of foreign exchange under section 8;

(d) The limit up to which any person may possess foreign currency or foreign coins under clause (a) of section 9;

(e) The class of persons and the limit up to which foreign currency account may be held or operated under clause *(b)* of section 9;

(f) The limit up to which foreign exchange acquired may be exempted under clause (d) of section 9;

(g) The limit up to which foreign exchange acquired may be retained under clause (e) of section 9;

(h) Any other matter which is required to be, or may be, specified.

Rules and Regulations to be Laid before Parliament

Every rule and regulation made under this Act shall be laid, as soon as may be after it is made, before each House of Parliament, while it is in session for a total period of thirty days which may be comprised in one session or in two or more successive sessions, and if, before the expiry of the session immediately following the session or the successive sessions aforesaid, both Houses agree in making any modification in the rule or regulation, or both Houses agree that the rule or regulation should not be made, the rule or regulation shall thereafter have effect only in such modified form or be of no effect, as the case may be; so, however, that any such modification or annulment shall be without prejudice to the validity of anything previously done under that rule or regulation.

Repeal and Saving

1. The Foreign Exchange Regulation Act, 1973 (46 of 1973) is hereby repealed and the Appellate Board constituted under sub-section (1) of section 52 of the said Act (hereinafter referred to as the repealed Act) shall stand dissolved.
2. On the dissolution of the said Appellate Board, the person appointed as Chairman of the Appellate Board and every other person appointed as Member and holding office as such immediately before such date shall vacate their respective offices and no such Chairman or other person shall be entitled to claim any compensation for the premature termination of the term of his office or of any contract of service.
3. Notwithstanding anything contained in any other law for the time being in force, no court shall take cognizance of an offence under the repealed Act and

no adjudicating officer shall take notice of any contravention under section 51 of the repealed Act after the expiry of a period of two years from the date of the commencement of this Act.

4. Subject to the provisions of sub-section (3) all offences committed under the repealed Act shall continue to be governed by the provisions of the repealed Act as if that Act had not been repealed.

5. Notwithstanding such repeal,—

   (a) Anything done or any action taken or purported to have been done or taken including any rule, notification, inspection, order or notice made or issued or any appointment, confirmation or declaration made or any licence, permission, authorization or exemption granted or any document or instrument executed or any direction given under the Act hereby repealed shall, in so far as it is not inconsistent with the provisions of this Act, be deemed to have been done or taken under the corresponding provisions of this Act;

   (b) Any appeal preferred to the Appellate Board under sub-section (2) of section 52 of the repealed Act but not disposed of before the commencement of this Act shall stand transferred to and shall be disposed of by the Appellate Tribunal constituted under this Act;

   (c) Every appeal from any decision or order of the Appellate Board under sub-section (3) or sub-section (4) of section 52 of the repealed Act shall, if not filed before the commencement of this Act, be filed before the High Court within a period of sixty days of such commencement:

   Provided that the High Court may entertain such appeal after the expiry of the said period of sixty days if it is satisfied that the appellant was prevented by sufficient cause from filing the appeal within the said period.

6. Save as otherwise provided in sub-section (3), the mention of particular matters in sub-sections (2), (4) and (5) shall not be held to prejudice or affect the general application of section 6 of the General Clauses Act, 1897 (10 of 1897) with regard to the effect of repeal.

The Conservation of Foreign Exchange

1. Short title, extent and commencement – (1) This Act may be called the Conservation of Foreign Exchange and Prevention of Smuggling Activities Act, 1974.
   (a) It extends to the whole of India.
   (b) It shall come into force on such date as the Central Government may, by notification in the Official Gazette, appoint.
2. Definitions- In this Act, unless the context otherwise requires,—
   (a) "Appropriate Government" means, as respects a detention order made by the Central Government or by an officer of the Central Government or a person detained under such order, the Central Government, and as respects a detention order made by a State Government or by an officer of a State Government or a person detained under such order, the State Government;
   (b) "Detention order" means an order made under section 3;
   (c) "Foreigner" has the same meaning as in the Foreigners Act, 1946 (31 of 1946);
   (d) "Indian customs waters" has the same meaning as in clause (28) of the Customs Act, 1962 (52 of 1962);
   (e) "Smuggling" has the same meanings as in clause (39) of section 2 of the Customs Act, 1962, and all its grammatical variations and cognate expressions shall be construed accordingly;
   (f) "State Government", in relation to a Union territory, means the Administrator thereof;

(g) Any reference in this Act to a law which is not in force in the State of Jammu and Kashmir shall, in relation to that State, be construed as a reference to the corresponding law, if any, in force in that State.

3. Power to make orders detaining certain persons –

(1) The Central Government or the State Government or any officer of the Central Government, not below the rank of a Joint Secretary to that Government, specially empowered for the purposes of this section by that Government, or any officer of the State Government, not below the rank of a Secretary to that Government, specially empowered for the purposes of this section by that Government, may, if satisfied, with respect to any person (including a foreigner), that, with a view to preventing him from acting in any manner prejudicial to the conservation or augmentation of foreign exchange or with a view to preventing him from

i. Smuggling goods, or

ii. Abetting the smuggling of goods, or

iii. Engaging in transporting or concealing or keeping smuggled goods, or

iv. Dealing in smuggled goods otherwise than by engaging in transporting or concealing or keeping smuggled goods, or

v. Harbouring persons engaged in smuggling goods or in abetting the smuggling of goods, it is necessary so to do, make an order directing that such person be detained:

[Provided that no order of detention shall be made on any of the grounds specified in this sub-section on which an order of detention may be made under section 3 of the Prevention of Illicit Traffic in Narcotic Drugs and Psychotropic Substances Act, 1988 or under section 3 of the Jammu and Kashmir

Prevention of Illicit Traffic in Narcotic Drugs and Psychotropic Substances ordinance, 1988.].

(2) When any order of detention is made by a State Government or by an officer empowered by a State Government, the State Government shall, within ten days, forward to the Central Government a report in respect of the order.

(3) For the purposes of clause (5) of article 22 of the Constitution, the communication to a person detained in pursuance of a detention order of the grounds on which the order has been made shall be made as soon as may be after the detention, but ordinarily not later than five days, and in exceptional circumstances and for reasons to be recorded in writing, not later than fifteen days, from the date of detention.

4. Execution of detention orders - A detention order may be executed at any place in India in the manner provided for the execution of warrants of arrest under the Code of Criminal Procedure, 1973 (2 of 1974).

5. Power to regulate place and conditions of detention - Every person in respect of whom a detention order has been made shall be liable -

(a) To be detained in such place and under such conditions including conditions as to maintenance, interviews or communication with others, discipline and punishment for breaches of discipline, as the appropriate Government may, by general or special order, specify; and

(b) To be removed from one place of detention to another place of detention, whether within the same State or in another State by order of the appropriate Government;

Provided that no order shall be made by a State Government under clause (b) for the removal of a person from one State to another State except with the consent of the Government of that other State.

5A. Grounds of detention severable – Where a person has been detained in pursuance of an order of detention under sub-section(1) which has been made on two or more grounds, such order of detention shall be deemed to have been made separately on each of such grounds and accordingly -

(a) Such order shall not be deemed to be invalid or inoperative merely because one or some of the grounds is or are -

i. Vague,

ii. Non-existent,

iii. not relevant,

iv. Not connected or not proximately connected with such person, or

v. Invalid for any other reason whatsoever, and it is not, therefore, possible to hold that the Government or officer making such order would have been satisfied as provided in sub-section (1) of section 3 with reference to the remaining ground or grounds and made the order of detention;

(b) The Government or officer making the order of detention shall be deemed to have made the order of detention under the said sub-section (1) after being satisfied as provided in that sub-section with reference to the remaining ground or grounds.]

6. Detention order not to be invalid or inoperative on certain grounds - No detention order shall be invalid or inoperative merely by reason -

a. That the person to be detained thereunder is outside the limited of the territorial jurisdiction of the Government or the officer making the order of detention, or

b. That the place of detention of such person is outside the said limits.

7. Powers in relation to absconding persons(1) If the appropriate Government has reason to believe that a person in respect of whom a detention order has been made has absconded or is concealing himself so that the order cannot be executed, the Government may -

   (a) Make a report in writing of the fact to a Metropolitan Magistrate or a Magistrate of the first class having jurisdiction in the place where the said person ordinarily resides; and thereupon the provisions of sections 82, 83, 84 and 85 of the Code of Criminal Procedure, 1973 (2 of 1974), shall apply in respect of the said person and his property as if the order directing that he be detained were a warrant issued by the Magistrate;

   (b) By order notified in the Official Gazette direct the said person to appear before such officer, at such place and within such period as may be specified in the order; and if the said person fails to comply with such direction, he shall, unless he proves that it was not possible for him to comply therewith and that he had, within the period specified in the order, informed the officer mentioned in the order of the reason which rendered compliance therewith impossible and of his whereabouts, be punishable therewith impossible and of his whereabouts, be punishable with imprisonment for a term which may extend to one year or with fine or with both.

   (2) Nothwithstanding anything contained in the Code of Criminal Procedure, 1973 (2 of 1974), every offence under clause(b) of sub-section (1) shall be cognizable.

8. Advisory Board- For the purposes of sub-clause (a) of clause (c) of clause (7) of article 22 of the Constitution,—

(a) the Central Government and each State Government shall, wherever necessary, constitute one or more Advisory Boards each of which shall consist of a Chairman and two other persons possessing the qualifications specified in sub-clause (a) of clause (4) of article 22 of the Constitution;

(b) Save as otherwise provided in section 9, the appropriate Government shall, within five weeks from the date of detention of a person under a detention order make a reference in respect thereof to the Advisory Board constituted under clause (a) to enable the Advisory Board to make the report under sub-clause (a) of clause (4) of article 22 of the Constitution;

(c) The Advisory Board to which a reference is made under clause (b) shall after considering the reference and the materials placed before it and after calling for such further information as it may deed necessary from the appropriate Government or from any person called for the purpose through the appropriate Government, from the person concerned, and if, in any particular case, it considers it essential so to do or if the person concerned desires to be heard in person, after hearing him person, prepare its report specifying in a separate paragraph thereof its opinion as to whether or not there is sufficient cause for the detention of the person concerned and submit the same within eleven weeks from the date of detention of the person concerned;

(d) When there is a difference of opinion among the members forming the Advisory Board the opinion of the majority of such members shall be deemed to be the opinion of the Board;

(e) A person against whom an order of detention has been made under this Act shall not be entitled to appear by any legal practitioner in any matter connected with the reference to the Advisory Board, and the proceedings of the Advisory Board and its report, excepting that part of the report in which the opinion of the Advisory Board is specified, shall be confidential;

(f) In every case where the Advisory Board has reported that there is in its opinion sufficient cause for the detention of a person, the appropriate Government may confirm the detention order and continue the detention of the person concerned for such period as it thinks fit and in every case where the Advisory Board has reported that there is in its opinion no sufficient cause for the detention of the person concerned, the appropriate Government shall revoke the detention order and cause the person to be released forthwith.

9. Cases in which and circumstances under which persons may be detained for period longer than three months without obtaining the opinion of Advisory Board- (1)Notwithstanding anything contained in this Act, any person (including a foreigner) in respect of whom an order of detention is made under this Act at any time before the 31st July, 1996, may be detained without obtaining, in accordance with the provisions of sub-clause (a) of clause (4) of article 22 of the Constitution, the opinion of an Advisory Board for a period longer than three months but not exceeding six months from the date of his detention, where the order of detention has been made against such person with a view to preventing him from smuggling goods or abetting the smuggling of goods or engaging in transporting or concealing or keeping smuggled goods and the Central Government or any Officer of the Central Government, not below the rank of an Additional Secretary to that Government, specially empowered for the purpose of this section by that Government, is satisfied that such person—

(a) Smuggles or is likely to smuggle goods into, out of or through any area highly vulnerable to smuggling; or

(b) Abets or is likely to abet the smuggling of goods into, out of or through any area highly vulnerable to smuggling; or

(c) Engages or is likely to engage in transporting or concealing or keeping smuggled goods in any area highly vulnerable to smuggling, and makes a declaration to that effect within five weeks of the detention of such person.

Explanation 1 - In this sub-section, "area highly vulnerable to smuggling" means, -

i. The Indian customs waters, contiguous to the State of Goa, Gujarat,Karnataka, Kerala, Maharashtra, Tamil Nadu and the Union territories of Daman and Diu and Pondicherry;

ii. The Inland area fifty kilometres in width from the coast of India falling within the territories of the States of Goa, Gujarat,Karnataka, Kerala, Maharashtra,Tamil Nadu and the Union territories of Daman and Diu and Pondicherry;

iii. The inland area fifty kilometres in width from the India-Pakistan border in the State of Gujarat, Jammu and Kashmir, Punjab and Rajasthan;

iv. The customs air port of Delhi; and

v. Such further or other Indian customs waters, or inland area not exceeding one hundred kilometres in width from any other coast or border of India, or such other customs station, as the Central Government may, having regard to the vulnerability of such waters, area or customs station, as the case may be, to smuggling, by notification in the Official Gazette, specify in this behalf.

Explanation 2 - (1) For the purposes of Explanation 1, "customs airport" and "customs station" shall have the same meaning as in clauses (10) and (13) of section 2 of the Customs Act, 1962 (52 of 1962), respectively.

(2) In the case of any person detained under a detention order to which the provisions of sub-section (1) apply, section 8 shall have effect subject to the following modifications, namely:

(i) In clause (b), for the words "shall, within five weeks", the words "shall, within four months and two weeks" shall be substituted;

(ii) In clause (c), -

(1) For the words "the detention of the person concerned", the words "the continued detention of the person concerned" shall be substituted;

(2) For the words "eleven weeks", the words "five months and three weeks" shall be substituted;

(iii) In clause (f), for the words "for the detention", at both the places where they occur, the words "for the continued detention" shall be substituted.

10. Maximum period of detention - The maximum period for which any person may be detained in pursuance of any detention order to which the provisions of section 9 do not apply and which has been confirmed under clause (f) of section 8 shall be a period of one year from the date of detention or the specified period, whichever period expires late and the maximum period for which any person may be detained in pursuance of any detention order to which the provisions of section 9 apply and which has been confirmed under clause (f) of section 8 read with sub- section (2) of section 9 shall be a period of two years from the date of detention or the specified period, whichever period expires later;

Provided that nothing contained in this section shall affect the power of the appropriate Government in neither case to revoke or modify the detention order at any earlier time.

Explanation In this section and section 10A - "specified period" means the period during which the Proclamation of Emergency issued under clause (1) of article 352 of the Constitution on the 3rd day of December, 1971 and the Proclamation of Emergency issued under that clause on the 25th day of June, 1975, are both in operation.

10A. Extension of period of detention—

(1) Notwithstanding anything contained in any other provision of this Act, the detention of every person detained under a detention order which has been confirmed under clause (f) of section 8 before the commencement of the Conservation of Foreign Exchange and Prevention of Smuggling Activities (Amendment) Act, 1976, and which is in force immediately before such commencement shall, unless his detention has been continued by the appropriate Government under the said clause for a period shorter than one year from the date of his detention, continue until the expiry of a period of one year from the date of his detention under such order or until the expiry of the specified period, whichever period expires later:

Provided that nothing contained in this sub-section shall affect the power of the appropriate Government to revoke or modify such detention order at any earlier time.

(2) Notwithstanding anything contained in any other provision of this Act, the detention of every person detained under a detention order which has been confirmed under clause (f) of section 8 read with sub-section (2) of section 9 before the commencement of the Conservation of Foreign Exchange and Prevention of Smuggling Activities

(Amendment) Act, 1976, and which is in force immediately before such commencement, shall, unless his detention has been continued by the appropriate Government under the said clause (f) read with the said sub-section (2) for a period shorter than two years from the date of his detention, continue until the expiry of a period of two years from the date of his detention under such order or until the expiry of the specified period, whichever period expires later:

Provided that nothing contained in this sub-section shall affect the power of the appropriate Government to revoke or modify such detention order at any earlier time.

11. Revocation of detention orders –

(1) Without prejudice to provisions of section 21 of the General Clauses Act, 1897 (10 of 1897), a detention order may, at any time, be revoked or modified -

a. Notwithstanding that the order has been made by an officer of a State Government, by that State Government or by the Central Government;

b. Notwithstanding that the order has been made by an officer of the Central Government or by a State Government, by the Central Government.

(2) The revocation of a detention order shall not bar the making of another detention order under section (3) against the same person.

12. Temporary release of persons detained –

(1) The Central Government may, at any time, direct that any person detained in pursuance of a detention order made by that Government or an officer subordinate to that Government or by a State Government or by an officer subordinate to a State Government, may be released for any

specified period either without conditions or upon such conditions specified in the directions as that person accepts, and may, at any time, cancel his release.

(1A) A State Government may, at any time, direct that any person detained in pursuance of a detention order made by that Government or by an officer subordinate to that Government may be released for any specified period either without conditions or upon such conditions specified in the direction as that person accepts, and may, at any time, cancel his release.

(2) In directing the release of any person under sub-section (1) or sub-section (1A) the Government directing the release may require him to enter into a bond with sureties for the due observance of the conditions specified in the direction.

(3) Any person released under sub-section(1) or sub-section(1A) shall surrender himself at the time and place, and to the authority, specified in the order directing his release or cancelling his release, as the case may be.

(4) If any person fails without sufficient cause to surrender himself in the manner specified in sub-section(3) he shall be punishable with imprisonment for a term which may extend to two years, or with fine, or with both.

(5) If any person released under sub-section(1) or sub-section(1A) fails to fulfill any of the conditions imposed upon him under the said sub-section or in the bond entered into by him, the bond shall be declared to be forfeited and any person bound thereby shall be liable to pay the penalty thereof.

(6) Notwithstanding anything contained in any other law and save as otherwise provided in this section, no person against whom a detention order made under this Act is in force shall be

released whether on bail or bail bond or otherwise.

12A. Special provisions for dealing with emergency - (1) Notwithstanding anything contained in this Act or any rules of natural justice, the provisions of this section shall have effect during the period of operation of the Proclamation of Emergency issued under clause (1) of article 352 of the Constitution on the 3rd day of December, 1971, or the Proclamation of Emergency issued under that clause on the 25th day of June, 1975, or a period of twenty four months from the 25th day of June, 1975, whichever period is the shortest.-

(2) When making an order of detention under this Act against any person after the commencement of the Conservation of Foreign and Prevention of Smuggling Activities (Amendment) Act, 1975, the Central Government or the State Government or, as the case may be, the officer making the order of detention shall consider whether the detention of such person under this Act is necessary for dealing effectively with the emergency in respect of which the Proclamations referred to in sub-section (1) have been issued (hereafter in this section referred to as the emergency) and if, on such consideration, the Central Government or the State Government or, as the case may be, the officer is satisfied that it is necessary to detain such person for effectively dealing with the emergency, that Government or officer may make a declaration to that effect and communicate a copy of the declaration to the person concerned:

Provided that where such declaration is made by an officer, it shall be reviewed by the appropriate Government within fifteen days from the date of making of the declaration and such declaration shall cease to have effect unless it is confirmed by that Government, after such review, within the said period of fifteen days.

(3) The question whether the detention of any person in respect of whom a declaration has been made under sub-section (2) continues to be necessary for effectively dealing with the emergency shall be reconsidered by the appropriate Government within four months from the date of such declaration and thereafter at intervals not exceeding four months, and if, one such reconsideration, it appears to the appropriate Government that the detention of the person is no longer necessary for effectively dealing with the emergency, the Government may revoke the declaration.

(4) In making any consideration, review or reconsideration under sub-section (2) or (3) the appropriate Government or officer may, if such Government or officer considers it to be against the public interest to do otherwise, act on the basis of the information and materials in its or his possession without disclosing the facts or giving an opportunity of making a representation to the person concerned.

(5) It shall not be necessary to disclose to any person detained under a detention order to which the provisions of sub-section (2) apply, the grounds on which the order has been made during the period the declaration made in respect of such person under that sub-section is in force, and, accordingly, such period shall not be taken into account for the purpose of sub-section (3) of section 3

(6) In the case of every person detained under a detention order to which the provisions of sub-section (2) apply, being a person in respect of whom a declaration has been made thereunder, the period during which such declaration is in

force shall not be taken into account for the purpose of computing -

i. The periods specified in clauses (b) and (c) of section 8

ii. The periods of "one year" and "five weeks" specified in sub-section (1), the period of "one year" specified in sub-section (2)(i), and the period of "six months" specified in sub-section (3), of section 9.

13. Protection of action taken in good faith- No suit or other legal proceeding shall lie against the Central Government or a State Government, and no suit, prosecution or other legal proceedings shall lie against any person, for anything in good faith done or intended to be done in pursuance of this Act.

14. Repeal—The Maintenance of Internal Security (Amendment) Ordinance, 1974 (11 of 1974), shall, on the commencement of this Act, stand repealed and accordingly the amendments made in the Maintenance of Internal Security Act, 1971 (26 of 1971), by the said Ordinance shall, on such commencement, cease to have effect.

Customs Valuation

In exercise of the powers conferred by Section 156 of the Customs Act, 1962 (52 of 1962), read with Section 22 of the General Clauses Act, 1897 (10 of 1897), and in supersession of the Customs Valuation Rules, 1963 except as respect things done or omitted to be done before such super session, the Central Government hereby makes the following rules, namely:—

1. Short title, commencement and application—

(1) (These rules may be called the Customs Valuation (Determination of Price of Imported Goods) Rules, 1988.

(2) They shall come into force on the 16th August, 1988.

(3) They shall apply imported goods where a duty of customs is chargeable by reference to their value.

2. Definitions– (1) In these rules, unless the context otherwise requires,-

1[(a) "Computed value" means the value of imported goods determined in accordance with rule 7A of these rules; (aa) " deductive value" means the value determined in accordance with rule 7 of these rules;]

(b) "Goods of the same class or kind", means imported goods that are within a group of range of imported goods produced by a particular industry of industrial sector and includes identical goods of similar goods;

(c) "Identical goods" means imported goods -

i. Which are same in all respects, including physical characteristics, quality and reputation as the goods being valued except for minor differences in appearance that do not affect the value of the goods;

ii. Produced in the country in which the goods being valued were produced; and

iii. produced by the same person who produced the goods, or where no such goods are available, goods produced by a different person, but shall not include imported goods where engineering, development work, art work, design work, plan or sketch undertaken in India were completed directly or indirectly by the buyer on these imported goods free of charge or at a reduced cost for use in connection with the production and sale for export of these imported goods;

(d) "Produced" includes grown, manufactured and mined;

(e) "Similar goods" means imported goods –

i. Which although not alike in all respects, have like characteristics and like component materials which enable them to perform the same functions and to be commercially interchangeable with the goods being valued having regard to the quality, reputation and the existence of trade mark;

ii. Produced in the country in which the goods being valued were produced; and

iii. Produced by the same person who produced the goods being valued, or where no such goods are available, goods produced by a different person, but shall not include imported goods where engineering, development work, art work, design work, plan or sketch undertaken in India were completed directly or indirectly by the buyer on these imported goods free of charge or at a reduced cost for use in connection with production and sale for export of these imported goods;

(f) "Transaction value" means the value determined in accordance with Rule 4 of these rules.

(2) For the purpose of these rules, persons shall be deemed to be " related " only if –

i. They are officers or directors of one another's businesses;

ii. They are legally recognized partners in business;

iii. They are employer and exployee;

iv. Any person directly or indirectly owns, controls or holds 5 percent or more of the outstanding voting stock or shares of both of them;

v. One of them directly or indirectly controls the other;

vi. Both of them are directly or indirectly controlled by a third person;

vii. Together they directly or indirectly control a third person; or

viii. They are members of the same family.

Explanation I– The term " person" also includes legal persons.

Explanation II—Persons who are associated in the business of one another in that one is the sole agent or sole distributor or sole concessionaire, however described, of the other shall be deemed to be related for the purpose of these rules, if they fall within the criteria of this sub-rule.

3. Determination of the method of valuation—For the purpose of these rules—
   i. The value of imported goods shall be the transaction value;
   ii. If the value cannot be determined under the provisions of clause (i) above, the value shall be determined by proceeding sequentially through Rules 5 to 8 of these rules.

1. Transaction value— (1) The transaction value of imported goods shall be the price actually paid or payable for the goods when sold for export to India, adjusted in accordance with the provisions of Rule 9 of these rules.

(2) The transaction value of imported goods under sub-rule (1) above shall be accepted provided that—

a. There are no restrictions as to the disposition or use of the goods by the buyer other than restrictions which are imposed or required by law or by the public authorities in India; or

- Limit the geographical area in which the goods may be resold; or
- Do not substantially affect the value of the goods;

a. The sale or price is not subject to same condition or consideration for which a value cannot be determined in respect of the goods being valued;

- no part of the proceeds of any subsequent resale, disposal or use of the goods by the buyer will accrue directly or indirectly to the seller unless an appropriate adjustment can be made in accordance with the provisions of Rule 9 of these rules; and
- the buyer and seller are not related, or where the buyer and seller are related, that transaction value is acceptable for customs purposes under the provisions of sub-rule below.

(3) (a) Where the buyer and seller are related, the transaction value shall be accepted provided that the examination of the circumstances of the sale of the imported goods indicate that the relationship did not influence the price.

(b) In a sale between related persons, the transaction value shall be accepted, whenever the importer demonstrates that the declared value of the goods being valued, closely approximates to one of the following values ascertained at or about the same time-

i. The transaction value of identical goods, or of similar goods, in sales to unrelated buyers in India;

ii. The deductive value for identical goods or similar goods;

iii. The computed value for identical goods or similar goods.]

Provided that in applying the values used for comparison, due account shall be taken of demonstrated difference in commercial levels, quantity levels, adjustments in accordance with the provisions of Rule 9 of these rules and cost incurred by the seller in sales in which he and the buyer are not related;

(c) Substitute values shall not be established under the provisions of clause (b) of this sub-rule.

1. Transaction of value of identical goods. - (1) (a) Subject to the provisions of Rule 3 of these rules, the

value of imported goods shall be the transaction value of identical goods sold for export to India and imported at or about the same time as the goods being valued.

(b) In applying this rule, the transaction value of identical goods in a sale at the same commercial level and in substantially the same quantity as the goods being valued shall be used to determine the value of imported goods.

(c) Where no sale referred to in clause (b) of sub-rule (1) of this rule, is found, the transaction value of identical goods sold at a different commercial level or in different quantities or both, adjusted to take account of the difference attributable to commercial level or to the quantity or both, shall be used, provided that such adjustments shall be made on the basis of the demonstrated evidence which clearly establishes the reasonableness and accuracy of the adjustments, whether such adjustment leads to an increase or decrease in the value. (2) Where the cost and charges referred to in sub-rule (2) of Rule 9 of these rules are included in the transaction value of identical goods, an adjustment shall be made, if there are significant differences in such costs and charges between the goods being valued and the identical goods in question arising from differences in distances and means of transport. (3) In applying this rule, if more than one transaction value of identical goods is found; the lowest such value shall be used to determine the value of imported goods.

6. Transaction value of similar goods—

(1) Subject to the provisions of Rule 3 of these rules, the value of imported goods shall be the transaction value of similar goods sold for export

to India and imported at or about the same time as the goods being valued.

(2) The provisions of clauses (b) and (c) of sub-rule (1), sub-rule (2) and sub-rule(3),of Rule 5 of these rules shall, mutatis mutandis, also apply in respect of similar goods.

Determination of value when transaction values is not available—If the value of imported goods cannot be determined under the provisions of rules 4, 5and 6, the value shall be determined under the provisions of rule 7 or, when the value cannot be determined under that rule, under rule 7A: Provided that at the request of the importer, and with the approval of the proper officer, the order of application of rules 7 and 7A shall be reversed.]

7. Deductive value—

(1) Subject to the provisions of Rule 3 of these rules, if the goods being valued or identical or similar imported goods are sold in India, in the condition as imported at or about the time at which the declaration for determination of value is presented, the value of imported goods shall be based on the unit price at which the imported goods or identical or similar imported goods are sold in the greatest aggregate quantity to persons who are not related to the sellers in India, subject to the following deductions:—

i. Either the commission usually paid or agreed to be paid or the additions usually made for profits and general expenses in connection with sales in India of imported goods of the same class or kind;

ii. The usual costs of transport and insurance and associated costs incurred within India;

iii. The customs duties and other taxes payable in India by reason of importation or sale of the goods.

(2) If neither the imported goods nor identical nor similar imported goods are sold at or about the same time of importation of the goods being valued, the value of imported goods shall, subject otherwise to the provisions of sub-rule (1) of this rule, be based on the unit price at which the imported goods or identical or similar imported goods are sold in India, at the earliest date after importation but before the expiry of ninety days after such importation.

(3) (a) If neither the imported goods not identical nor similar imported goods are sold in India in the conditions as imported, then, the value shall be based on the unit price at which the imported goods, after further processing, are sold in the greatest aggregate quantity to persons who are not related to the seller in India (b) In such determination, due allowance shall be made for the value added by processing and the deductions, provided for in items (i) to (iii) of sub-rule (1) of this rule.

Computed value—Subject to the provisions of rule 3, the value of imported goods shall be based on a computed value, which shall consist of the sum of:

a. The cost of value of materials and fabrication or other processing employed in producing the imported goods;

b. An amount for profit and general expenses equal to that usually reflected in sales of goods of the same class or kind as the goods being valued which are made by producers in the country of exportation for export to India;

c. Rhe cost or value of all other expenses under sub-rule (2) of rule 9 of these rules.]

8. Residual method—(1) Subject to the provisions of Rule 3 of these rules, where the value of imported goods cannot be determined under the provisions of

any of the preceding rules, the value shall be determined using reasonable means consistent with the principles and general provisions of these rules and sub-section (1) of Section 14 of the Customs Act, 1962 (52 of 1962) and on the basis of data available in India. (2) No value shall be determined under the provisions of (5) this rule on the basis of-

i. The selling price in India of the goods produced in India;
ii. A system which provides for the acceptance for customs purposes \ of the highest of the two alternative values;
iii. The price of the goods on the domestic market of country of exportation; [(iii a) the cost of production other than computed values which have been determined for identical or similar goods in accordance with the provisions of rule 7A.]
iv. The price of the goods for the export to a country other than India;
v. Minimum customs values; or
vi. Arbitrary or fictitious values.

9. Cost and services— (1) In determining the transaction value, there shall be added to the price actually paid or payable for the imported goods,-
   (a) The following cost and services, to the extent they are incurred by the buyer but are not included in the price actually paid or payable for the imported goods, namely:
      i. Commissions and brokerage, except buying commissions;
      ii. the cost of containers which are treated as being one for customs purposes with the goods in question;
      iii. the cost of packing whether for labour or materials;

(b) The value, apportioned as appropriate, of the following goods and services where supplied directly or indirectly by the buyer free of charge or at reduced cost for use in connection with the production and sale for export of imported goods, to the extent that such value has not been included in the price actually paid of payable, namely:

i. Materials, components, parts and similar items incorporated in the imported goods;

ii. Tools, dies, moulds and similar items used in the production of the imported goods;

iii. Materials consumed in the production of the imported goods;

iv. Engineering, development, art work, design work, and and plans and sketches undertaken elsewhere than in India and necessary for the production of the imported goods;

(c) Royalties and license fees related to the imported goods that the buyer is required to pay, directly or indirectly, as a condition of the sale of the goods being valued, to the extent that such royalties and fees are not included in the price actually paid or payable.

(d) The value of any part of the proceeds of any subsequent resale, disposal or use of the imported goods that accrues, directly or indirectly, to the seller;

(e) All other payments actually made or to be made as a condition of sale of the imported goods, by the buyer to the seller, or by the buyer to a third party to satisfy an obligation of the seller to the extent that such payments are not included in the price actually paid of payable.

(2) For the purposes of sub-section (1) and sub section (1A) of section14 of the Customs Act, 1962 (52 of 1962) and these rules, the value of the imported goods shall be the value of such goods, for delivery

at the time and place of importation and shall include—

a. The cost of transport of the imported goods to the place of importation;

b. Loading, unloading and handling charges associated with the delivery of the imported goods at the place of importation; and

c. The cost of insurance:

   i. Where the coast of transport referred to in clause (a) is not ascertainable, such cost shall be twenty percent of the free on board value of the goods;

   ii. The charges referred to in clause (b) shall be one per cent of the free on board value of the goods plus the coast of transport referred to in clause (a) plus the coast of insurance referred to in clause (c);

   iii. Where the coast referred to in clause (c) is not ascertainable, such cost shall be 1.125% of free on board value of the goods;

Provided further that in the case of goods imported by air, where the cost referred to in clause (a) is ascertainable, such cost shall not exceed twenty per cent of free on board value of the goods:

Provided also that where the free on board value of the goods is not ascertainable, the coasts referred to in clause (a) shall be twenty per cent of the free on board value of the goods plus cost of insurance for clause (i) above and the cost referred to in clause (c) shall be 1.125 % of the free on board value of the goods plus cost of transport for clause (iii) above].

(3) Additions to the price actually paid or payable shall be made under this rule on the bases of objective and quantifiable data.

(4) No addition shall be made to the price actually paid or payable in determining the value of the imported goods except as provided for in this rule.

10. Declaration by the importer–

(1) The importer or his agent shall furnish –

a. A declaration disclosing full and accurate details relating to the value of imported goods; and

b. Any other statement, information or document including an invoice of the manufacturer or producer of the imported goods where the oops are imorted from or through a person other than the manufacturer or producer, as considered necessary by the proper officer for determination of the value of imported goods under these rule.]

(2) Nothing contained in these rules shall be construed as restricting or calling into question the right of the proper officer of customs to satisfy himself as to the truth or accuracy of any statement, information, document or declaration presented for valuation purposes.

(3) The provisions of the Customs Act, 1962 (52 of 1962) relating to confiscation, penalty and prosecution shall apply to cases where wrong declaration, information, statement or documents are furnished under these rules.

10A. Rejection of declared value - (1) When the proper officer has reason to doubt the truth or accuracy of the value declared in relation to any imported goods, he may ask the importer of such goods to furnish further information including documents or other evidence and if, after receiving such further information, or in the absence of a response of such importer, the proper officer still has reasonable doubt about the truth or accuracy of the value so declared, it shall be deemed that the value of such imported goods cannot be determined under the provisions of sub-rule (1) of rule 4.(2) At the request of and importer, the proper officer, shall intimate the importer in writing the grounds for doubting the truth or accuracy of the value declared in relation to goods imported by such importer and provide a reasonable opportunity of being heard, before taking a final decision under sub-rule (1).]

11. Settlement of dispute— In case of dispute between the importer and the proper officer of customs valuing the goods, the same shall be resolved consistent with the provisions contained in sub-section (1) of Section 14 of the Customs Act, 1962 (52 of 1962).
12. Interpretative Notes— The interpretative notes specified in the Schedule to these rules shall apply for the interpretation of these rules.
    1. Substituted by M.F. (D.R) Notification No.26/95-Cus.(N.T.),dated 24-4-1995.
    2. Inserted by M.F.(D.R.) Notification No.26/95-Cus,(N.T.), dated 24-4-1995.
    3. Inserted by M.F.(D.R.) Notification No.26/95-Cus.(N.T.), dated 24-4-1995.
    4. Inserted by M.F.(D.R.) Notification No.26/95-Cus.(N.T.),dated 24-4-1995
    5. Substituted by M.F.(D.R.)F.No.528/167/88-Cus.,(TV)/ICD, dated 6-9-1988.
    6. Inserted by M.F.(D.R.)Notification No.26/95-Cus.(N.T.),dated 24-4-95
    7. Substituted by M.F.(D.R.)Notification No.39/90(N.T.)-Cus., dated 5-7-1990
    8. Substituted (w.e.f.1-10-1991) by M.F.(D.R.) Notification No.67/91 Cus. (N.T.), dated 1-10-1991.
    9. Inserted by M.F.(D.R.)Notification No.10/98-Cus.(N.T.),dated 19-2-1998.

The Schedule

General Note:

Use of generally accepted accounting principles

1. " Generally accepted accounting principles" refer to the recognized consensus or substantial authoritative

support within a country at a particular time as to which economic resources and obligations shall be recorded as assets and liabilities, which changes in assets and liabilities should be recórded, how the assets and liabilities and changes in them should be measured, what information should be disclosed and how it should be disclosed and which financial statements should be prepared. These standards may be broad guidelines of general application as well as detailed practices and procedures.

Notes to Rules

Note to Rule 2

In Rule 2(2) (v), for the purposes of these rules, one person shall be deemed to control another when the former is legally or operationally in a position to exercise restraint or direction over the latter.

Note to Rule 4

Price actually Paid or Payable

The price actually paid or payable is the total payment made or to be made by the buyer to or for the benefit of the seller for the imported goods. The payment need not necessarily take the form of a transfer of money. Payment may be made way of letters of credit or negotiable instruments. Payment may be made directly or indirectly. An example of an indirect payment would be the settlement by the buyer, whether in whole or in part, of a debt owed by the seller.

Activities undertaken by the buyer on his own account, other that those for which an adjustment is provided in Rule 9, are not considered to be and indirect payment to the seller, even though they might be regarded as of benefit to the seller. The costs of such activities shall not, therefore, be added to the price actually paid or payable in determining the value of imported goods.

The value of imported goods shall not include the following charges or costs provided that they are distinguished from the price actually paid or payable for the imported goods: Charges for construction, erection, assembly, maintenance or technical assistance, undertaken after importation on imported goods such as industrial plant, machinery or equipment;

a. The cost of transport after importation;

b. Duties and taxes in India.

The price actually paid or payable refers to the price for the imported goods. Thus the flow of dividends or other payments from the buyer to the seller that do not relate to the imported goods are not part of the customs value.

Rule 4(2)(a)(iii)

Among restrictions which would nòt render a price actually paid or payable unacceptable are restrictions which do not substantially affect the value of the goods. An example of such restrictions would be the case where a seller requires a buyer of automobiles no to sell or exhibit them prior to a fixed date which represents the beginning of a model year.

Rule 4(2)(b)

If the sale or price is subject to some condition or consideration for which a value cannot be determined with respect to the goods being valued, the transaction value shall not be acceptable for customs purposes. Some examples of this include:

a. The seller establishes the price of the imported goods on condition that the buyer will also buy other goods in specified quantities;

b. The price of the imported goods is dependent upon the price or prices at which the buyer of the imported goods sells other goods to the seller of the imported goods;

c. The price is established on the basis of a form of payments extraneous to the imported goods, such as where the imported goods are semi-finished goods which have been provided by the seller on condition that he will receive a specified quantity of the finished goods.

However, conditions or considerations relating to the production or marketing of the imported goods shall to result in rejection of the transaction value. For example, the fact that the buyer furnishes the seller with engineering and plans undertaken in India shall not result in rejection of the transaction value for the purposes of Rule 4. Likewise, if the buyer undertakes on his own account, even though by agreement with the seller, activities relating to the marketing or the imported goods, the value of these activities is not part of the value of imported goods nor shall such activities result in rejection of the transaction value.

Rule 4(3)

1. Rule 4(3) (a) and Rule 4(3) (b) provide different means of establishing the acceptability of a transaction value.
2. Rule 4(3) (a) provides that where the buyer and the seller are related, the circumstances surrounding the sale shall be examined and the transaction value shall be accepted as the value of imported goods provided that the relationship did not influence the price. It is not intended that there should be an examination of the circumstances in all cases where the buyer and the seller are related. Such examination will only be required where there are doubts about the acceptability of the price. Where the proper officer of customs has no doubts about the acceptability of the price, it should be accepted without requesting further information from the importer. For example, the proper officer of customs may have previously examined the relationship, or he may already have detailed information concerning the buyer and the seller, and may already be satisfied from such examination or information that the relationship did not influence the price.
3. Where the proper officer of customs is unable to accept the transaction value without further inquiry, he should give the importer an opportunity to supply

such further detailed information as may be necessary to enable him to examine the circumstances surrounding the sale. In this context, the proper officer of customs should be prepared to examine relevant aspects of the transaction, including the way in which the buyer and seller organize their commercial relations and the way in which the price in question was arrived at, in order to determine whether the relationship influenced the price. Where it can be shown that the buyer and seller, although related under the provisions of Rule 2(2), buy from and sell to each other as if they were not related, this would demonstrate that the price had not been influenced by the relationship. As example of this, if the price had been settled in a manner consistent with the normal pricing practices of the industry in question or with the way the seller settles prices for sales to buyers who are not related to him, this would demonstrate that the price had not been influenced by the relationship. As a further example, where it is shown that the price is adequate to ensure recovery of all costs plus a profit which is representative of the firm's overall profit realized over a representative period of time (e.g. on an annual basis) in sales of goods of the same class or kind, this would demonstrate that the price had not been influenced.

4. Rule 4(3)(b) provides an opportunity for the importer to demonstrate that the transaction value closely approximates to a "test" value previously accepted by the proper offer of customs and is therefore acceptable under the provisions of rule 4. Where a test under rule 4(3) (b) is met, it is not necessary to examine the question of influence under [Rule 4(3)(a)]. If the proper officer of customs has already sufficient information to be satisfied, without further detailed inquiries, that one the tests provided in rule 4(3)(b) has been met, there is no reason for him to require the importer to demonstrate that the test can

be met. In rule 4(3)(b) the term " unrelated buyers" means buyers who are not related to the seller in any particular case.

Rule 4(3)(b)

A number of factors must be taken into consideration in determining whether one value " closely approximates" to another value. These factors include the nature of the imported goods, the nature of the industry itself, the season in which the goods are imported, and whether the difference in value is commercially significant. Since these factors may vary from case to case, it would be impossible to apply a uniform standard such as a fixed percentage, in each case. For example, a small difference in value in a case involving one type of goods could be unacceptable while a large difference in a case involving another type of goods might be acceptable in determining whether the transaction value closely approximates to the "test" values set forth in rule 4(3)(b).

Notes to Rule 5

1. In applying rule 5, the proper officer of customs shall, wherever possible, use a sale of identical goods at the same commercial level and in substantially the same quantities as the goods being valued. Where no such sale is found, a sale of identical goods that takes place under any one of the following three conditions may be used:
   a. A sale at the same commercial level but in different quantities;
   b. A sale at a different commercial level but in substantially the same quantities; or
   c. A sale at a different commercial level and in different quantities.
2. Having found a sale under any one of these three conditions adjustments will then be made, as the case may be, for:
   a. Quantity factors only;
   b. commercial level factors only; or

(c) both commercial level and quantity factors.

3. For the purposes of rule 5, the transaction value of identical imported goods means a value, adjusted as provided for in rule 5(1)(b) and (c) and rule 5(2), which has already been accepted under rule 4.
4. A condition for adjustment because of different commercial levels or different quantities is that such adjustment, whether it leads to an increase or a decrease in the value, be made only on the basis of demonstrated evidence that clearly establishes the reasonableness and accuracy of the adjustment, e.g. valid price lists containing prices referring to different levels or different quantities. As an example of this, if the imported goods being valued consist of a shipment of 10 units and the only identical imported goods for which a transaction value exists involved a sale of 500 units, and it is recognized that the seller grants quantity discounts, the required adjustment may be accomplished by resorting to the seller's price list and using that price applicable to a sale of 10 units. This does not require that a sale had to have been made in quantities of 10 as long as the price list has been established as being bona fide through sales at other quantities. In the absence of such an objective measure, however, the determination of a value under the provisions of rule 5 is not appropriate.

Note to Rule 6

1. In applying rule 6, the proper officer of customs shall, wherever possible, use a sale of similar goods at the same commercial level and in substantially the same quantities as the goods being valued. For the purpose of rule 6, the transaction value of similar imported goods means the value of imported goods, adjusted as provided for in rule 6(2) which has already been accepted under rule 4.

2. All other provisions contained in note to rule 5 shall mutatis mutandis also apply in respect of similar goods.

Note to Rule 7

1. The term "unit/price at which.... Goods are sold in the greatest aggregate quantity" means the price at which the greatest number of units is sold in sales to persons who are not related to the persons from whom they buy such goods at the first commercial level after importation at which such sales take place.
2. As an example of this, goods are sold from a price list which grants favourable unit prices for purchases made in larger quantities.

Sale quantity Unit price Number of sales Total quantity sold at each price1-10 units 100 10 sales of 5 units, 65.5 sales of 3 units 11-25 units 95 5 sales of 11 units. 55 over 25 units 90 1 sale of 30 units 80

1 Sale of 50 Units

The greatest number of units sold at a price is 80, therefore, the unit price in the greatest aggregate quantity is 90.

- As another example of this, two sales occur, in the first sale 500 units are sold at a price of 95 currency units each. In the second sale 400 units are sold at a price of 90 currency units each. In this example, the greatest number of units sold at a particular price is 500, therefore, the unit price n the greatest aggregate quantity is 95.
- A third example would be the following situation where various quantities are sold at various prices.

 a. Sales sale quantity Unit price

40 units 100	30 units 90
15 units 100	50 units 95
25 units 105	35 units 90
5 units 100	

b. Total quantity sold Unit price

65 90	50 95
60 100	25 105

In this example, the greatest number of units sold at a particular price is 65, therefore, the unit price in the greatest aggregate quantity is 90.

1. Any sale in India, as described in paragraph 1 above to a person who supplies directly or indirectly free of charge or at reduced cost for use in connection with the production and sale for export of the imported goods any of the elements specified in rule 9(1) (b), should not be taken into account in establishing the unit price for the purposes of rule 7.
2. It should be noted that "profit and general expenses" referred to in rule 7(1) should be taken as a whole. The figure for the purposes of this deduction should be determined on the basis of information supplied by or on behalf of the importer unless his figures are inconsistent with those obtaining in sales in India, of imported goods of the same class or kind. Where the importers figures are inconsistent with such figures, the amount for profit and general expenses may be based upon relevant information other than that supplied by or on behalf of the importer.
3. The "general expenses" include the direct and indirect costs of marketing the goods in question.
4. Local taxes payable by reason of the sale of the goods for which deduction is not made under the provisions of rule 7(1)(iii) shall be deducted under the provisions of rule 7(1)(i).
5. In determining either the commissions or the usual profits and general expenses under the provisions of rule 7(1), the question whether certain goods are "of the same class or kind" as other goods must be determined on a case-by-case basis by reference to the circumstances involved. Sales in India, of the

narrowest group or range of imported goods of the same class or kind, which includes the goods being valued, for which the necessary information can be provided, should be examined. For the purposes of rule 7 "goods of the same class or kind" includes goods imported from the same country as the goods being valued as well as goods imported from other countries.

6. For the purposes of rule 7(2) the "earliest date" shall be the date by which sales of the imported goods or of identical or similar imported, goods are made in sufficient quantity to establish the unit price.

7. Where the method in rule 7(3) is used, deductions made for the value added by further processing shall be based on objective and quantifiable data relating to the cost of such work. Accepted industry formulas, recipes, methods or construction, and other industry practices would form the basis of the calculations.

8. It is recognized that the method of valuation provided for in rule 7(3) would normally not be applicable when, as a result of the further processing, the imported goods lose their identity. However there can be instances where, although the identity of the imported goods is lose their identity. However there can be instances where, although the identity of the imported goods is lost, the value added by the processing can be determined accurately without unreasonable difficulty. On the other hand, there can also be instances where the imported goods maintain their identity but form such a minor elements in the goods sold in the country of importation that the use of this valuation method would be unjustified. In view of the above, each situation of this type must be considered on a case-by-case basis.

Note to Rule 7A

1. As a general rule, value of imported goods is determined under these rules on the basis of

information readily available in India. In order to determine a computed value, however, it may be necessary to examine the costs of producing the goods being valued and other information which has to be obtained from outside India. Furthermore, in most cases, the producer of the goods will be outside the jurisdiction of the proper officer. The use of the computed value method will generally be limited to those cases where the buyer and seller are related, and the producer is prepared to supply to the proper officer the necessary costing and to provide facilities for any subsequent verification which may be necessary.

2. The "cost or value" referred to in clause (a) of rule 7A is to be determined on the basis of information relating to the production of the goods being valued supplied by or on behalf of the producer. It is to be based upon the commercial accounts of the producer, provided that such accounts are consistent with the generally accepted accounting principles applied in the country where the goods are produced.
3. The "cost or value" shall include the cost of elements specified in clauses (1)(a)(ii) and (1)(a)(iii) of rule 9. It shall also include the value, apportioned as appropriate under the provisions of the relevant note to rule 9, of any element specified in rule 9(1)(b) which has been supplied directly or indirectly by the buyer for use in connection with the production of the imported goods. The value of the elements specified in rule 9(1)(b)(iv) which are undertaken in India shall be included only to the extent that such elements are charged to the producer. It is to be understood that no cost or value of the elements referred to in this paragraph shall be counted twice in determining the computed value.
4. The "amount for profit and general expenses" referred to in clause (b) of rule 7A is to be determined

on the basis of information supplied by or on behalf of the producer unless the producer's figures are inconsistent with those usually reflected in sales of goods of the same class or kind as the goods being valued which are made by producers in the country of exportation for export to India.

5. It should be noted in this context that the "amount for profit and general expenses" has to be taken as a whole. It follows that if, in any particular case, the producer's profit figure is low and his general expenses are high, the producer's profit and general expenses taken together may nevertheless be consistent with that usually reflected in sales of goods of the same class or kind. Such a situation might occur, for example, if a product were being launched in India and the producer accepted a nil or low profit to offset high general expenses associated with the launch. Where the producer can demonstrate a low profit on his sales of the imported goods because of particular commercial circumstances, his actual profit figures should be taken into account provided that he has valid commercial reasons to justify them and his pricing policy reflects usual pricing policies in the branch of industry concerned. Such a situation might occur for example, where producers have been forced to lower prices temporarily because of an unforeseeable drop in demand, or where they sell goods to complement a range of goods being produced in India and accept a low profit to maintain competitivity. Where the producer's own figures for profit and general expenses are not consistent with those usually reflected in sales of goods of the same class or kind as the goods being valued which are made by producers in the country of exportation for export to India, the amount for profit and general expenses may be based upon relevant information other than that supplied by or on behalf of the producer of the goods.

6. The "general expenses" referred to in clause(b) of rule 7A covers the direct and indirect costs of producing and selling the goods for export which are not included under clause (a)of rule 7A.
7. Whether certain goods are "of the same class or kind" as other goods must be determined on a case-by-case basis with reference to the circumstances involved. In determining the usual profits and general expenses under the provisions of rule 7A, sales for export to India of the narrowest group or range of goods, which includes the goods being valued, for which the necessary information can be provided, should be examined. For the purposes of rule 7A "goods of the same class or kind" must be from the same country as the goods being valued.

Note to Rule 8

1. Value of imported goods determined under the provisions of rule 8 should to the greatest extent possible, be based on previously determined customs values.
2. The methods of valuation to be employed under rule 8 may be those laid down in (rules 4 to 7A), inclusive, but a reasonable flexibility in the application of such methods would be in conformity with the aims and provision of rule 8.
3. Some examples of reasonable flexibility are as follows:
    a. Identical goods — The requirement that the identical goods should be imported at or about the same time as the goods being valued could be flexibly interpreted; identical imported goods produced in a country other than the country of exportation of the goods being valued could be the basis for customs valuation; customs values of identical imported goods already determined under the provisions of (rules 7 and 7A) could be used.

b. Similar goods – The requirement that the similar goods should be imported at or about the same time as the goods being valued could be flexibly interpreted; similar imported goods produced in a country other than the country of exportation of the goods being valued could be the basis for customs valuation; customs values of similar imported goods already determined under the provisions of (rules 7 and 7A) could be used.

c. Deductive method – The requirement that the goods shall have been sold in the "condition as imported" in rule 7(1) could be flexibly interpreted; the ninety days requirement could be administered flexibly.

Note to Rule 9

In rule 9(1)(a)(i), the term "buying commissions" means fees paid by an importer to his agent for the service of representing him abroad in the purchase of the goods being valued.

Rule 9(1)(b)(ii)

1. There are two factors involved in the apportionment of the elements specified in rule 9(1)(b)(ii) to the imported goods - the value of the element itself and the way in which that value is to be apportioned to the imported goods. The apportionment of these elements should be made in a seasonable manner appropriate to the circumstances and in accordance with generally accepted accounting principles.

2. Concerning the value of the element, if the importer acquires the element from a seller not related to him at a given cost, the value of the element is that cost. If the element was produced by the importer or by a person related to him, its value would be the cost of producing it. If the element had been previously used by the importer, regardless of whether it had been

acquired or produced by such importer, the original cost of acquisition or production would have to be adjusted downward to reflect its use in order to arrive at the value of the element.

3. Once a value has been determined for the element it is necessary to apportion that value to the imported goods. Various possibilities exist. For example, the value might be apportioned to the first shipment if the importer wishes to pay duty on the entire value at one time. As another example, the importer may request that the value be apportioned over the number of units produced up to the time of the first shipment. As a further example, he may request that the value be apportioned over the entire anticipated production where contracts or firm commitments exists for that production. The method of apportionment used will depend upon the documentation provided by the importer.

4. As an illustration of the above, an importer provides the producer with a mould to be used in the production of the imported goods and contracts with him to buy 10,000 units. By the time of arrival of the first shipment of 1,000 units the producer has already produced 4,000 units. The importer may request the proper officer of customs to apportion the value of the mould over 1,000 units, 4,000 units or 10,000 units.

Rule 9(1)(b)(iv)

1. Additions for the elements specified in rule 9(1)(b)(iv) should be based on objective and quantifiable data. In order to minimize the burden for both the importer and proper officer of customs in determining the values to be added, data readily available in the buyer's commercial record system should be used in so far as possible.

2. For those elements supplied by the buyer which were purchased or leased by the buyer, the addition would

be the cost of the purchase or the lease. No addition shall be made for those elements available in the public domain, other than the cost of obtaining copies of them.

3. The case with which it may be possible to calculate the values to be added will depend on a particular firm's structure and management practice, as well as its accounting methods.
4. For example, it is possible that a firm which imports a variety of products from several countries maintains the records of its design centre outside the country of importation in such a way as to show accurately the costs attributable to a given product. In such cases, a direct adjustment may appropriately be made under the provisions of rule 9.
5. In another case, a firm may carry the cost of the design centre outside the country of importation as a general overhead expense without allocation to specific products. In this instance, an appropriate adjustment could be made under the provisions of rule 9 with respect to the imported goods by apportioning total design centre costs over total production benefiting from the design centre and adding such apportioned cost on a unit basis to imports.
6. Variations in the above circumstances will, of course, require different factors to be considered in determining the proper method of allocation.
7. In cases where the production of the element in question involves a number of countries and over a period of time, the adjustment should be limited to the value actually added to that element outside the country of importation.

Rule 9(1)(c)

1. The royalties and license fees referred to in rule 9(1) (c) may include among other things, payments in

respect to patents, trademarks and copyrights. However, the charges for the right to reproduce the imported goods in the country of importation shall not be added to the price actually paid or payable for the imported goods in determining the customs value.

2. Payments made by the buyer for the right to distribute or resell the imported goods shall not be added to the price actually paid or payable for the imported goods if such payments are not a condition of the sale for export to the country of importation of the imported goods.

Rule 9(3)

Where objective and quantifiable data do not exist with regard to the additions required to be made under the provisions of rule 9, the transaction value cannot be determined under the provisions of rule 4. As an illustration of this, a royalty is paid on the basis of the price in a sale in the importing country of a litre of particular product that was imported by the kilogram and made up into a solution after importation. If the royalty is based partially on the imported goods and partially on other factors, which have nothing to do with the imported goods (such as when the imported goods are mixed with domestic ingredients and are no longer separately identifiable, or when the royalty cannot be distinguished from special financial arrangements between the buyer and the seller), it would be inappropriate to attempt to make an addition for the royalty. However, if the amount of this royalty is based only on the imported goods and can be readily quantified, an addition to the price actually paid or payable can be made.

1. Substituted by M.F. (D.R.) Letter F.No 528/167/88-Cus.(TU/ICD), dated 28.10.1988.
2. Inserted by M.F.(D.R.) Notification No.26/95-Cus.(N.T.),dated 24-4-1995.
3. Subsitituted by M.F.(D.R.) Notification No.26/95-Cus.(N.T.),dated 24-4-1995.

4. Subsitituted by M.F.(D.R.)Notification No.26/95-Cus.(N.T.),dated 24-4-1995.
5. Substituted by M.F.(D.R.)Notification No.26/95-Cus.(N.T.),dated 24-4-95.

Smugglers And Foreign Exchange Manipulators

An Act to provide for the forfeiture of illegally acquired properties of smugglers and foreign exchange manipulators and for matters connected therewith or incidental thereto; Whereas for the effective prevention of smuggling activities and foreign exchange manipulations which are having a deleterious effect on the national economy it is necessary to deprive persons engaged in such activities and manipulations of their ill-gotten gains; And whereas such persons have been augmenting such gains by violations of wealth-tax, income-tax or other laws or by other means and have thereby been increasing their resources for operating in a clandestine manner; And whereas such persons have in many cases been holding the properties acquired by them through such gains in the names of their relatives, associates and confidants. Be it enacted by Parliament in the Twenty-sixth Year of the Republic of India as follows:

1. Short title, Extent and Commencement

1. This act may be called the Smugglers and Foreign Exchange Manipulators (Forfeiture of Property) Act, 1976.
2. It extends to the whole of India except the State of Jammu and Kashmir.
3. It shall be deemed to have come into force on the 5th day of November, 1975.

2. Application

(1) The provisions of this Act shall apply only to the persons specified in sub-section (2).

(2) The persons referred to in sub-section (1) are the following, namely:

(a) Every person:

(i) Who has been convicted under the Sea Customs Act, 1878 (8 of 1878), or the Customs Act, 1962 (52 of 1962), of an offence in relation to goods of a value exceeding one lakh of rupees; or

(ii) Who having been convicted under the Sea Customs Act, 1878 (8 of 1878), or the Customs Act, 1962 (52 of 1962), has been convicted subsequently under either of those Acts; or

(iii) Who having been convicted under the Foreign Exchange Regulation Act, 1947 (7 of 1947), or the Foreign Exchange Regulation Act, 1973 (46 of 1973), has been convicted subsequently under either or those Act;

(b) Every person in respect of whom an order of detention has been made under the Conservation of Foreign Exchange and Prevention of Smuggling Activities Act, 1974 (52 of 1974):Provided that-

(i) Such order of detention, being an order which the provisions of section 9 or section 12A of the said Act do not apply, has not been revoked on the report of the Advisory Board under section 8 of the said Act or before the receipt of the report of the Advisory Board or before making a reference to the Advisory Board; or

(ii) Such order of detention, being an order to which the provisions of section 9 of the said Act apply, has not been revoked before the expiry of the time for, or on the basis of, the review under sub-section (3) of section 9 or on the report of the Advisory board under section 8, read with sub-section (2) of section 9, of the said Act; or

(iii) Such order of detention, being an order to which the provisions of section 12A of the said Act apply, has not been revoked before the expiry of the time for, or on the basis of, the first review under sub-section (3) of that section, or on the basis of the report of the Advisory Board under section 8, read with sub-section (6) of section 12A, of that Act; or

(iv) Such order of detention has not been set aside by a Court of competent jurisdiction;

(c) Every person who is a relative of person referred to in clause (a) or clause (b);

(d) Every associate of a person referred to in clause (a) or clause (b);

(e) Any holder (hereafter in this clause referred to as the present holder) of any property which was at any time previously held by a person referred to in clause (a) or clause (b) unless the present holder or, as the case may be, any one who held such property after such person and before the present holder, is or was a transferee in good faith for adequate consideration.

Explanation 1

For the purposes of sub-clause (i) of clause (a), the value of any goods in relation to which a person has been convicted of an offence shall be the wholesale price of the goods in the ordinary cause of trade in India as on the date of the commission of the offence.

Explanation 2

For the purposes of clause (c), "relative", in relation to a person, means:

(i) Spouse of the person;

(ii) Brother or sister of the person;

(iii) Brother or sister of the spouse of the person;

(iv) Any lineal ascendant or descendant of the person;

(v) Any lineal ascendant or descendant of the spouse of the person;

(vi) Spouse of a person referred to in clause (ii), clause (iii), clause (iv) or clause (v);

(vii) Any lineal descendant of a person referred to in clause (ii) or clause (iii).

Explanation 3

For the purposes of clause (d), "associate", in relation to a person, means-

(i) Any individual who, had been or is residing in the residential premises (including out-houses) of such person;

(ii) Any individual who had been or is managing the affairs or keeping the accounts of such person;

(iii) Any association of persons, body of individuals, partnership firm, or private company within the meaning of the Companies Act, 1956 (1 of 1956), of which such person had been or is a member, partner or director;

(iv) Any individual who had been or is a member, partner or director of an association of persons, body of individuals, partnership firm or private company referred to in clause (iii) at any time when such person had been or is a member, partner or director of such association, body, partnership firm or private company;

(v) Any person who had been or is managing the affairs, or keeping the accounts, of any association of persons, body of individuals, partnership firm or private company referred to in clause (iii);

(vi) The trustee of any trust, where,-

(a) The trust has been created by such person; or

(b) The value of the assets contributed by such person (including the value of the assets, if any, contributed by him earlier) to the trust amounts, on the date on which the contribution is made, to not less than twenty per cent of the value of the assets of the trust on that date;

(vii) Where the competent authority, for reasons to be recorded in writing, considers that any properties of such person are held on his behalf by any other person, such other person.

Explanation 4:

For the avoidance of doubt, it is hereby provided that the question whether any person is a person to whom the provisions of this Act apply may be determined with reference to any facts, circumstances or events (including any conviction or detention) which occurred or took place before the commencement of this Act

2A. Act not to Apply to Certain Persons

On and from the commencement of the provisions of the Narcotic Drugs and Psychotropic Substances Act, 1985 (61 of 1985), the provisions of this Act shall not apply to persons in relation to whom any order, or proceeding, may be made or taken under that Chapter.

3. Definitions

1. In this Act, unless the context otherwise requires,

"Appellate Tribunal" means the Appellate Tribunal for Forfeited Property constituted under section 12;

"competent authority" means an officer of the Central Government authorised by it under sub-section (1) of section 5 to perform the functions of a competent authority under this Act;

"illegally acquired property", in relation to any person to whom this Act applies, means-

(i) Any property acquired by such person, whether before or after the commencement of this act, wholly or partly out of or by means of any income, earnings or assets derived or obtained from or attributable to any activity prohibited by or under any law for the time being in force relating to any matter in respect of which Parliament has power to make laws; or

(ii) Any property acquired by such person, whether before or after the commencement of this Act, wholly or partly out of or by means of any income, earnings or assets in respect of which any such law has been contravened; or

(iii) Any property acquired by such person, whether before or after the commencement of this Act, wholly or partly out of or by means of any income, earnings or assets the source of which cannot be proved and which cannot be shown to be attributable to any act or thing done in respect of any matter in relation to which Parliament has no power to make laws; or

(iv) Any property acquired by such person, whether before or after the commencement of this Act, for a consideration, or by any means, wholly or partly traceable to any property referred to in sub-clauses (i) to (iii) or the income or earnings from such property and includes-any property held by such person which would have been, in relation to any previous holder thereof, illegally acquired property under this clause if such previous holder had not ceased to hold it, unless such person or any other person who held the property at any time after such previous holder or, where there are two or more such previous holders, the last of such previous holders is or was a transferee in good faith for adequate consideration; any property acquired by such person, whether before or after the commencement of this Act, for a consideration, or by any means, wholly or partly traceable to any property falling under item (A), or the income or earnings therefrom; "prescribed" means prescribed by rules made under this Act; "property" includes any interest in property, movable or immovable; "trust" includes any other legal obligation. (2) Any reference in this Act to any law which is not in force in any area shall, in relation to that area, be construed as a reference to the corresponding law, if any, in force in that area. (3) Any reference in this Act to any officer or authority shall, in relation to any area in which there is no officer or authority with the same designation, be construed as a reference to such officer or authority as may be specified by the central Government by notification in the Official Gazette.

4. Prohibition of Holding Illegally Acquired Property

(1) As from the commencement of this Act, it shall not be lawful for any person to whom this Act applies to hold any illegally acquired property either by himself or through any other person on his behalf.

(2) Where any person holds any illegally acquired property in contravention of the provisions of sub-section (1), such property shall be liable to be forfeited to the Central Government in accordance with the provisions of this Act.

5. Competent Authority

(1) The Central Government may, by order published in the Official Gazette, authorise as many officers of the Central Government (non below the rank of a Joint Secretary to the Government), as it thinks fit, to perform the functions of the competent authority under this Act.

(2) The competent authorities shall perform their functions in respect of such persons or classes or persons as the Central Government may, by order, direct.

6. Notice of Forfeiture

(1) If, having regard to the value of the properties held by any person to whom this Act applies, either by himself or through any other person on his behalf, his known sources, of income, earnings or assets, and any other information or material available to it as a result of action taken under section 18 or otherwise,

the competent authority has reason to believe (the reasons for such belief to be recorded in writing) that all or any of such properties are illegally acquired properties, it may serve a notice upon such person (hereinafter referred to as the person affected) calling upon him within such time as may be specified in the notice, which shall not be ordinarily less than thirty days, to indicate the sources of his income, earnings or assets, out of which or by means of which he has acquired such property, the evidence on which he relies and other relevant information and particulars, and to show cause why all or any of such properties, as the case may be, should not be declared to be illegally acquired properties and forfeited to the Central Government under this Act.

(2) Where a notice under sub-section (1) to any person specifies any property as being held on behalf of such person by any other person, a copy of the notice shall also be served upon such other person.

7. Forfeiture of Property in Certain Cases:

(1) The competent authority may, after considering the explanation, if any, to the show-cause notice issued under section6, and the materials available before it and after giving to the person affected (and in a case where the person affected holds any property specified in the notice through any other person, to such other person also) a reasonable opportunity of being heard, by order, record a finding whether all or any of the properties in question are illegally acquired properties.

(2) Where the competent authority is satisfied that some of the properties referred to in the show-cause notice are illegally acquired properties but is not able to identify specifically such properties, then, it shall be lawful for the competent authority to specify the properties which, to the best of its judgment, are illegally acquired properties and record a finding accordingly under sub-section (1).

(3) Where the competent authority records a finding under this section to the effect that any property is illegally acquired property, it shall declare that such property shall, subject to the provisions of this Act, stand forfeited to the central Government free from all encumbrances.

(4) Where any shares in a company stand forfeited to the Central Government under this Act, then, the company shall, notwithstanding any thing contained in the Companies Act, 1956 (1 of 1956), or the articles of association of the company, forthwith register the Central Government as the transferee of such shares.

8. Burden of Proof

In any proceedings under this Act, the burden of proving that any property specified in the notice served under section 6 in not illegally acquired property shall be on the person affected.

9. Fine in Lieu of Forfeiture

(1) Where the competent authority makes declaration that any property stands forfeited to the Central Government under section 7 and it is a case where the source of only a part, being less than one-half, of the income, earnings or assets with which such property was acquired has not been proved to the satisfaction of the competent authority, it shall make an order giving an option to the person affected to pay, in lieu of forfeiture, a fine equal to one and one-fifth times the value of such part.

Explanation:

For the purposes of this sub-section, the value of any part of income, earnings or assets, with which any property has been acquired, shall be,-

(a) In the case of any part of income of earnings, the amount of such part of income of earnings;

(b) In the case of any part of assets, the proportionate part of the full value of the consideration for the acquisition of such assets.

(2) Before making an order imposing a fine under sub-section (1), the person affected shall be given a reasonable opportunity of being head.

(3) Where the person affected pays the fine due under sub-section (1), within such time as may allowed in that behalf, the competent authority may, by order, revoke the declaration of forfeiture under section 7 and thereupon such property shall stand released.

10. Procedure in Relation to Certain trust Properties

In the case of any person referred to in clause (vi) of Explanation 3 to sub-section (2) of section 2, if the competent authority, on the basis of the information and materials available to it, has reason to believe (the reasons for such belief to be recorded in writing) that any property held in trusts in illegally acquired property, it may serve a notice upon the author of the trust or, as the case may be, the contributor of the assets out of or by means of which such property was acquired by the trust and the trustees, calling upon them within such time as may be specified in the notice which shall not ordinarily be less than thirty days, to explain the source of the money or other assets out of or by means of which such property was acquired or, as the case may be, the source of the money or other assets which were contributed to the trust for acquiring such property and thereupon such notice shall be deemed to be a notice served under section 6 and all other provisions of this Act shall apply accordingly.

Explanation:

For the purposes of this section "illegally acquired property", in relation to any property held in trust, includes-

(i) Any property which if it had continued to be held by the author of the trust of the contributor of such property to the trust would have been illegally acquired property in relation to such author or contributor;

(ii) Any property acquired by the trust out of any contributions made by any person which would have been illegally acquired property in relation to such person had such person acquired such property out of such contributions.

11. Certain transfers to be Null and Void

Where after the issue of a notice under section 6 or under section 10, any property referred to in the said notice is transferred by any mode whatsoever such transfer shall, for the purposes of the proceedings under this Act, be ignored and if such property is subsequently forfeited to the Central Government under section 7, then, the transfer of such property shall be deemed to be null and void.

12. Constitution of Appellate Tribunal

(1) The Central Government may, be notification in the Official Gazette, constitute an Appellate Tribunal to be called the Appellate Tribunal for Forfeited Property consisting of a Chairman and such number of other members (being officers of the Central Government not below the rank of a Joint secretary to the Government) as the Central Government thinks fit, to be appointed by that Government for hearing appeals against the orders made under section 7, sub-section (1) of section 9 or section 10.

(2) The Chairman of the Appellate Tribunal shall be a person who is or has been or is qualified to be a judge of the Supreme Court or of a High Court.

(3) The terms and conditions of service of the Chairman and other members shall be such as may be prescribed.

(4) Any person aggrieved by an order of the competent authority made under section 7, sub-section (1) of

section 9 or section 10, may, within forty-five days from the date on which the order is served on him, prefer an appeal to the Appellate Tribunal.

Provided that the Appellate Tribunal may entertain any appeal after the said period of forty-five days, but not after sixty days, from the date aforesaid if it is satisfied that the appellant was prevented by sufficient cause from filling the appeal in time.

(5) On receipt of an appeal under sub-section (4), the Appellate Tribunal may, after giving an opportunity to the appellant to be heard, if he so desires, and after making such further enquiry as it deems fit, confirm, modify or set aside the order appealed against.

(6) The powers and functions of the Appellate tribunal may be exercised and discharged by Benches consisting of three members and constituted by the Chairman of the Appellate Tribunal.

(6A)Notwithstanding anything contained in sub-section (6), where the Chairman considers it necessary so to do for the expeditious disposal of appeals under this section, he may constitute a Bench of two members and a Bench so constituted may exercise and discharge the powers and functions of the Appellate Tribunal:

Provided that if the members of a Bench so constituted differ on any point or points, they shall state the point or points on which they differ and refer the same to a third members (to be specified by the chairman) for hearing on such point or points and such point or points shall be decided according to the opinion of that member.

(7) The Appellate Tribunal may regulate its own procedure.

(8) On application to the Appellate Tribunal and on payment of the prescribed fee, the Tribunal may

allow a party to any appeal or any person authorised in this behalf by such party to inspect at any time during office hours, any relevant records and registers of the Tribunal and obtain a certified copy of any part thereof.

13. Notice Or order not to be Invalid For error in Description

No notice issued or served, no declaration made, and no order passed, under this Act shall be deemed to be invalid by reason of any error in the description of the property or person mentioned therein if such property or person is identifiable from the description so mentioned.

14. Bar of Jurisdiction

No order passed or declaration made under this Act shall be appealable except as provided therein and no civil court shall have jurisdiction in respect of any matter which the Appellate Tribunal or any competent authority is empowered by or under the Act to determine, and no injunction shall be granted by any Court or other authority in respect of any action taken or to be taken in pursuance of any power conferred by or under this Act.

15. Competent Authority and Appellate Tribunal to have Powers of Civil court

The competent authority and the Appellate tribunal shall have all the powers of a civil court while trying a suit under the Code of Civil Procedure, 1908 (5 of 1908), in respect of the following maters, namely:

(a) Summoning and enforcing the attendance of any person and examining him on oath;

(b) Requiring the discovery and production of documents;

(c) Receiving evidence on affidavits;

(d) Requisitioning any public record or copy thereof from any court or office;

(e) Issuing commissions for examination of witnesses or documents;

(f) Any other matter which may be prescribed.

16. Information to Competent Authority

(1) Notwithstanding anything contained in any other law, the competent authority shall have power to require any officer or authority of the central Government or a State Government of a local authority to furnish information in relation to such persons, points or matters as in the opinion of the competent authority will be useful for, or relevant to, the purposes of this Act.

(2) Any officer of the Income-tax Department, the Customs Department or the Central Excise Department or any officer of Enforcement appointed under the Foreign Exchange Regulation Act, 1973 (46 of 1973), may furnish suo motu any information available with him to the competent authority if in the opinion of the officer such information will be useful to the competent authority for the purposes of this Act.

17. Certain Officers to Assist Competent Authority and Appellate Tribunal

For the purposes of any proceedings under this Act, the following officers are hereby empowered and required to assist the competent authority and the Appellate Tribunal, namely:

(a) Officers of the Customs Department;

(b) Officers of the Central Excise Department;

(c) Officers of the Income-tax Department;

(d) Officers of Enforcement appointed under the Foreign Exchange Regulation Act, 1973 (46 of 1973);

(e) Officers of Police;

(f) Such other officers of the Central of State Government as are specified by the Central Government in this behalf by notification in the Official Gazette.

18. Power of Competent Authority to Require Certain Officers to Exercise certain Powers:

(1) For the purposes of any proceedings under this Act or the initiation of any such proceedings, the competent authority shall have power to cause to be conducted any inquiry, investigation or survey in respect of any person, place, property, assets, documents, books of account or any other relevant matters.

(2) For the purposes referred to in sub-section (1), the competent authority may, having regard to the nature of the inquiry, investigation or survey, require an officer of the Income-tax Department to conduct or cause to be conducted such inquiry, investigation or survey.

(3) Any officer of the Income-tax Department who is conducting or is causing to be conducted any inquiry, investigation or survey required to be conducted under sub-section (2), may, for the purpose of such inquiry, investigation or survey, exercise any power (including the power to authorise the exercise of any power) which may be exercised by him for any purpose under the Income-tax Act, 1961 (43 of 1961), and the provisions of the said Act shall, so far as may be, apply accordingly.

19. Power to Take Possession:

(1) Where any property has been declared to be forfeited to the Central Government under this Act, or where the person affected has failed to pay the fine due under sub-section (1) of section 9 within the time allowed therefore under sub-section (3) of the section, the competent authority may order the person affected as well as any other person who may be in possession of the property to surrender or deliver possession thereof to the competent authority or to any person duly authorised by it in this behalf within thirty days of the service of the order.

(2) If any person refuses or fails to comply with an order made under sub-section (1), the competent authority may take possession of the property and may for that purpose use such force as may be necessary.

(3) Notwithstanding anything contained in sub-section (2), the competent authority may, for the purpose of taking possession of any property referred to in sub-section (1), requisition the service of any police officer to assist the competent authority and it shall be the duty of such officer to comply with such requisition.

20. Rectification of Mistakes

With a view to rectifying any mistakes apparent from the record, the competent authority or the Appellate Tribunal, as the case may be, may amend any order made by it within a period of one year from the date of the order:

Provided that if any such amendment is likely to affect any person prejudicially, it shall not be made without giving to such person a reasonable opportunity of being heard.

21. Findings under other Laws not Conclusive for Proceedings under this Act

No finding of any officer of authority under any other law shall be conclusive for the purposes of any proceedings under this act.

22. Service of Notices and Orders

Any notice or order issued or make under this Act shall be served:

(a) By tendering the notice or order or sending it by registered post to the person for whom it is intended or to his agent;

(b) If the notice or order cannot be served in the manner provided in clause (a), by affixing it on a conspicuous place in the property in relation to which the notice or order is issued or made, or on some conspicuous part of the premises in which the person for whom it is intended is known to have last resided or carried on business or personally worked for gain.

23. Protection of Action taken in Good Faith

No suit, prosecution or other proceeding shall lie against the Central Government or any Officer of the Central or State Government for any thing which is done, or intended to be done, in good faith, in pursuance of this Act or the rules made thereunder.

24. Act to have Overriding Effect

The provisions of this Act shall have effect notwithstanding any thing inconsistent therewith contained in any other law for the time being in force.

25. Provisions of the Act not to Apply to Certain Properties Help in Trust

Nothing contained in this Act shall apply in relation to any property held by a trust or an institution created or established wholly for public, religious or charitable purposes if:

(i) Such property has been so held by such trust or institution from a date prior to the commencement of this Act.

(ii) Such property is wholly traceable to any property held by such trust or institution prior to the commencement of this Act.

26. Power to Make Rules

(1) The Central Government may, by notification in the Official Gazette, make rules to carry out the provisions of this Act.

(2) In particular and without prejudice to the generality of the foregoing power, such rules may provide for all or any of the following matters, namely:

(a) The terms and conditions of service of the chairman and other members of the Appellate Tribunal under sub-section (3) of section 12;

(aa) the fees which shall be paid for the inspection of the records and registers of the Appellate Tribunal or for obtaining a certified copy of any part thereof under sub-section (8) of section 12;

(b) the powers of a civil court that may be exercised by the competent authority and the Appellate Tribunal under clause (f) of section 15;

(c) any other matter which has to be, or may be, prescribed.

Chapter 4

Tracking Transaction at Hotels

TRACKING TRANSACTION

An advanced computer-based electronic security management system is instrumental in making the Mirage Resort Hotel a progressive facility. Security has assumed an increasingly important role in the hotel business. The larger the facility and the more diverse the features, services, and amenities, the more demanding the need for comprehensive security management. Nowhere is this more evident than at a 100-acre entertainment complex like the Mirage Resort Hotel in Las Vegas, where security concerns are heightened by the cash-intensive casino operation.

The creation of a fully integrated security environment at the Mirage represents an exciting new dimension in security management. Opened in 1989, the desert resort is among the most progressive facilities of its type. The Mirage has three 30-story towers and more than 3,000 rooms, including suites, villas, and bungalows with private pools. Two ballrooms, at 20,000- and 40,000-square feet, are available for special events, and meeting rooms can handle groups up to 5,000 people. The complex includes waterfalls, an erupting volcano, a tropical plant atrium, and an artificial coral reef aquarium with sharks and tropical fish. Also available for the enjoyment of guests and visitors are natural animal habitats: one for a pair of rare Royal White tigers, the other for six Atlantic Bottlenose dolphins.

An array of entertainment, recreational, and shopping opportunities are featured, including a 1,500-seat theater and around-the-clock casino operations. Guests can find restaurants, health and fitness centres, interconnected lagoon-shaped swimming pools, boutiques, and lounges. Special events such as prize fights and boat and auto shows compound the importance of security.

Security control in a gaming resort as large and complex as the Mirage is a demanding and never-ending challenge. Sophisticated security controls are in force in the casino, where millions of dollars are transacted every hour in games, including slot machines, video poker, keno, craps, blackjack, baccarat, and poker. Strict compliance with gaming laws and established casino procedures is controlled by close supervision, surveillance, and carefully monitored audits.

An advanced computer-based electronic security management system, the Polaroid ID-2000 Plus, plays a central role in supporting the Mirage's integrated security environment. The system has proven to be a formidable management tool. Designed for expansion, the modular system is a core component in the recording and payroll programme.

The system combines advanced data base, computer, and electronic imaging technologies. It provides, for example, a streamlined ID card and badge production capability and a responsive, economical way to manage employee-related security information.

The system also serves as an auditing aid to track activities, such as the number of meals served to employees in the cafeteria each day. Swipe readers at cash registers in the cafeteria make the process fast and efficient.

Specific information about the resort's 7,000 employees is input, stored, and retrieved by the digital electronic security management system. It captures image data, including colour portraits and signatures; generates photo ID cards and management reports; and communicates with other data bases. Report-generating capabilities simplify the tracking of ID cards that have been issued for active and former employees. The system also facilitates the monitoring of staff levels.

The electronic production and data base system is connected to a file server in the computer centre. Several sites are now on-line by means of a local area network (LAN) using standard Ethernet connections and Novell network software. Additional terminals or systems can be added for expansion. One of the locations integrated by the LAN is the ID card and badge production centre in the human resources department. New employees are processed and badged at this location; other areas on the network use the system to validate employee security information.

Verification terminals are installed in the security and finance departments, casino surveillance, and the casino cash cage. Authorized individuals can validate, on-screen, employee photos, signatures, and related data. Although verification information is easily obtained by entering an employee number, access to the complete data base is limited to supervisory personnel. Information available for access includes the employee's full name, signature sample, colour portrait, ID number, job title, work location, and date of hire or termination. The individual's affiliation as a Mirage employee or corporate employee is shown.

Powering the system is a high-speed 386 CPU using special workstation software, which incorporates password authorization and an internal audit trail to prevent system abuse. Using an optional 180 megabyte magnetic disk, the Mirage system can store approximately 14,000 full-colour portraits or 11,500 portraits and signatures. Optional storage modules, including larger capacity magnetic disk drives and optical disk drives, are available.

Active files, including signatures, colour portraits, and related textual information, are safely stored in digital format on the hard disk. Safety backups of the complete system are made on magnetic tape by the computer centre at least three times a week. If an employee is terminated or quits, the photo and signature files are deleted to save storage space. Text files, however, are stored indefinitely.

Information systems helped define the requirements and objectives of the departments involved. The system has improved productivity on several operating levels. Working closely with Polaroid engineers, information systems developed a maintenance strategy with flexible service levels and contingency provisions for priority service in designated areas. If emergency maintenance service is required, downtime in critical operations will be minimized.

Producing more than 6,000 ID CARDS a year could be an expensive, time-consuming operation. For the Mirage's human resources department, however, it is merely routine.

Human resources is responsible for processing new employees, issuing new ID cards and badges, replacing damaged or lost badges, and responding to the continuing need for special events badges. To handle the challenges of ID card production the company relies on the production speed and efficiency of the computer-based security management system.

"Compared to the marathon effort involved in producing new ID cards when the Mirage first opened," reflects Monalee Stockner, human resources supervisor, "normal day-to-day activities are calm." ID cards were produced for more than 7,000 employees by the human resources team, with assistance from several temporary employees and a few of the management system devices on loan from Polaroid.

Employee processing and imaging activities were completed during a five-day whirlwind operation involving 10- to 12-hour shifts. Cards were assembled at night. According to Stockner, "Without the speed and automated features of the computerized production system, the job could not have been done as quickly, economically, or efficiently."

The electronic production workstation includes an operator console consisting of a colour video camera, electronic flash lighting, portrait and text monitors, keyboard, and a signature capture device. A colour film recorder, film cutter, laminator, and print development timers are included in the output unit.

Information acquisition for an ID card, including text entries and video imaging of the subject's portrait and signature, takes less than five minutes per person. The badge is given to the employee the same day. Temporary special event IDs are produced for employees assigned to such activities as large parties, banquets, conventions, and prize fights. Since the Mirage was opened, more than 50,000 employee ID cards have been produced.

An operator can enter employee information and capture, digitally store, and retrieve high-fidelity colour portraits and signatures or access data from existing computer data bases. A freeze-frame feature allows the operator to preview and freeze the subject's video portrait before the card is made.

A built-in signature capture camera stores signatures from a signed signature card. At the touch of a button the system electronically merges the digitized video portrait, signature, text, and multicolour Mirage logo contained in the software package.

Information entered is contained on a new-hire document prepared by the employee's department. It includes pertinent information about the employee, his or her job title, and where he or she works.

ID cards can be produced in many of visual formats. More than a dozen variations are used by the Mirage to distinguish between different personnel classifications and affiliations. These include Mirage employees, corporate staff, and contractors. Special formats have also been developed for restricted areas or for temporary use at special events.

Although the electronic security management system can automatically assign sequential employee numbers, human resources prefers to control this function. In this way, blocks of numbers can be reserved for special applications in the system.

When the employee number is entered, a bar code representing the number is automatically generated and printed on an adhesive-back label by a printer. Inexpensive, hard-copy, black-and-white thermal reference images can also be produced in seconds by a printer at the production station.

With a single keystroke, electronically assembled images for two separate employee badges are exposed on a sheet of instant colour print film. Development takes about a minute. Prints are then die-cut and inserted into a special laminate sandwich with a printed insert containing card use guidelines and the bar code label. The envelope is then permanently sealed. The finished card is attractive, durable, and virtually tamperproof. After lamination the bar code is verified with a test device, which displays the employee number.

Remotely Located Verication

Terminals integrated through the LAN facilitate employee recognition, signature validation, and confirmation of employment status.

In addition to the information verification capabilities of the production workstation, data verification terminals on the network provide valuable information for security and management-related functions.

Security staff. Responsible for the safety of patrons and protection of the Mirage's physical assets, the security staff also plays an active role in maintaining guest relations and providing emergency services.

The 275-person security staff, larger than the police departments of many small cities, operates around the clock. Security's responsibilities include controlling access in restricted areas, knowing the location of employees in emergencies, and monitoring property removal.

"The ability to access an employee's security records in seconds, to determine where they can be located, saves valuable time in an emergency," says Jennifer Keeney, security coordinator. "We can locate an employee quickly, for example, should there be an emergency at home, without having to make lots of phone calls and be faced with unnecessary delays. We can see what the person looks like and even get fast thermal prints to help our staff recognize the person. In emergencies, visual recognition is extremely important, especially with a work force involving thousands of people."

Photo ID badges need not be worn in most areas. Employees can carry the ID card in a wallet or purse. In instances where individuals are not recognized by security personnel at employee entrances or in restricted areas, they will be asked to show their ID card. ID information for new hires or terminated employees is available at all verification terminals on a same-day basis.

In yet another important function, the ability to compare signatures with samples stored in the security management system's digital memory has streamlined the Mirage's property removal procedures. Because signatures of people authorized to approve property passes can be easily validated, it is now easier to control the removal of property. Thermal prints of authorized signatures for property removal forms are kept on file and current at various security stations.

Casino surveillance. Rapid information verification is critical for the casino surveillance group. Operating around the clock, 365 days a year, a team of trained observers keeps a watchful eye on cash transactions, operational procedures, and dealer interactions with patrons.

Patricia Cipolla, director of surveillance, is emphatic about the importance of security control. "Our job," she states, "is to protect the Mirage's assets and its patrons. We watch the money and the way the games are run. Any deviation in established procedures signals that something may be wrong."

Ceiling-mounted video cameras can record the activities at any game in the casino. Videotapes of randomly selected games or those being monitored are available for review on video monitors located in the surveillance area.

Should a transaction involving markers, redemption slips, bills, and credits, or a dealer's performance deviate from established guidelines, information about the dealer can be accessed instantly. Since the videotape can be seen in normal or close-up modes, surveillance specialists start the process by zooming in on the dealer's name badge. By entering the name at the verification terminal, employee information is instantly displayed, including a colour portrait and signature sample.

If irregularities are observed, other than what appears to be an honest mistake, the surveillance team may continue monitoring the dealer. A random check of a particular table could, for example, reveal a disparity between the dealer's photo and the name shown on the badge. This disparity would be checked out immediately with a casino supervisor.

In other instances, the dealer's name may not appear on the casino schedule for the shift. The disparity could be attributed to a last-minute schedule change, which can be easily verified by calling the floor supervisor. Occasionally, casino accounting is advised that an audit of documents pertaining to a particular game may be warranted.

"Instant access to employee information, especially ID pictures, makes our job a lot easier," says Cipolla. "It often took hours or days to scour through computer printouts to pinpoint the person involved in a specific transaction. The task can now be done in minutes. The search process, which also involved phone calls to casino supervisors, wasted valuable time, was cumbersome, and expensive."

Casino accounting. Casino accounting operates two shifts a day and is responsible for important audit functions for the Mirage's gaming activities. The department is responsible for maintaining the casino's operational integrity and for strict compliance with established procedures.

Timely information about gaming activities and people who authorize transactions is necessary for effective management. "The most important piece of information available," comments Robert Galvin, casino accounting manager, "is an employee's ID number. For us, it provides the means to access a key piece of data, employee signature samples."

The accounting department's data verification terminal provides instant access to information needed for transaction audits. Matching photos to names or comparing signature samples with those appearing on documents is extremely helpful.

Cash cage. Because of the large amounts of money involved, the casino cash cage may require complete ID verification, including signatures and photos of unfamiliar people. In the past, matching signatures on cash disbursement forms or receipts to signature cards took hours or even days to accomplish. It now takes minutes.

Performing rapid searches of information with specific parameters, such as name, employee number, title, department, and job description, has resulted in significant productivity improvement.

"Immediate access to essential information," says Galvin, "has resulted in better control, increased audit speed, and reduced labour hours. Since we've been linked to the security management system, productivity has improved dramatically." The verification terminal, also used by internal auditing and gaming control board personnel, allows greater audit frequency and improved monitoring of money flow.

An innovative time and attendance system, to be fully implemented by early 1993, is being phased into the Mirage's operations on a controlled schedule. The ambitious undertaking is expected to produce enormous cost savings and efficiency improvements while providing significant benefits for both employees and management. As an integral part of a comprehensive management control system, badges provide the media for time clock entries.

According to Ernie Pearce, director of information systems, "The new time and attendance system, now in use by several departments, is one of the most progressive programmes to be introduced at the Mirage. The sophisticated, computerized time-keeping and payroll system improves the interaction between supervisors and the work force. It also eliminates many of the payroll-related transaction errors that inconvenienced employees and wasted valuable company time.

"The ability to use the benefits of the security management system's large data base, along with the photo ID badge as a clock entry system," continues Pearce, "provides important functional and economic advantages."

Using sophisticated computer-based time clocks with bar code readers, the new system integrates employee work-time and payroll information with the security management data base. In this way, a long-standing information gap has been bridged. The new, high-tech computer-based clocks—to be located at every work location—will allow employees to use their ID cards to log in and out in a virtually error-free system.

The "smart" clocks are programmed with all the necessary operating parameters. These include authorized clock locations for different departments, employees' normal start and stop times, and overtime pay scales, including holidays, IRS regulations, and applicable union rules.

The new system will improve efficiency and minimize transaction discrepancies, such as illegible manual entries. It will also eliminate time-keeping problems for people working at remote locations or whose work locations vary.

In the past, bar codes have been used only to track the number of meals served in the cafeteria. With the new time-keeping system, however, they will play a more significant role in overall efficiency.

An opaque strip covering the bar code prevents tampering and reduces the likelihood that copies could be used to fool the clocks. Appearing opaque to the eye and to copy machines, the protected bar code is scanned without difficulty by bar code readers. Applied to the inside of the laminate envelope, the strip is considered tamperproof.

The Mirage's electronic security management system, which has been in operation for more than two years, has provided cost-effective solutions for a variety of problems. Software-driven and modular, important upgrades can be achieved simply by replacing a disk or a module.

The combined data base, management, and electronic imaging system is easy to use, requires minimal training, and is inexpensive to operate. During its first 18 months of operation the system was on-line 24 hours a day, seven days a week, with virtually trouble-free performance.

An international company was preparing to evacuate 15 expatriate employees and dependents from a country that had suffered an earthquake. When it came time to meet at the departure point, 25 people showed up. Those arranging for the evacuation had not known that two technical teams were in the country supporting clients at the time. The additional evacuees, who had heard of the evacuation informally from individuals at the local office, disrupted the company's plan.

There were not enough vehicles to get everyone to the airport in one trip, and there were not enough seats on the airplane that had been reserved. The other employees had made their way to the departure point hoping to get a seat because the local office employee did not tell them of the limited transportation or inform them that it would be safer to wait in the hotel until other transportation could be arranged.

The company evacuated the 15 people originally expected at that time, and the additional 10 employees were flown out two days later. This meant that an evacuation that should have been completed in approximately 12 hours— from when the employees and dependents arrived at the rendezvous point until they actually departed—ended up lasting 60 hours. Fortunately, everyone was able to get out safely, but the delay could have been disastrous.

As companies seek new business in far-flung markets, their employees increasingly need to travel and work around the globe. Companies must be prepared to help these employees through any contingencies, including earthquakes, civil unrest, and other crises.

While some risks are greater in developing countries, emergency situations requiring evacuation can arise anywhere. For instance, Singapore, a relatively safe and natural-disaster-free city, suffered from severe smog in 1999 as the result of forest fires that were raging in nearby Indonesia. The conditions made the city unbearable and forced many foreign personnel to evacuate. Other examples of such incidents include an earthquake in Taiwan, civil unrest in Indonesia, a coup in Fiji, and the invasion of Kuwait—all of which necessitated the evacuation of international personnel.

Most companies with international operations have detailed plans in place for evacuating their expatriate personnel should the local security situation deteriorate or in case of a natural disaster. But as the case highlighted at the beginning of this article illustrates, these plans often fail to address the evacuation of another category of employees; Those who are visiting on a business trip when a disaster strikes.

The evacuation of international travelers often falls between the travel advisory service, which provides employees with information on areas where it might be dangerous to travel, and evacuation planning efforts, which focus on expatriate personnel based in the country. Many companies do not even know how many employees are visiting a particular international location. In the event of an emergency, they might spend hours, if not days, trying to determine which employees are there.

This problem especially affects companies that are organized along functional lines rather than geographically. It is not uncommon for an in-country office to report to a certain department, such as marketing. Personnel from other departments might travel in and out of the country without ever contacting the local office.

To avoid confusion, companies must coordinate their travel security and international evacuation programmes. Corporate security should serve as a central point for activity and information related to evacuation planning, coordinating the role of other players in the travel process, such as internal departments, travel service providers, employees, host country offices, and hotels.

How travel information is collected, maintained, and distributed will vary among companies. Generally, however, security should not bother with routine tracking of employee travel plans. Instead, the security department can enlist the help of various internal departments to ensure that it is able to locate employees on travel in an emergency. For example, security should ask human resources or travel service providers to collect the data on employee travel. In an emergency, security will know that it can turn to this resource for the information.

Security may want to ask the company's public relations department to communicate the details of the travel and evacuation plan to staff as part of the internal communications programme.

Travel Service Provider

A company's travel service provider, whether a company employee or outside firm, can play an important role in gathering information about employees traveling abroad. Generally, these firms keep detailed records for billing purposes, and those records can help the security department to determine the location of employees when needed. The travel service company could also provide weekly or daily reports of which employees are traveling and to where.

In addition to regular reports, the travel service provider should be able to give the company access to its staffs travel records 24 hours a day in case of an emergency. Many companies have erroneously assumed that they could get the necessary staff location information from travel service providers in an emergency.

The provider can also be required to book only designated hotels, perhaps ones where corporate security has verified the safety and security of the facility. In addition, because travel itineraries often change while employees are on the road, if the travel service provider has an office in a host country, employees can contact it to change hotel and flight reservations rather than going directly to the hotel or airline. This means that the changes will immediately be keyed into the system, and the information can be distributed to the corporate security department or another internal point of contact, such as human resources. In addition, the provider can be asked to include emergency telephone numbers and procedures with each airline ticket issued to employees.

The security department should periodically audit the programme for tracking employee travel to make sure that the records are being kept and that the contact telephone numbers and other information are all up to date. It also might be useful to test the programme under simulated conditions.

At the same time, security needs to keep the travel agent advised of any high-risk areas so that he or she can caution current or future travelers or, in serious cases, refer them back to security. In companies where there is an approval system for travel, those responsible for approving travel requests must be brought into the system so that they don't approve travel to "no-go" areas.

Employees

In many cases, employees make their own travel changes by contacting the airline or hotel directly, or they use the hotel concierge or business centre. Employees should be required to advise a designated corporate contact or the travel service provider of these changes.

Some companies now require employees to submit weekly movement sheets listing travel destinations and contact details for the week to come. It is generally advisable to include these schedules with some other form of business report, such as the employees' weekly progress or sales reports, to increase the level of compliance.

One multinational telecommunications company, which has employees traveling to more than 20 countries every day of the year, implemented a Web-based itinerary tracking system to allow employees to update their travel schedules online. Employees can use any computer with Internet access to enter the password-protected site and update their information.

Host Country Offices

The company's offices abroad are also important players in the security process. Though it would be difficult for international offices to report all of the internal travel movements of visiting employees, they should at least be required to track which employees are visiting their countries and where they are staying. This task can be made easier by requiring the traveling employees to check in with the local office or to go there to connect to the computer network or access their corporate e-mail account.

If the local offices will be responsible for making in-country travel and accommodation arrangements for visiting employees, they should be required to use only designated hotels and they should be asked to provide contact information for hotels and transportation providers as well as other reservation details to headquarters.

One company with several international offices encouraged travelers to check in with the local offices by setting up workstations specifically for travelers and providing technical support to help them connect to the corporate mail system. This approach worked well, especially in the countries where local communications were unreliable.

However, the company neglected to put in place a system for the local office to report to headquarters about the travelers in the country. When an earthquake struck, the main office did not know how many employees were in the vicinity of the earthquake or how to locate them. The information was available at the local office, but it was unreachable.

At a minimum, international offices should be required to monitor the internal travel of visitors if a situation shows signs of deteriorating, even if they do not track which employees are visiting their country during normal times. They should also be able to locate and provide assistance, including evacuation, for visiting employees.

Similarly, headquarters or travel vice providers should notify the host country office when employees plan to travel there, though in practice this depends on the company. For instance, if another division of the company runs the host country office, the traveler's division might not even have the contact details for the host country office. Also intra-office politics plays a role.

Host Country Hotels

The hotels that employees use while traveling play an important part in the security process. A strong business relationship between a company and the hotel can be key. The more nights per year that the company contracts for, the more willing a hotel will be to comply with additional security demands. For instance, contracts with hotels can require them to report to a designated corporate contact when employees are staying there and to provide assistance to the employees in case of an emergency. Also, hotels can be expected to provide basic medical care through a contracted doctor as well as emergency cash.

Larger hotels that employ a full-time security manager are preferable. The hotel security manager can be given procedures to follow for corporate employees if an evacuation is necessary. These procedures should provide detailed instructions on how and to where employees should be evacuated.

Any reporting procedures and phone numbers for relevant contacts should also be given to the hotel's security manager. Obviously, there will be costs associated with services such as evacuating employees, and arrangements for payment must be made with the hotel.

Nonresident Situations

An international nonprofit organization was holding a conference with 150 delegates in a country where it did not have a representative office. The organization had been meticulous with its evacuation planning for all the countries where it had offices, but it failed to draw up a plan for the conference locale. As a result, when civil unrest suddenly erupted, the organization struggled to get everyone out of the area safely.

All the delegates had come from different parts of the world on many different airlines, and they were staying at hotels scattered around the city. When the company tried to get the delegates out, gathering them together and trying to book 150 people on about 20 different airlines initially proved to be an impossible task. Later, the organization decided to prioritize the flights to four airlines, choosing the most available and reliable and issuing new tickets for the delegates who were not originally scheduled to depart on those flights.

The delegates should have been required to travel on certain airlines (this would also have been cheaper because they would have received a preferential rate), and they should have been booked into fewer hotels that were closer together. Also, arrangements could have been made with the airlines to assist with an evacuation.

If security had done a risk assessment, the organization would have known that the potential for civil unrest was high. In such a case, even if the group did not change the venue, it could have required that delegates fly into a neighbouring country so that everyone could then take the same charter flight to the conference city, which would have made evacuation much easier.

As this case illustrates, special plans are needed for countries where the company does not have a permanent presence but to which company employees travel regularly or in large numbers. When problems occur in such areas, employees will have no support from a local office that, even without prior notice, typically has some vehicles, houses, cash, and local employees who know their way around.

A traveller to a country without a company office would have to rely on the embassy, if there is one, the hotel, and in some cases, the client he or she was visiting. But the company can smooth the way by providing contact information to authorities, such as the embassy, and by making prior arrangements with hotels and other resources.

Plan preparation. Though it is nearly impossible to draw up separate plans for every country to which company employees travel, a basic threat assessment will determine which of these countries are a high risk. Plans should be created for these countries first. Then, more generic plans should be written and distributed.

The plans should provide instructions for what to do in case of an emergency, factors to consider when trying to leave the country, and resources where employees can seek assistance. Appropriate actions might include traveling in groups, keeping small denominations of cash to give away at roadblocks for the purpose of extortion, traveling in two vehicles in case one breaks down, getting to the airport early, and repeatedly checking that an airplane seat has not been "mistakenly" given to someone else. In addition, evacuees should carry only limited luggage, keeping documents and valuables in a hand-carried bag in case they lose or have to abandon their luggage. Telephone numbers for the police, embassies, airlines, the travel service provider, and other sources of assistance should also be included.

Local Contacts

Corporate security might consider contracting with local security companies in international locations to provide assistance in an emergency. An agreement can be made with a local security company whereby it will locate, secure, and, if necessary, evacuate the company's employees in the host country for a set fee or agreed upon hourly rate. These companies can also provide assistance to the traveling employee for minor emergencies, such as a lost passport or traffic accident. While this might also he done in locations where the company has a permanent facility, it is especially useful if the company does not maintain an office in the country.

Communications

Some local security companies with strong emergency response capabilities may also have satellite communications, which means they might be among the few groups reachable immediately following a disaster. Being able to speak with someone in the country to get firsthand information about local conditions and the well-being of employees is key.

Not being able to reach traveling staff or a local office after receiving news of a disaster can often result in the company activating its crisis management team and spending hours working on numerous scenarios and outcomes, only to find out that employees have escaped unscathed.

Travel Claims

Back at company headquarters or the employee's home office, the department responsible for reimbursing travel expenses is in the position to assist with the enforcement of travel security policies. One obvious option is for the company to refuse to reimburse employees for accommodations other than those approved by security. The department can also ensure that employees use the company's travel service provider and not their own travel agent by paying the travel service provider directly.

One U.S.-based multinational firm was able to increase employee use of designated international hotels by contracting with the hotel chain to pay the employees their per diem allowances. The company did not reimburse general travel expenses for accommodation, meals, and incidentals but instead paid a daily allowance via the hotels. The choice was simple. If employees wanted the money, they would have to use the designated hotel. The system achieved almost 100 percent compliance.

It will often be necessary, however, for traveling employees to pay for a number of expenses themselves. Typically, the best approach is to issue the employee a corporate credit card with sufficient limits to pay for several air tickets, rent vehicles, and so forth. But in countries with deteriorating security situations, cash is king.

After an earthquake or other natural disaster, there may not be electrical power to run ATM machines or the point-of-sales machines required to process credit card transactions. Telephone lines may be down or congested, making telephone authorization for a credit card transaction impossible. During civil unrest, merchants may be reluctant to accept credit cards for fear of not being reimbursed by local banks for the transactions.

Traveling employees should, therefore, be required to carry enough cash with them at all times to pay for meals, taxis, and "exit taxes," which are often collected by groups that set up roadblocks on the roads leading to international airports.

The best approach is for the traveller to keep a small "mugger's toll" where it can be quickly accessed and to hide the rest on one's person. Cash should be both in local currency and U.s. dollars and should be in small denominations.

Corporate travel is unavoidable. And in a world where both natural and man-made disasters are increasing in number, close encounters with crises are also inevitable. But security can ensure that those situations do not result in loss of life by coordinating the company's travel and emergency response plans and getting all parties to understand the importance of compliance.

In 1998, governments and international organizations continued their active efforts to increase regulatory and criminal enforcement of various laws to stem the tide of transnational crime. These efforts were reflected in the criminalization of various business and financial transactions, the imposition of new due diligence measures on the private sector and the concomitant weakening of privacy and confidentiality laws, strengthened penalties for non-compliance with regulatory efforts, and new law enforcement techniques, such as undercover sting operations, wiretapping, expanded powers to search homes and businesses, and controlled deliveries. So obtrusive are many of the law enforcement techniques and the privatization of law enforcement, whereby governments transfer their responsibilities to the private sector, that many professionals engaged in international transfer of wealth counseling analogized the trends to those in Aldous Huxley's A Brave New World (or perhaps the Steve Miller Band's rendition).

This discussion outlines the trends in six areas and draws some practice pointers from the trends. Section II will discuss the activities of international organizations that are driving much of the strategy, framework, and minimum standards for the development of an international anti-money laundering regime. Increasingly, international organizations, both of a universal and a more regional level, are consciously trying to build alliances and networks with each other and the private sector.

In Section III, selective elements of the substantive law of anti-money laundering are considered in the context of recent developments, such as the continued erosion of secrecy and the imposition of increased due diligence requirements. Section IV discusses major case and miscellaneous developments, such as the failure of Russian offshore banks in Antigua.

Section V highlights the growth of international tax enforcement, the increased reporting requirements and unilateral extraterritorial application of the law, the increasing bilateral and multilateral cooperation, and the new traps for the wary due to tax enforcement developments.

In Section VI, international asset forfeiture trends are highlighted. These activities pose a much graver threat to the ability of clients to do business internationally than ten years ago. The goal of immobilizing the assets of transnational criminals has become increasingly the watchword. While the rights of innocent third parties are protected in principle, it sometimes takes a lot of money and professional acumen for such persons to obtain due process.

Section VII focuses on criminal cooperation mechanisms. Section VIII discusses the use of international human rights provisions as a shield for defendants, fiduciaries, and intermediaries in the context of international anti-money laundering and financial crime cases.

As an introductory matter, the life cycle of money laundering is important to grasp. It has three cycles:

(1) Placement, whereby the criminal has enormous amounts of dirty money in the form usually of cash that he needs to place or initiate in a way that neither law enforcement nor the private sector will identify as the proceeds of crime;

(2) Layering, which involves the creation of many layers between the dirty money and the ultimately cleaned money through the use of offshore vehicles, such as trusts in secrecy jurisdictions, in tandem with multiple, entitles, such as companies, and secrecy mechanisms, such as nominees, stamen, bearer shares, and sophisticated structuring; and

(3) Integration is achieved when the criminal has transformed the dirty money through enough layers of the laundering cycle that a legitimate banker, lawyer, or fiduciary, even one with cutting edge due diligence, would never suspect the criminal source of the money.

Integration means that, in 1999, the money of the many heirs of Joseph Kennedy, the famous former bootlegger during the prohibition days, now is not questioned. Indeed, the money even finances federal elections (e.g., of the U.S. President, Senate, and House). In Colombia, the money of the Cali cartel has been integrated for two or three decades into the leading pharmaceutical companies, soccer teams, and also the financing of political elections (e.g., the

United States imposed sanctions due to the financing of Samper's election).

Much of the emphasis of the politics of international anti-money laundering is to try to deprive criminals—especially transnational criminals—and organized crime of the fruits of the crimes and the means of their committing more crimes. Another goal is to allocate the seized proceeds to governments and law enforcement. Hence, the economics and politics of anti-money laundering are to redistribute economics and power of crime. To help with the fight, governments and international organizations have solicited the collaboration of the private sector to prevent money laundering through know-your-customer and identifying and reporting to law enforcement suspicious transactions.

DEVELOPMENTS OF INTERNATIONAL ORGANIZATIONS

Multilateral organizations have set the framework for anti-money laundering standards, mechanisms, and institutions. The United Nations pioneered the 1988 Vienna Convention Against the Trafficking in Illegal Narcotic and Psychotropic Substances, which contains the requirements to criminalize money laundering and immobilize the assets of persons involved in illegal narcotics trafficking.

In 1989, the G-7 Economic Summit Group established the Financial Action Task Force (FATF), which operates out of the Office of Economic Cooperation and Development (OECD) headquarters in Paris. FATF has issued a set of forty recommendations (Forty Recommendations) that concern legal requirements, financial and banking controls, and external affairs. FATF operates through a Caribbean FATF (CFATF) and is in the process of establishing a similar group in Asia. It issues an annual report that provides an overview of progress and problems in international anti-money laundering.

The G-10 Basle Group of Central Banks has actively provided guidelines for central bank supervisors and regulatory controls. As mentioned below, on September 23, 1997, the Basle Group issued guidelines on supervision.

Regionally, the Council of Europe's 1991 Convention on Laundering, Search, Seizure and Confiscation of Assets has become the major international convention that obligates signatory governments to cooperate against anti-money laundering from all serious crimes.

The European Union, as a signatory to the 1988 Vienna Drug Convention and due to its own actions to combat financial crimes against the Communities, issued a 1991 Anti-Money Laundering Directive that it is poised to strengthen. As mentioned below, it is now in the process of an initiative against cybercrimes.

An important regional organization in the anti-money laundering has been the Inter-American Drug Abuse Control Commission (CICAD). At its meeting on November 4-7, 1997, CICAD anti-money laundering experts recommended an ongoing assessment of compliance with standards and the creation of national financial intelligence units (FIUs). National governments and international organizations are striving to create mechanisms to monitor regularly compliance with international standards.

Because the recent FATF annual reports and topologies provide cutting-edge discussions of the status of money laundering trends, they are discussed next.

A. FATF 1997 Annual Report

In June 1997, the Financial Action Task Force on Money Laundering issued its annual report for 1996-97. The report highlighted the annual survey of money laundering methods and countermeasures covering a global overview of trends and techniques. These methods included the increased use by money launderers of non-bank financial institutions, especially bureaux de change, remittance businesses and non-financial professionals. Special attention was devoted to the money laundering threats of new payment technologies.

The work of the FATF in 1996-97 focused on three main areas: "(i) reviewing money laundering methods and countermeasures; (ii) monitoring the implementation of anti-money laundering measures by its members; and (iii) undertaking an external relations programme[] to promote the widest possible international action against money laundering."

Reviewing Money Laundering Methods and Countermeasures: A significant achievement of FATF during 1996-97 was the annual survey of money laundering methods and countermeasures. The survey provides a global overview of trends and techniques, especially the issue of money laundering through new payment technologies, such as smart cards and banking through the Internet. FATF reviewed the issue of electronic fund transfers and examined ways to improve the appropriate level of feedback that should be provided to reporting financial institutions.

Trends in FATF Members: While drug trafficking remains the single largest source of illegal proceeds, non-drug related crime is increasingly important. The most noticeable trend is the continuing increase in the use by money launderers of non-bank financial institutions and of non-financial businesses relative to banking institutions. The trend reflects the increased level of compliance by banks with anti-money laundering measures. The survey noted, "Outside the banking sector, the use of bureaux de change or money remittance businesses remains the most frequently cited threat."

FATF members have continued to expand their money laundering laws, covering non-drug related predicate offenses, improving confiscation laws, and expanding the application of their laws in the financial sector in order to apply preventive measures to non-bank financial institutions and non-financial businesses.

FATF discussed money laundering threats that may be inherent in the new e-money technologies, of which there are three categories: stored value cards, Internet/network based systems, and hybrid systems. Important features of the systems that will affect this threat are: (1) the value limits imposed on accounts and transactions; (2) the extent to which stored value cards become inoperable with Internet-based systems; (3) the possibility that stored value cards can transfer value between individuals; (4) the consistency of intermediaries in the new payment systems; and (5) the detail in which account and transaction records are kept.

Future issues include the need to review regulatory regimes, the availability of adequate records, and "the difficulties in detecting and in tracking or identifying unusual patterns of financial transactions." Since the application of new technologies to electronic payment systems is still in its infancy, law enforcement and regulators must continue to cooperate with the private sector. Then authorities may understand the issues that must be considered and addressed as the market and technologies mature.

Olicy Issues: Electronic Fund Transfers. As a result of difficulties in tracing illicit funds routed through the international funds transfer system, the Society for Worldwide Interbank Financial Telecommunications (SWIFT) board "issued a broadcast to its members and participating banks encouraging users to include full identifying information for originators and beneficiaries in SWIFT field tags 50 (Ordering Customer) and 59 (Beneficiary)." Many countries have acted to encourage compliance within their financial communities with the SWIFT broadcast message.)

To strengthen the body of information on identifying the true originating parties in transfers, SWIFT has devised a new optional format (MT103) for implementation after November 1997. The message format will have a new optional message field for inputting all data "relating to the identification of the sender and receiver (beneficiary) of the telegraphic transfer." Additionally, "SWIFT has issued guidance to users of its current system to describe where such information may appear in the MT 100 format." FATF has helped SWIFT devise the new mechanism and is encouraging the use of the new message format.

Providing Feedback to Financial Institutions. FATF recommends that at least the recipient of a suspicious transactions report should acknowledge receipt thereof. If the report is then subject to a fuller investigation, the institution could be advised of either the agency that is going to investigate the report or the name of a contact officer. If a case is closed or completed, the sending institution should receive timely information on the decision or result. Further cooperative exchange of information and ideas is required for the partnership between units that receive suspicious transaction reports, general law enforcement, and the financial sector to work more effectively.

Estimate of Magnitude of Money Laundering. Because of insufficient data, FATF has created an ad hoc group that "will consider the available statistical information and other information concerning the proceeds of crime and money laundering." This ad hoc group will also "define the parameters of a study on the magnitude of money laundering and agree on a methodology and a timetable for the study."

Monitoring the Implementation of Anti-Money Laundering Measures: As part of FATF's work, its members have pledged to monitor the implementation of its Forty Recommendations through a two-pronged approach consisting of (1) "an annual self-assessment exercise," and (2) "more detailed mutual evaluation process under which each member is subject to an onsite examination."

As a result of Turkey's failure to implement FATF's recommendations, FATF issued a public statement, in accordance with Recommendation 21, that Turkey, a member country, was insufficiently in compliance with the Forty Recommendations. Recommendation 21 states that "[f]inancial institutions should give special attention to business relations and transactions with persons, including companies and financial institutions, from countries that do not or insufficiently apply" the Forty Recommendations. On November 19, 1996, Turkey enacted Law no. 4208 on the Prevention of Money Laundering. As a result, FATF decided to lift the application of Recommendation 21.

In 1995, after completing its first round of mutual evaluations of whether all members had adequately implemented the Forty Recommendations, a second round of mutual evaluations was conducted. The second round focused on the effectiveness of members' anti-money laundering measures in practice. Mutual evaluations of Australia, the United Kingdom, Denmark, the United States, Austria, and Belgium occurred in 1996-97.

Asset Confiscation and Provisional Measures. The FATF Secretariat conducted a study evaluating members' confiscation measures and found that an effective confiscation mechanism should encompass a range of serious offenses and should act in appropriate cases to confiscate proceeds of crime where it is held in the name of third parties. Countries should also consider widening confiscation laws to permit confiscation without conviction in certain cases, or the more limited alternative of freezing, and where possible, confiscation action against absconders and fugitives from justice.

For most members, the crucial issue was the burden of proof upon the government and whether it can be eased or reversed. Countries have enacted or considered the following measures: "applying an easier standard of proof than the normal criminal standard; reversing the burden of proof and requiring the defendant to prove that his assets are legitimately acquired; and enabling courts to confiscate the proceeds of criminal activity other than the crimes of which the defendant is immediately convicted." Further options are to provide the court with discretion to confiscate a convicted drug trafficker's assets or to require the court to order the confiscation of all assets that are disproportionate to the person's legitimate income. Mutual legal assistance problems include instances arising from questionable members that have ratified the relevant international conventions or do not have the necessary domestic legislation in effect. Relatively limited mutual assistance experience exists among members in the confiscation field, and asset sharing and coordinating seizure and confiscation proceedings are still emerging.

Customer Identification. Because of the comparatively weaker regimes for customer identification in non-bank financial institutions and bureaux de change, these institutions have become more attractive routes for money launderers. Refinements are required for overseas and nominee accounts. In addition, refinements are required for the structuring of large non-financial business intermediaries and situations in which no face-to-face contact between the customer and the financial institution exists. The issue of customer identification arises in the context of rapid development of electronic transactions and financial services through new technologies.

External Relations: In external relations, FATF encourages countries to adopt and implement the FATF Recommendations and monitors and reinforces this process. FATF also cooperates and coordinates with all the international and regional organizations concerned with counter-money laundering measures. Finally, it pursues a flexible approach, "tailoring external relations activity to the circumstances of the region or countries involved."

FATF will embark upon more initiatives to encourage the adoption and implementation of the Forty Recommendations. FATF is working to develop a long-term strategic plan in collaboration with other relevant international organizations.

In 1996, FATF adopted both a policy and rules for "assessing the implementation of anti-money laundering measures in nonmember governments." The development of a mutual evaluation procedure should encourage countries and jurisdictions not only to develop anti-money laundering laws, but also to improve countermeasures already in existence. Hence, FATF has worked with other international organizations such as CFATF, the Council of Europe, and the

Offshore Group of Banking Supervisors (OGBS) to develop countermeasures.

In 1996 and 1997, important counter-money laundering developments included the establishment of the Asia/Pacific Group on Money Laundering and the Southern and Eastern African Money Laundering Conference. FATF has supported existing bodies rather than starting new initiatives. The new global project of the U.N. Drug Control Programme/U.N. Crime Prevention and Criminal Justice Division (UNDCP/UNCPCJD) on money laundering will help implement these measures through training and technical assistance.

In the Caribbean, FATF supported the endorsement of the Memorandum of Understanding (MOU) at the 1996 Ministerial meeting of the CFATF. CFATF finalized mutual evaluation reports of the Cayman Islands and Trinidad & Tobago, and planned six evaluation visits for 1997. CFATF also started its typologies exercise, whereby it will "develop and share among its members the latest intelligence on money laundering and other financial crime techniques used in the Caribbean region and elsewhere."

In April 1997, the Finance Ministers of the Asia Pacific Economic Cooperation (APEC) issued a ministerial statement welcoming the establishment of the Asia/Pacific Group on Money Laundering. FATF stated that the endeavor required urgent funding from FATF members and those of the Asia/Pacific Group on Money Laundering.

Finally, from October 1-3, 1996, representatives of thirteen African countries attended a conference on anti-money laundering and agreed on a proposal to establish a Southern and Eastern African Financial Action Task Force.

B. FATF 1998 Annual Report

In June 1998, the Financial Action Task Force on Money Laundering released its annual report for 1997-98. The ninth round of FATF was chaired by Belgium and was marked by the elaboration of a five year plan for 1999-2004, highlighted by a decision to broaden the FATF network and the scope of its work, and to strengthen the review of money laundering trends and countermeasures.

Trends and Future Mission of FATF: The most noticeable trend is the continuing increase in the use by money launderers of non-bank financial institutions and of non-financial businesses relative to banking institutions. The trend reflects the increased level of compliance by banks with anti-money laundering measures. Outside the banking sector, the use of bureaux de change or money remittance businesses remain the most frequently cited.

In 1994, five years after the 1989 G-7 Summit established FATF, its members decided that the Task Force—which is not a permanent international organization—should continue its work for a further five years until 1999. Moreover, it was agreed in 1994 that no final decision on the future of FATF would be taken until 1997-98.

By mid-1999, it is expected that every FATF member will have experienced two evaluations of their anti-money laundering systems. While the first round of evaluations dealt with the issue of whether all members had adequately implemented the Forty Recommendations, the second round concerns the effectiveness of the anti-money laundering system in each member country. FATF organized "missions and seminars in nonmember countries to promote awareness of the money laundering problem" and encourage countermeasures. Although FATF's Forty Recommendations have gained some international recognition, a large number of countries still have not implemented anti-money laundering systems.

FATF has succeeded in achieving an international consensus on the money laundering countermeasures, in persuading many countries to implement the measures, and in establishing a "network" of money laundering experts in each of the FATF members. FATF has improved the flow of information both at the domestic level and internationally.

The first major task in the future that the report outlined is "to establish a world-wide anti-money laundering network and to spread the FATF's message to all continents and regions of the globe." To accomplish the task, FATF will expand its membership to "strategically important countries which already have certain key anti-money laundering measures in place... and are politically determined to make a full commitment towards the implementation of the Forty Recommendations, and which could play a major role in their regions in the process of combating money laundering." FATF will also develop regional bodies emulating FATF, and will cooperate closely with relevant international organizations such as the U.N. bodies and the International Financial Institutions.

The second major task will be to improve the implementation of the Forty Recommendations in FATF members. The focus will be to "ensure that all members have implemented the revised Forty Recommendations in their entirety and in an effective manner." Hence, the existing monitoring mechanisms will receive a renewed assessment focusing on the 1996 Recommendations. This assessment will involve

An enhanced self-assessment process; and a third round of simplified mutual evaluations for all FATF members starting in 2001, focusing exclusively on compliance with the revised parts of the Recommendations, the areas of significant deficiencies identified in the second round, and generally the effectiveness of the countermeasures.

The third main task will be to strengthen the review of money laundering trends and countermeasures. Because money laundering is an evolving activity, FATF members must follow laundering trends and techniques and assess the effectiveness of the FATF recommendations. The geographical scope of the future typologies exercises must be extended. The close monitoring of trends will enable FATF to anticipate and react to the trends by elaborating countermeasures. 2.

Monitoring the Implementation of Anti-Money Laundering Measures.

Much of FATF's work consists of monitoring the implementation by its members of the Forty Recommendations. FATF members are committed to the discipline of multilateral surveillance and peer review. Member countries have their implementation of the recommendations monitored through a two-pronged approach comprised of (1) "an annual self-assessment exercise," and (2) a "more mutual evaluation process under which each member is subject to an on-site examination."

The 1997-98 self-assessment process consisted of each member providing information concerning the status of their implementation of the Forty Recommendations. The information is then compiled and analyzed, providing the basis for assessing to what extent the Forty Recommendations have been implemented.

With respect to legal issues, all members have enacted laws criminalizing drug money laundering. All but three FATF members have criminalized laundering of the proceeds of range of crimes in addition to drug trafficking. The report notes that "the overall level of compliance will improve considerably when Japan, Luxembourg, and Singapore have extended their drug money laundering offenses to serious crimes," which all three are in the process of doing.

"A number of members still must take measures in relation to confiscation and provisional measures, both domestically and pursuant to mutual legal assistance." In regard to domestic confiscation, nineteen members are in full compliance, and six in partial compliance. For mutual legal assistance, seventeen members are in full compliance, five in partial compliance, and three are out of compliance (Canada, Greece and the United States). Urgent action by some FATF members is required to bring themselves into compliance with the relevant recommendations.

Slight improvement occurred in the 1997-98 implementation of the FATF recommendations on financial issues. Major improvements occurred in relation to two new recommendations that were introduced in 1996, namely Recommendation 13 dealing with the need to monitor laundering using new technologies, and Recommendation 25 on shell corporations. However, non-bank institutions still are not properly implementing the recommendations at the same level as the banking sector.

While nearly all FATF members "comply fully with customer identification and record-keeping requirements for banks... some persistent gaps in coverage with respect to certain categories of non-bank financial institutions" still exist. Serious concerns exist regarding the anonymous passbooks for residents in Austria that FATF is pursuing through the FATF noncompliance procedures.

The requirement for financial institutions to report suspicious transactions and related measures has received "very satisfactory" implementation in relation to banks and almost as good for non-bank financial institutions. However, improvement is required with respect to non-bank financial institutions, especially in countries such as Canada, Iceland, and the United States.

The report also discusses the mutual evaluations of Canada, Switzerland, the Netherlands, Germany, Italy, Norway, Japan, and Greece.

A section of the report concerning the application of the FATF policy for non-complying members covers, inter alia, the failure of Austria to abolish anonymous passbooks for Austria residents and a series of concerns on Canadian countermeasures. The proposed Canadian countermeasures include mandatory suspicious transaction reporting, penalizing failures to file a report and filing a false report, as well as a "tipping-off" offense, the establishment of a new financial intelligence unit, protection from criminal and civil liability for any person or body that makes a report, and establishing a cross border reporting system for currency and monetary instruments.

Reviewing Money Laundering Methods and Countermeasures: FATF performed a further survey of money laundering methods and countermeasures that provides a global overview of trends and techniques. The issues of money laundering through new payments technologies—smart cards, banking through the Internet—and of the non-financial businesses and remittance companies were discussed. The survey also considered the issues of how to "improve the appropriate level of feedback which should be provided to reporting financial institutions, and the continuation of work on estimating the magnitude of money laundering." Moreover, FATF convened a second meeting with representatives of the world's financial sector trade institutions.

With respect to new technology—for example, e-cash—the report concluded that much work remains before all the related money laundering dangers can be clearly identified and before any possible specific countermeasures can be considered. FATF has also directed its attention toward money laundering in sectors such as insurance or money changing. In connection with the latter, consideration is given to the consequences of the conversion of European currencies into the Euro.

With respect to providing feedback to financial institutions, the FATF guidelines are not mandatory because they recognize "that ongoing law enforcement investigations should not be put at risk that secrecy laws in some countries may prevent their financial intelligence unit from disclosing significant feedback, and that general privacy laws can also limit feedback." Hence, the guidelines are designed to assist financial intelligence units, law enforcement and other government bodies involved in the receipt, analysis, and investigation of suspicious transaction reports, and in the provision of feedback to reporting institutions on those reports. The guidelines suggest that at least regulatory authorities make available sanitized cases to reporting institutions, and "each case could include a description of the fact, a summary of the result, a description of the inquiries made by the FIU if appropriate, and a description of the lessons to be learned from the reporting and investigative procedures that were adopted in the case." Additionally, new money laundering methods, as well as trends in existing techniques, are described and identified and the guidelines provide that institutions are advised of such trends and techniques.

The guidelines also consider means for providing general feedback, such as "annual reports, regular newsletters, videos, electronic information systems such as websites, electronic databases or message systems, meetings with institutions, conferences and workshops, and working or liaison groups." The report notes that specific feedback is more difficult to provide than general feedback due to legal and practical concerns, such as potential jeopardy to ongoing law enforcement investigations and resource limitations, and secrecy laws relating to the financial intelligence or general privacy laws. Still, whenever possible, specific feedback should include acknowledgment by the FIU of receipt of the report and advice to the institution that a particular agency will investigate the report when this occurs and if the investigation would not be adversely affected. "If a case is closed or completed, whether because of a concluded prosecution, because the report was found to relate to a legitimate transaction or for other reasons," the institution should be notified of that decision or result.

FATF's External Relations and Other International Initiatives: As the third component of its mission, FATF undertakes external relations actions designed to raise awareness in nonmember countries or regions on the need to prevent or combat money laundering, and offers the Forty Recommendations as a basis for doing so.

In September 1997, FATF's external relations included a mission to Cyprus, resulting in Cyprus undergoing a joint Council of Europe/Offshore Group of Banking Supervisors

(OGBS) mutual evaluation of Cyprus' money laundering system in the spring of 1998. In October 1997, FATF helped organize a conference in St. Petersburg to complement a high-level mission to Moscow in 1996. Various new and proposed countermeasures are in place and in the works in Russia.

FATF-style regional bodies are active. CFATF has grown to twenty-four states and has instituted measures to ensure the effective implementation of, and compliance with, the Forty Recommendations.

The CFATF Secretariat monitors members' implementation of the Kingston Ministerial Declaration through the following activities: self-assessment of the implementation of the Recommendations; an on-going programme of mutual evaluation of members; coordination of, and participation in, training and technical assistance programmes; biannual plenary meetings for technical representatives; and annual Ministerial meetings.

The report notes that "supported by, and in collaboration with UNDCP, the CFATF Secretariat has developed a regional strategy for technical assistance and training to aid effective investigation and prosecution of money laundering and related asset forfeiture cases." In 1997-98, three mutual evaluation reports were discussed and six on-site visits occurred. A timetable was set for the remaining mutual evaluations. In July 1997, the Working Party meeting of the Asia/Pacific Group on Money Laundering (APG) made progress. It currently consists of sixteen members that "have started to exchange information and to examine the strengths and weaknesses of their systems through the mechanism of jurisdiction reports." Measures have been proposed to improve technical assistance and training, strengthen mutual legal assistance and improve cooperation with the financial sector.

FATF adopted a policy for assessing the implementation of anti-money laundering measures in non-member governments. The procedure will encourage countries and territories not only to implement anti-money laundering measures, but also to improve the countermeasures already in place. In this regard, the FATF assessed the CFATF, the Council of Europe and the OGBS's mutual evaluation procedures as being in conformity with its own principles. As the latter is comprised of representatives of banking supervisory authorities, the FATF has sought formal political endorsement of the procedures and the forty Recommendations from those governments of the members of the OGBS that are not represented in either the CFATF or the FATF.

FATF cooperates with other international organizations. In this regard, the U.N. Office for Drug Control and Crime Prevention (UNODCCP) has started the Global Programme Against Money Laundering (GPML), a research and technical cooperation programme. In the context of the GPML, the UNODCCP organized several important international anti-money laundering events in 1997-1998, including awareness-raising seminars for West Africa in Ivory Coast, and for South Asian countries plus Myanmar and Thailand. On June 8-10, 1998, the U.N. General Assembly on international narcotics trafficking adopted a political declaration in which U.N. members undertake to make special efforts against the laundering of money linked to drug trafficking. The declaration recommends that states that have not yet done so adopt by the year 2003 national anti-money laundering legislation and programmes in accordance with relevant provisions of the 1988 Vienna Convention Against the Traffic in Illicit Narcotic and Psychotropic Substances, and a package of countermeasures that were adopted at the same session. The Commonwealth Heads of Government recently has held summits calling for concerted anti-money laundering actions. At its June 1998 London meeting, it considered four main items:

1. Improving domestic coordination through national interdisciplinary coordinating structure;
2. The special problems of dealing with money laundering in countries with large parallel economies;

3. Strengthening regional initiatives for more effective implementation of anti-money laundering measures; and
4. Self-evaluation of progress made in implementing anti-money laundering measures in the financial sector.

The Inter-American Development Bank has held meetings and is starting to become involved in anti-money laundering activities, such as training, supporting dialogue with the private sector, and funding programmes).

The Organization of American States (OAS)/Inter-American Drug Abuse Control Commission (CICAD) have a group of experts that meets twice a year. In May 1998, it "approved a training programme for judges, prosecutors, FIU personnel and law enforcement. It also undertook to amend the model regulations to expand the predicate offence for money laundering and to provide for the establishment of national forfeiture funds." It finished a directory of contact points to effect information exchange and mutual legal assistance that would be accessible through OAS's webpage.

The expansion of the FATF network and of the scope of its countermeasures will mean that launderers will use their power and know-how to try to take advantage of globalization and new technology, and to identify and exploit jurisdictions whose systems are vulnerable. For a five-year assessment, noticeably absent in the discussion is the use of international relations and particularly international-regime theory, including the rise and fall of linkages that make regimes rise and fall, and the targeting of key elements within such regimes. Additional limitations that exacerbate the absence of this element of its strategic planning are the temporal—its existence is limited to five years—and informal commitments—FATF is still not a formal entity. Given the threats arising from money laundering, one would think the world community would make commitments commensurate with the threats, but then progress in evolving international enforcement regimes can be slow.

During 1996-97, progress was made in combating money laundering, both within and outside the FATF membership. Implementation of the Forty Recommendations by FATF has again improved and the monitoring mechanisms have been further strengthened and refined. The international anti-money laundering activities undertaken by FATF and other international organizations have increased.

On June 23-24, 1997, the Egmont Group, composed of specialists in financial investigation from thirty-six countries and seven international organizations, including Interpol and Europol, approved at its fifth meeting a declaration of principles to harmonize policies and intensify its efforts in combating money laundering.(134) The Spanish Executive Service of the Commission to Prevent Money Laundering and Financial Offenses organized the meeting at the Bank of Spain.

Among the principles agreed upon were the following: (1) the stimulation of exchanges among various FIUs; (2) the adoption of a programme of communication among FIUs through the Internet; (3) the holding and development of regional workshops or seminars for their members and their units and sub-units; and (4) the study of a formal structure to maintain the continuation and consolidation of the Egmont group and the articulation of procedures for FIUs and their counterparts.

The Egmont Group was established on June 9, 1995, at the palace of Egmont-Arenberg in Brussels as a result of an international movement directed at the promulgation in all countries of a norm pertaining to the prevention of money laundering and the establishment in each state of an organization to fulfill the obligations imposed on FIUs. The Egmont Group does not constitute an international organization or set forth hard law obligations under an international agreement, but rather provides an informal means for interested entities to meet and cooperate voluntarily.

The conclusions of the meeting indicate that Spanish norms on preventing money laundering and collaboration among credit entities, banks, and savings and loan associations, have gained momentum. Sepblac took action during 1989 on 1,530 cases on various fronts. In the matter of international business transactions, Sepblac verified the fulfillment of requirements of enterprises owned by foreign shareholders. In so doing, it discovered the manipulation in the formation of stock exchange prices. Furthermore, Sepblac observed foreign loans that hide increases of capital in Spanish affiliate enterprises abroad.

In the matter of money laundering, Seplac transmitted and finalized 412 cases in 1998, 58 of which were referred to the antidrug prosecutor, 54 to the special anti-corruption prosecutor, 10 to different judicial authorities, and 43 to police authorities. The remaining cases were shelved without further investigation or prosecution. Sepblac also investigated, among other activities, suspicious dealings in sectors such as jewelry and precious metals, the importation of vehicles, contraband tobacco, hotel businesses, the industry of information technology and products, value added tax fraud, and casinos.

The work of the Egmont Group and Sepblac indicate the emergence and coalescence of a financial enforcement regime, of which money laundering is an important component. The cooperation within the Egmont Group exemplifies the role of informal cooperation and its impact on the formation and growth of national enforcement activities.

The achievement of a financial enforcement regime has occurred within the goals and activities of both formal organizations and obligations—such as the U.N. Drug Programme, the 1988 U.N. Vienna Convention Against the Traffic in Illicit Narcotic and Psychotropic Substances and the European Union, and the 1991 EU Anti-Money Laundering Directive—and informal organizations and undertakings—such as FATF and its Forty Recommendations, and the Caribbean FATF and its additional recommendations.

On December 10, 1997, at a meeting in Washington, D.C., ministers from eight industrialized governments agreed to combat cybercrime with enhanced technology and a harmonized crime legislation. The arrangements to cooperate against cybercrime result from the ongoing discussions among the G-7 nations, that is, the G-7 Economic Summit countries—plus the European Union and Russia. In particular, the governments agreed to cooperate in investigations and enforcement actions involving cyber criminals.

The G-8 countries agreed on a series of principles, such as denying a safe haven to abusers of information technology. Just as important will be the establishment of a network and contacts to assist in investigating and arresting perpetrators of cybercrimes, including computer hackers, online peddlers of child pornography, drug traffickers, organized crime, and people who use computer networks to perpetrate illicit activities.

The ministers agreed on the following steps:

1. Ensuring that law enforcement is properly staffed and trained to fight cybercrime;
2. Developing improved means to quickly trace attacks coming through computer networks; allocating the same time and resources to the prosecution of cybercriminals who have attacked other countries as would be allocated for domestic attacks, if extradition is not possible due to nationality;
3. Ensuring the preservation of electronic evidence and developing solutions for transborder searches and computer searches involving data whose location is not known to officials;
4. Cooperating with the private sector to develop new solutions for preserving and collecting critical evidence;
5. Accelerating the process by which traffic data from communications carriers can be obtained;
6. Ensuring expeditious responses to mutual assistance requests, in appropriate cases, by voice, fax, or e-mail communications followed by written confirmation, if needed;

7. Encouraging, the development of international standards for reliable and secure telecommunications and data processing technologies;
8. Using compatible forensic standards to retrieve and authenticate electronic data; and
9. Including cybercrime issues when negotiating mutual assistance agreements or arrangements.

A 1996 survey of the Computer Security Institute revealed that forty-two percent of Fortune 500 companies had experienced an unauthorized use of their computer systems during the last year.

While U.S. Attorney General Janet Reno has said that the action plan does not require new legislation by the United States, wiretap laws must be adjusted to accommodate the digital era. All ministers promised to review their legal systems, "to ensure that [their laws] appropriately criminalize abuses of telecommunications and computer systems and promote the investigation of high crimes."

During the week of the meeting, the vulnerability of the Internet to such crimes was emphasized when hackers broke into computers at Yahoo!, one of the most popular sites on the World Wide Web, and threatened to infect users' computers with a damaging computer virus unless an alleged hacker was released from jail.

Many cyber crimes involve fraudulent pyramid schemes distributed by electronic mail. Another fraud includes tricking Internet users into relinquishing passwords that can be used to access their accounts. The G-8 agreement is an effort by national governments to enable international criminal cooperation developments to keep pace with technology and its use by transnational criminals.

On September 23, 1997, the Basle Committee on Banking Supervision, the central bank organ of the G-10 countries, agreed on a final version of supervision principles to strengthen the supervisory regime. While the new guide contains no substantive changes, the text has gained support. For example, delegates attending the Denver Summit endorsed it.

The Committee also obtained comments from many countries outside the group, including Chile, China, the Czech Republic, Hong Kong, Mexico, Russia, and Thailand. In addition, bankers and banking regulators from Argentina, Brazil, Hungary, India, Indonesia, South Korea, Malaysia, Poland, and Singapore contributed to the summit.

Major financial countries have been asked to endorse the two principles by no later than October 1998. The principles "outline the basic elements of a banking supervisory system including licensing and structure, prudential regulations and requirements, methods of ongoing banking supervision, information requirements, the formal powers of supervisors and cross-border banking." A compendium of laws accompanies the regulations that banks are requested to update on a regular basis.

The Basle Core Principles aim to provide a basic reference with which supervisory and other public authorities worldwide may supervise all of the banks within their jurisdictions. Central banks that endorse the principles will review and update their own current supervisory arrangements in accordance with the principles.

The Committee urged national legislators to ensure that required changes in the law be enacted quickly. Since the measures outlined in the principles took one and a half years to coordinate, and since they are minimum requirements, the Committee observes that many countries may want to tighten their own rules further than the principles require. The Committee pledged technical assistance and training for regulatory agencies from non-G-10 countries that want to take advantage of the principles.

The continued review and strengthening of global and domestic financial supervisory mechanisms has become more urgent in a globalized world in which transnational crime and organized groups operate. Increasingly, international organizations and groups, such as the Basle Committee, the FATF, the World Bank Group, and Interpol, are exchanging information and cooperating among themselves to complement their regulatory and enforcement frameworks.

On April 24, 1997, members of the European Parliament (MEPs) proposed to enact legislation against certain cybercrimes, namely pornography, paedophilia, and racist material. The measures will include establishing teams of cyberpolice to monitor the Internet, requiring industry self-regulation, and concluding international enforcement cooperation agreements. The European Union also scheduled for July 6-8, 1997 a ministerial conference on global information networks that was intended to lead to a declaration on regulatory principles.

The MEPs will try to strike a balance between protecting the public from obscenity and respecting an individual's right to free speech and privacy. The United States, Germany and France have regulated the Internet, but with limited success. The French and German authorities have focused on Internet service providers. For instance, Karlheinz Moewes, the chief officer of the Munich police, heads the first German force to combat Internet crime. His team of five Internet police investigated 110 cases of child pornography worldwide in 1996. They patrol the Internet on a regular basis, searching for child pornography and trying to follow and penetrate groups of paedophiles.

In Belgium and the United Kingdom, similar law enforcement groups operate. For instance, in the United Kingdom the teams cooperate with the Internet Service Providers Association, which blocks access if illegal sites are discovered. The difficulty is that the persons responsible for perpetrating the crimes may be outside the European Union and in remote parts of the world where law enforcement cooperation is not effective.

MEPs have called on the European Commission to propose a common framework for self-regulation and to agree on a code of good behaviour. According to EU Industrial Affairs Commissioner Martin Bangemann, the EU must introduce binding measures on service providers, with penalties. MEPs believe that service providers must be liable for illicit material on their systems.

In April 1997, German authorities charged the managing director of CompuServe in Bavaria with providing access to pornographic and racist material. The situation is seen as a test case. Service providers contend that they should be treated like telecommunications companies, who are not prosecuted when criminals use their lines.

French MEP Pierre Pradier wants to make users responsible because families can use software devices to screen criminal and harmful material.

One problem is the classic issue of whether the law can keep up With the technology. Undoubtedly, the European Union and other major powers will need to update their laws constantly. Meanwhile, criminal organizations are likely to search for, identify, and utilize the states that intentionally or accidentally have the lowest law and regulatory regime.

At its meeting on November 4-7, 1997 in Lima, Peru, CICAD, a brânch of the OAS, made several decisions and recommendations of importance to international enforcement, including steps to undertake an ongoing assessment of money laundering in the hemisphere, the creation of national FIUs, and measures to strengthen the training of officials and the exchange of information and reciprocal judicial assistance.

Creation of Financial Intelligence Units

The CIAD recommended to CICAD the amendment of the Model Regulations as follows:

In accordance with the law, each member state shall establish or designate a central agency responsible for receiving, requesting, analyzing and disseminating to the competent authorities, disclosures of information relating to financial transactions that are required to be reported pursuant to these Model Regulations or that concern suspected proceeds of crime.

The recommendation explains that the objective is to receive and analyze information so that it can be utilized by the competent authorities. The entities can be referred to variously as Financial Intelligence Units, Financial Investigation Units, Financial Information Units, or Financial Analysis Units. Depending on its location in the governmental structure of a country, FIUs may assume one of the following modes as identified by the Egmont Group: a police model; a judicial model; a mixed police and judicial model; or an administrative model.

Ongoing Assessment of the Plan of Action of Buenos Aires

After discussing the results of responses to a questionnaire on the status of anti-money laundering regulations in twenty-one CICAD countries, the CICAD Group of Experts determined that the top two priority areas on which to focus their efforts for the immediate future would be (1) the training of officials, and (2) strengthening the exchange of information and reciprocal judicial assistance.

Training should focus on officials who work in FIUs or in other entities—whose purpose is to receive and analyze information, investigate on the basis thereof, or both—transactions that appear to involve money laundering. Training also is required for investigators on the applicable investigation methods and techniques for money laundering offenses and on methods of presenting evidence regarding money laundering before the courts or other competent entities.

Moreover, training is required for prosecutors and judges to ensure full understanding of the offense, the importance of stringent conviction and. prosecution, evidence in money laundering cases, international cooperation among judges for mutual legal assistance purposes (especially in exchanging the probative elements of the offense), the importance of seizure, confiscation pending trial, ultimate forfeiture of laundered assets and instrumentalities, and the difficulties in securing convictions.

Training also is required for officials of supervisory and regulatory agencies responsible for overseeing financial institutions. In this connection, training should be focused on the development and application of the appropriate control systems over financial institutions. It should also include training with respect to reporting systems for required cash and suspicious transaction reports, on the authority and law under which the agency operates, and on comparative approaches in other countries.

The Group of Experts will organize an informal working group for the purpose of identifying a training programme based on the priority areas identified in the Group's discussion and the replies to the questionnaire. The Group discussed the difficulties in investigating and proving money laundering, especially due to its transnational nature that complicates, in particular, investigation and issues of proof. These aspects require a high level of international cooperation, formal and informal, that must be efficient and effective. There must exist a reciprocal capability to seize and freeze assets as well as to provide for their confiscation when they are situated in a country other than where the investigation and trial are occurring.

The Group noted the importance of studies to facilitate the compilation, systematization, and diffusion of information on applicable national and international norms to identify the appropriate central authorities to give effect to the intended cooperation. For their next meeting, the Group of Experts agreed to consider the applicability of developing a manual on these matters that would set out the applicable laws and contact points in the various administrations in CICAD member states. The Executive Secretariat will develop a model outline for such a manual for the next meeting of the Group. To assist in this work, CICAD members will provide an explanatory report on these measures and identify the competent authorities.

The Group of Experts agreed that a typologies exercise will become part of their ongoing agenda. For the next meeting certain countries would prepare, on a voluntary basis, a report on their experience in detecting money laundering typologies.

On May 12-14, 1998, the OAS-CICAD met and agreed to strengthen anti-money laundering enforcement efforts. This section outlines the Commission's initiatives.

a. *Training:* The Group approved a training plan based on modules for the training of judges, prosecutors, FIU personnel, and law enforcement officials. Wherever possible, the training plan would be implemented on a sub-regional basis, following a needs assessment and diagnosis to determine the priorities of each country or region.

b. *Amendments to the Model Regulations:* To bring the model regulations approved in May 1992 in line with the broad international policy guidelines, especially those contained in the Summit of the Americas Plan of Action of Buenos Aires of 1995, the model regulations will incorporate the concept of "serious offenses," so that anti-money laundering laws and regulations are designed to counteract serious crimes rather than just drug violations. As a result, the title of the regulations was modified to read Model Regulations Concerning Laundering Offenses Connected to Illicit Drug Trafficking, Related and Other Serious Offenses. As defined, "serious offenses" means "those defined by the legislation of each country, including, for example illegal activities that relate to organized crime, terrorism, illicit trafficking of arms, persons or body organs, corruption, fraud, extortion and kidnapping."

Another change is that under new Article 7(d) CICAD members will "facilitate the sharing of the objects of the forfeiture or the proceeds from their sale, on a basis commensurate with participation, with the country or countries that assisted or participated in the investigation or legal proceedings that resulted in the objects being forfeited." In addition, new Article 7(f) obligates members to "promote and facilitate the creation of a national forfeiture fund to administer the objects of forfeiture and to authorize their use or allocation to support programmes for judicial management [and] training," as well as for counterdrug efforts and related programmes.(185)

The group adopted a proposal by St. Lucia to amend Article 10, [sections] 1(b) to broaden the definition of financial institutions to include businesses authorized to conduct "offshore" financial activities. The group deferred until the next meeting action on proposals of St. Lucia to add collective investment funds, such as mutual funds and unit trusts, to Article 9(2).

c. *Manual on Information Exchange for Anti-Laundering and Mutual Assistance:* Consideration was given to the information page that could become a valuable tool for all countries in facilitating points of contact for information exchange and mutual legal assistance. The pages would be accessible through CICAD's webpage and would be kept current.

   The United States discussed the operation of the Egmont website system as an example of how secure information exchanges are occurring among the FIU Egmont members. Eventually, the CICAD system may be set up for secure information exchange.

d. *Cooperation with the CICAD Working Group on the Multilateral Evaluation Mechanism:* The Group of Experts agreed that they would offer their assistance and technical capabilities to the CICAD Working Group on the Multilateral Evaluation Mechanism.

The assistance would permit the experts can help with anti-money laundering evaluation, so that once the OAS members agree to undertake multilateral evaluations of the member's counter drug policies.

e. *Permanent Council Working Group:* The Group of Experts reviewed the draft resolution to the OAS General Assembly of the Permanent Council Working Group—that was established to consider the desirability of an Inter-American convention against money laundering. The Experts will advise the working group of their own views on a convention from its technical perspective.

Analysis

The expansion of the anti-money laundering efforts in the Western Hemisphere to include serious crimes rather than just drug trafficking brings this group current with practice in the rest of the world. The consideration of a multilateral evaluation mechanism, the exchange of information, training, and even a convention are all efforts to strengthen compliance and indicate broader political agreement and acceptance of the purposes of anti-money laundering.

The ongoing assessment, the establishment of FIUs, and the typologies exercise are small steps towards cooperation in hemispheric anti-money laundering enforcement. Meaningful and effective cooperation, harmonization of laws and standards, and effective establishment of an anti-money laundering regime must await the establishment of a proper network. A solid legal infrastructure with funding for professionals is needed for intensive and daily work on compliance with conventions and resolutions, harmonization of laws, collaboration on common approaches to mechanisms and technology, and common approaches to operational problems. At present, the governments and international organizations in the Western Hemisphere are searching for ways to develop ad hoc solutions to individual criminal problems, such as anti-money laundering.

SUBSTANTIVE LAW OF ANTI-MONEY LAUNDERING

Since the initiation of international anti-money laundering efforts in the mid-1980s, various substantive requirements have been established: the requirement to criminalize money laundering activities; the requirement that covered persons must know-their-customer; the requirement to identify and report to authorities suspicious transactions; the requirement to freeze, trace, seize, and ultimately forfeit the proceeds and instrumentalities of money laundering crimes; the requirement of covered persons to have a compliance officer and to train employees; the requirement for covered persons to have outside audits the compliance of their organization with anti-money laundering standards; and the prohibition of secrecy as a reason for a country and covered persons to refuse to follow any of the anti-money laundering obligations.

In U.S. law, the main provisions of anti-money laundering are found in Titles 12, 18 and 31 of the U.S. Code. The Bank Secrecy Act of 1970 (BSA) was a precursor to anti-money laundering. It was intended to deter laundering and the use of secret foreign bank accounts. It established an investigative "paper trail" for large currency transactions by establishing regulatory reporting standards and requirements, such as the Currency Transaction Report requirement. This requirement early distinguished the United States from other countries' approach to anti-money laundering. The BSA imposed civil and criminal penalties for noncompliance with its reporting requirements. It was designed to improved the detection and investigation of criminal, tax, and regulatory violations. A unique aspect of U.S. anti-money laundering laws that other countries are starting to emulate is the simultaneous use of anti-money laundering, tax, regulatory, and even criminal, – especially organized crime – goals.

The Money Laundering Control Act of 1986, which was part of the Anti-Drug Abuse Act of 1986, created three new criminal offenses for money laundering activities by, through, or to a financial institution: (1) knowingly helping launder money; (2) knowingly engaging – including by being willfully blind—in a transaction of more than $10,000 that involves property from criminal activity; and (3) structuring transactions to avoid the BSA reporting.

The Anti-Drug Abuse Act of 1988 strengthened anti-money laundering by: significantly increasing civil, criminal and forfeiture sanctions for laundering crimes and BSA violations, including forfeiture of "any property, real or personal, involved in a transaction or attempted transaction in violation of laws" relating to the filing of Currency Transaction Reports, money laundering, or structuring transactions; requiring stronger and more precise identification and recording of cash purchases of certain monetary instruments; allowing the Treasury Department to require financial institutions to file additional, geographically targeted reports; requiring the Treasury Department to negotiate bilateral international agreements covering the recording of large U.S. currency transactions and the sharing of such information; and increasing the criminal sanction for tax evasion when money from criminal activity is involved.

In 1992, the Housing and Community Development Act of 1992 made changes in anti-money laundering laws. It strengthened penalties for financial institutions violating anti-money laundering laws, and allows regulators to close or seize institutions by appointing a conservator or receiver or terminating the institution's charges. Regulators can suspend or remove institution-affiliated parties who have violated the BSA or been indicted for money laundering or criminal activity under the BSA. It forbids any individual convicted of money laundering from unauthorized participation in any federally insured institutions.

Under the Annunzio-Wylie Act, the Treasury must issue regulations requiring national banks and other depository institutions to identify which of their account holders—other than other depository institutions or regulated broker dealers—are non-bank financial institutions, such as money transmitters or check cashing services. Treasury, along with the Federal Reserve, must promulgate regulations requiring financial institutions and other entities that cash checks, transmit money, or perform similar services to maintain records of domestic and international wire transfers that are useful in law enforcement investigations. Under the Act, the U.S. Government has established a BSA Advisory Group that includes representatives from the Departments of Treasury as well as Justice, and the Office of National Drug Control Policy and other interested persons and financial institutions. The group was created for the purpose of developing a harmonious private-public cooperation on anti-money laundering.

Under the Annunzio-Wylie Act, Treasury can require financial institutions to adopt anti-money laundering programmes that include: internal policies, procedures, and controls; designation of a compliance officer; and continuation of an ongoing employee training programme; and an independent audit function to test the adequacy of the programme.

Treasury can require any financial institution, or any financial institution employee, to report suspicious transactions relevant to possible violation of law or regulation under the protection from civil suit arising from such reports by virtue of a "safe harbor." The American Bankers' Association and the banking industry had long sought such a safe harbor.

Under the Act, a financial institution or employee may be prosecuted for "tipping off" – that is, if they disclose, to the subject of a referral or a grand jury subpoena, that a criminal referral has been filed or a grand jury investigation has been started concerning a possible crime of money laundering and BSA laws. Officers who improperly disclose information concerning a grand jury subpoena for bank records are subject to prosecution.

A. The 1998 U.S. Money Laundering Act: Fostering Partnerships and Better Targeting

Before adjourning in 1998, Congress considered and almost enacted the Money Laundering Deterrence Act of 1998.

On October 5, 1998, it passed in the House, but died in the Senate. Because it has the support of the Administration and many other people, the bill is worth considering. It would amend title 31 of the U.S. Code to improve methods for preventing financial crimes, and for other purposes. It amends Title 31 of the U.S. Code to improve methods for preventing financial crimes.

Section 2 notes that organized crime groups are continually devising new methods to launder money, "including the use of financial service providers that are not depository institutions, such as money transmitters and check cashing services, the purchase and resale of durable goods," and the exchange of black market foreign currency. The involvement of international criminal enterprises engaged in money laundering is complex, diverse, and fragmented. Many foreign gangs and groups have financial management and organizational infrastructures that are highly sophisticated and difficult to track because of the globalization of the financial service industry.

Section 2 lists as the purposes of the Act to provide the law enforcement community with the necessary legal authority to combat money laundering, to broaden the law enforcement community's access to transactional information already being collected" in a non-financial trade or business, and " to expedite the issuance by the Secretary of the Treasury of regulations designed to deter money laundering activities at certain types of financial institutions." Section 3 amends the suspicious activity reporting requirements in the Bank Secrecy Act to facilitate the flow of financial regulatory agencies.

Subsection (a) broadens the "safe harbor" provisions of 31 U.S.C. [sections] 5318 to independent public accountants who file Suspicious Activity Reports (SAR). It is hoped that accountants conducting audits and routine examinations of a financial institution's books and records will report wrongdoing. Subsection (b) limits the circumstances under which the filing of a SAR may be disclosed. Subsection (c) "provides financial institutions with immunity from liability when making employment references that include suspicion of a prospective employee's possible involvement in a violation of law or regulation," unless the financial institution knows such suspicion "to be false or if the institution acts with malice or reckless disregard for the truth in making such a reference." Subsection (d) makes SARs available to self-regulatory organizations as defined by the Securities and Exchange Act of 1934.

Section 4 expands the scope of the summons authority under 31 U.S.C. [sections] 5318(b)(1) from merely "investigations for the purpose of civil enforcement" of the Bank Secrecy Act to "examinations to determine compliance with the Bank Secrecy Act, as well as investigations relating to reports filed pursuant to the Act." The èxpanded summons authority will help in the case of non-depository institutions whose activities are not subject to regulatory oversight.

Section 5 "clarifies existing statutory language making it illegal to violate reporting requirements mandated by a geographic targeting order issued by the Secretary of the Treasury or the funds transfer record-keeping rules." Section 6 eliminates Treasury Secretary's obligation "to report to Congress on the status of states' adoption of uniform laws regulating money transmitters." The Treasury Department's recently promulgated regulations for Money Services Businesses, which include money transmitters, has rendered this directive unnecessary.

Section 7 "exempts Bank Secrecy Act reporting requirements, including those imposed by geographic targeting orders, from consideration under the Paperwork Reduction Act."

Section 8 "transfers from the Internal Revenue Code to the Bank Secrecy Act the requirement that any person engaged in a trade or business (other than financial institutions required to report under the Bank Secrecy Act) file a report with the Federal government on cash transactions in excess of $10,000." Reports made pursuant to this requirement "provide law enforcement authorities with a paper trail that can help identify a lifestyle that is not commensurate with an individual's known sources of legitimate income."

Under prior law, non-financial institutions had to report cash transactions exceeding $10,000 to the Internal Revenue Service (IRS) on IRS Form 8300. Because such reports must be filed pursuant to the Internal Revenue Code, Form 8300 information is considered tax return information. As such, it may not be disclosed to any persons or used in any manner not authorized by the Internal Revenue Code. Authorized disclosures of Form 8300 information are subject to the procedural and recordkeeping requirements of Section 6103 of the Internal Revenue Code. For example, Section 6103(p)(4)(E) requires agencies seeking Form 8300 information to file a report with the Secretary of the Treasury that describes the procedures established and utilized by the agency for ensuring the confidentiality of the information.

The IRS requires that agencies requesting Form 8300 information file a "Safeguard Procedures Report," which must be approved by the IRS before such information can be released. While the IRS uses Form 8300 to identify individuals who may be engaged in tax evasion, the information collected on the form can also be useful to other law enforcement agencies investigating other financial crimes, including money laundering. Form 8300 information can be instrumental in helping law enforcement authorities trace cash payments by drug traffickers and other criminals for luxury cars, jewelry, and other expensive merchandise. However, Form 8300s are not accessible to law enforcement authorities and, as a result of the above-mentioned restrictions under Section 6103, they cannot be retrieved electronically from a database maintained by the Treasury Department.

The change will make the reports much more accessible. Section 9 requires that within 120 days of enactment the Treasury must promulgate know-your-customer regulations for financial institutions. The regulations have been under discussion and study among Federal banking and financial regulatory agencies, including the Treasury Department, the Federal Reserve Board of Governors, the Office of the Comptroller of the Currency, and the Federal Deposit Insurance Corporation. The regulations "are intended to assist financial institutions in verifying that their customers' funds are derived from legitimate sources." Section 10 extends the statute of limitations period from one to two years in forfeitable fungible property in bank accounts under 18 U.S.C. [sections] 984. It provides that all bank deposits are fungible and authorizes the forfeiture of money held to prove that the money in the account on one day is the "same money" as was in the account on a prior occasion.

Section 11 requires the Treasury Secretary, in consultation with "federal banking agencies" and within one year of enactment of [the law], to prepare a report on the nature and extent of private banking activities in the U.S.; regulatory efforts to monitor private banking activities and ensure that they are conducted in compliance with the Bank Secrecy Act; and policies and procedures of depository institutions that are designed to ensure that private banking activities are conducted in compliance with the Bank Secrecy Act.

Section 12 requires the Treasury Secretary, to prescribe regulations requiring financial institutions to maintain all accounts in such a way as to ensure that the name of an account holder and the number of the account are associated with all account activity of the account holder, and to ensure that all such information is available for purposes of account supervision and law enforcement.

Section 13 "expresses the sense of the Congress that the Secretary of the Treasury should make available to all Federal, State and local law enforcement agencies and financial regulatory agencies the full contents of the electronic database of reports required to be filed under the Bank Secrecy Act." Section 14 "directs the Secretary of the Treasury, in consultation with appropriate Federal law enforcement authorities, to develop criteria... to identify areas outside the [United States] in which money laundering activities are concentrated, and to designate any areas so identified as foreign high intensity money laundering areas."

Section 15 "authorizes the doubling of criminal penalties for Bank Secrecy Act violations committed with respect to a transaction involving a person in, a relationship maintained in, or transport of a monetary instrument involving a foreign country known to have been designated as a foreign high intensity money laundering area" pursuant to Section 14, which refers to the portions of the Department of State's annual International Narcotics Strategy Control Report that identifies foreign countries that serve as safe havens for money laundering.

B. Erosion of Secrecy

For professionals involved in the international transfer of wealth techniques, financial privacy is an important principle. Fiduciaries have obligations under law—both common law and statutory law in some countries—contract, and ethics to uphold confidentiality. Increasingly, in the era of globalization and since the start of the anti-money laundering regime in the mid-1980s, secrecy is sometimes overridden by obligations of banks, financial institutions, solicitors, and other covered persons to "know their customer" (or client) and identify and report suspicious transactions.

Two developments indicate the fragility and nature of exceptions to bank secrecy: the initiatives to rectify the Nazi gold losses and the intensive efforts by liquidators of a Cayman bank to recover computer bank records turned over by its former chairman and managing director to the U.S. Government.

Swiss Foreign Minister Reassures Swiss Bankers on Secrecy: One of the exceptions to bank and business secrecy has been the effort to ascertain the extent of wrongdoing and pay compensation to the victims of the Holocaust. The effort is sometimes referred to as the Nazi gold debacle. The various investigations, agreements, and lawsuits all have succeeded in overcoming bank secrecy in Switzerland and other countries, and demonstrate yet another exception to such secrecy. In this context, the Swiss Government has tried to assure its investors about its efforts to maintain legitimate secrecy.

On September 5, 1997, Flavio Cotti, Switzerland's foreign minister, assured Swiss bankers that the Swiss Government would not buckle to international demands to dilute Switzerland's bank secrecy laws, one of the main factors for Switzerland's dominance in the private banking business. His remarks were made during the annual meeting of the Swiss Bankers Association (SBA) in Berne and were designed to reassure Swiss bankers that Swiss authorities are aware of the financial risks facing the banks in the aftermath of growing criticism of the banks' wartime role in dealing with the accounts of Holocaust victims and looted Nazi gold.

According to Cotti, the Swiss Government would ensure that the Swiss banking industry remains a "central pillar of the Swiss economy." The banking sector generates ten percent of gross domestic product, employs 108,000 people, and contributes eleven percent of tax revenues.

Cotti complimented Swiss bankers for helping improve Switzerland's international image and for the "extraordinary speed" with which they had prepared a "package of measures comparable to no other." In addition, Cotti noted that the issue of "unfair tax competition" had assumed greater significance and that "Swiss banking secrecy and other laws supporting the Swiss financial centre had become frequent targets of criticism at OECD meeting."

Cotti also discussed the role of the Swiss banking community in accepting assets of "dubious origin from heads of state." In this connection, the Swiss Government had responded in an "active and efficient manner" in 1997 to block the Swiss bank accounts of ex-President Mobutu. The lessons from this and other cases is that "[t]he efficiency of Switzerland's financial centre attracts assets of criminal or dubious origin and it was in the deepest interests of the financial centre to keep such monies at a distance."

Ultimately, the lifting of bank secrecy helped facilitate the agreement announced on August 12, 1998, whereby representatives of Swiss commercial banks and Holocaust survivors reached a settlement, in which the banks agreed to "pay $1.25 billion in reparations to victims of the Nazi era, in exchange for the dismissal of three class action suits... and recommendations by the victims groups that the state and local authorities cancel plans to impose sanctions."

Cotti's remarks and the lifting of bank secrecy to resolve the controversy over the claims of Holocaust victims indicate the transition that the Swiss government and private sector are undergoing with respect to bank secrecy, vetting to exclude illegitimate money, the new anti-money laundering regime concerning "know-your-customer", "identifying and reporting suspicious transactions", "criminalizing money laundering", and freezing and forfeiting illegal proceeds and the instrumentalities of the same. The transition becomes more complex when governments, international organizations, non-governmental organizations, and public opinion assess and impose moral judgments about the private sector and the government's role during World War II nearly forty years later.

A case involving an effort by the Cayman Government to reclaim computer bank records obtained from a former managing director and target of a U.S. law enforcement proceeding provides a perspective of the practical limitations of bank secrecy in an increasingly shrinking world. On May 7, 1997, the U.S. District Court for the District of New Jersey issued an order denying a petition by liquidators of a Cayman bank seeking the return of its computer bank records that its former chairman and managing director had turned over to the U.S. Government. The managing director was a target of a law enforcement proceeding when he "voluntarily" turned over the documents. The liquidator then filed a petition for the return of property pursuant to Federal Rule of Criminal Procedure 41(e). On January 18, 1995, the Cayman Government appointed an interim controller to take control of the affairs of the offshore bank. At the time, the offshore bank had approximately 1,000 clients, including corporations, trusts and individuals, some of which were U.S. residents.

On January 24, 1994, the Cayman Government revoked the offshore bank's "category `B' Bank & Trust company licenses" and closed the bank. The Cayman Government also filed a petition for an order to wind-up the affairs of the offshore bank due to "serious irregularities" identified in the conduct of the offshore bank's business. On February 10, 1995, the Grand Court of the Cayman Islands ordered the offshore bank "wound up" (liquidated).

On June 21, 1996, a federal grand jury in Newark, New Jersey returned a multi-count indictment charging the individual defendant and others with conspiracy and money laundering. FBI agents subsequently arrested the individual defendant.

In June 1996, the individual defendant gave the FBI a tape containing "copies of certain computer back-up tapes containing detailed financial and operating records of the [Offshore] Bank." The individual defendant voluntarily gave the tape to the Federal Bureau of Investigation (FBI) "without the issuance of a warrant, subpoena or other compulsory process." It remains in the possession of the U.S. Government.

The FBI contacted the Royal Cayman Islands Police and sought assistance in its efforts to gain access to the information stored on the tape. On August 6, 1996, Christopher Johnson, the liquidator, "filed a formal, written complaint of the `theft' of the tape to the Cayman Police." The petition focused on the inevitability of the eventual transferal of the tape to the IRS "for the purpose of investigating and, where appropriate, prosecuting any bank clients subject to U.S. taxation."

The Advisory Committee's Report for Rule 41(e) of the Federal Rules Criminal Procedure provides "that an aggrieved person may seek return of property that has been unlawfully seized, and a person whose property has been lawfully seized may seek return of property when aggrieved by the Government's continued possession of it." Moreover, Rule

41(e) allows a court to "order either the originals or copies of seized documents be returned to their owner and permit the Government access and/or use of the information." Using four factors in entertaining a Rule 41(e) motion, the court denied the order.

The first factor is "whether the Government displayed a callous disregard for the constitutional rights of the petitioner." The Cayman liquidator and government did not meet the test. The Johnson court noted that the U.S. Government had no role in the procurement of the tape. Instead, the individual defendant voluntarily provided the tape to the U.S. Government. Since there was no U.S. Government involvement in the procurement of the tape, no constitutional rights were at issue in the instant case. Thus, the Johnson court held that the rights afforded by the Fourth Amendment are "wholly inapplicable to a `search or seizure, even an unreasonable one, effected by a private individual not acting as an agent of the Government or with the participation or knowledge of any government official.'"

Because the documents were voluntarily given to the U.S. Government, the latter's "use of the tape in its investigation of the suspected tax evasion scheme and other suspected financial crimes connected to the offshore bank and in future prosecutions will not violate the constitutional rights of the offshore bank or any of its clients." The second factor the Johnson court considered was whether the petitioner had an individual interest in and need for the property he wanted returned. The court found against the petitioner, stating that the petitioner already possessed the information contained on the tape and, hence, its return did not appear necessary for petitioner to carry on the offshore bank's business.

That the offshore bank was in liquidation and apparently would be defunct shortly invalidated the claim that petitioners did not need the tape to undertake their duties.

The Johnson court found unpersuasive the speculative argument that the use of the tape may expose the offshore bank to "numerous complaints and claims" because U.S. nationals are in any event "required to reveal the existence of foreign bank accounts and report certain foreign transactions." The reporting requirement meant that the U.S. nationals lacked a reasonable expectation of privacy in the offshore bank records.

Upon consideration of the third factor, the Johnson court found that the offshore bank would not suffer "irreparable harm" if the tape was not returned, since the offshore bank's licenses have been revoked and the bank was in liquidation.

The court also considered and rejected the fourth factor, whether the petitioners had an adequate remedy at law. Even if the petitioner was able to establish that the bank would suffer irreparable harm, the court found that the exercise of equitable jurisdiction to forbid the Government the use of the tape was not justified. Generally, even when the U.S. Government improperly has possession of evidence, and when the aggrieved party's Rule 41(d) motion is successful, courts have permitted the Government to retain copies of the evidence.

The Johnson court rejected the petitioners' argument that the doctrine of international comity requires the suppression of the tapes. While comity is "the spirit of cooperation in which a domestic tribunal approaches the resolution of cases touching the laws and interests of other sovereign states," it must yield to domestic policy. In particular, the Johnson court stated that no country will suffer the law of another to interfere with its own to the injury of its citizens. Here, the court noted that the U.S. Government declared that the information on the tape constitute "significant evidence" of a "widespread tax evasion scheme" and has "initiated multiple investigations concerning suspected criminal activities by customers of the Offshore bank."

The Johnson court rejected the arguments that disclosure of the information contained on the tape to U.S. Government agencies, such as the IRS, may expose the offshore bank to numerous complaints and claims. The court noted that, notwithstanding the Cayman Government's claim that its Mutual Legal Assistance in Criminal Matters Treaty enabled the United States to obtain the information on the tapes from it on request, the U.S. Government is not able to obtain information on pure tax matters under the Cayman-U.S. MLAT.

In rejecting the arguments of the petitioner under international comity, the Johnson court found the speculative arguments regarding harm that may result to the offshore bank and the banking industry of the Cayman Government insufficient to overcome the interest of the United States in its ongoing criminal investigation. The case represents a setback to Cayman secrecy and indicates the practical limitations of secrecy. Any person who relies on secrecy of one country now must factor into the equation the limitations that may eventually eliminate the confidentiality on which it seeks to rely.

Due Diligence

Since the mid-1980s, a major component of international anti-money laundering efforts has been due diligence requirements. These requirements include: the duty to know-your-client, the duty to identify and report to authorities suspicious transactions, the requirement to appoint a compliance officer with access to the top executives of an organization, the duty to train employees on anti-money laundering, and the duty to ensure that anti-money laundering obligations are properly audited so that any violations will be detected and remedied. Increasingly, those bodies covered by due diligence include nonbank financial institutions, such as money transmitters. In addition, the requirements for bank and financial supervisors to monitor and audit continue to multiply. On November 19, 1998, the release by the British Government of its report on financial services in the Channel Islands initiated a number of changes in due diligence to prevent and combat money laundering.

In its November 1998 report on problems in international financial services in the Channel Islands, the British Government called for reforms, many of which presage similar reforms it will demand from other offshore territories. The so-called Edwards report—named for its author, a former top official at the British Treasury—reviews financial supervision in the Channel Islands (consisting of Guernsey, Jersey, and the Isle of Man) and calls on them to strengthen restrictions on offshore companies and start cooperating with foreign financial investigations.

Lord Williams, a British Home Office minister, subsequently agreed to chair a series of meetings with the three territories starting in January 1999, to follow up on the list of proposed reforms in the Edwards report.

The Edwards Report applauds the efforts of the islands, which are self-governing dependencies of the British crown, to strengthen standards in their 350 million [pounds sterling] financial industry. The report notes that one-third of investments come from U.K. residents. However, the report contains detailed recommendations for major reforms focusing especially on the rules for establishing offshore companies and trusts used to shelter assets from tax or from outside scrutiny. While all three islands have accepted the recommendations generally, they resist a number of specific recommendations—such as requiring companies to file audited accounts, and, in the case of the Isle of Man, vetting companies established on the island—in the hope that new measures to control company agents will solve the problem.

The report calls on all of the islands to improve the regulation of companies and company directors. The islands' low tax rates and relatively flexible regulatory controls have attracted large numbers of international companies. Approximately 100,0000 companies are incorporated in the islands, especially in the Isle of Man. Many more are administered from, but not incorporated in, the islands. According to former Minister Edwards, company regulation requires tightening in all three islands. The priority for the authorities in all three islands is to cooperate fully with other countries in the pursuit of financial crime and money laundering.

In recent years, several high profile financial court cases have called attention to the Channel Islands' regulatory procedures. For example, in 1998 Bank Cantrade was forced to pay fines of $3 million because one of its traders had misled investors by showing profits of $15 million on foreign currency transactions when he had actually lost $11 million. In 1995, when the Barings merchant bank failed, "the bank's Guernsey subsidiary had lent deposits well in excess of its capital base and was technically insolvent. However, the unit was not declared insolvent while the authorities tried to find a buyer."

According to the Edwards Report, these and other cases indicate the need for more on-site inspections of financial institutions as well as the need some kind for of reform, moratorium, or administration procedures as in the United Kingdom to assist them in dealing with insolvency. The report also calls for a financial ombudsman to deal with customer complaints.

The Edwards Report recommends that the Isle of Man strengthen its regulation of companies. Thousands of companies are incorporated in the Isle of Man and thousands more are administered from Guernsey and Jersey, if not actually incorporated there. Most of the companies are private and formed by non-residents or trusts to hold assets or interests outside the islands. The Isle of Man has no system to vet new companies that want to register or for persons to obtain disclosure about the companies already registered.

For Guernsey, the Edwards report calls for dealing with the problem of nominee directors—the so called "Sark lark." This phenomenon involves residents of Sark, a small island under Guernsey's jurisdictions, who sit as directors on many different company boards. While the population of Sark is only 575, the total directorships held amount to approximately 15,000. Three residents hold between 1,600 and 3,000 directorships each.

Guernsey has started to crack down on "false domiciles," whereby islanders were responding to phone calls for companies located elsewhere. However, the island has resisted divesting residents of their directorships.

In general, the islands reacted positively to the Edwards report. However, bankers complained that the report's recommendations would erode client confidentiality. The financial industry is likely to oppose and resist many of the detailed changes, including comprehensive customer compensation schemes in Jersey and Guernsey, and some changes in trust law.

The Edwards report recommends the establishment of a confidential hotline for whistle blowers, such as the person who reported improprieties in Cantrade, but was ignored by his superiors. Jersey authorities are considering providing statutory protection for such informers.

The Jersey Bankers Associations has indicated that it favours the release of information to other authorities where the latter are investigating crimes. However, they worry about "areas which potentially affect the fine dividing line between protecting [their] clients' confidentiality and the disclosure of information about customer affairs to authorities outside the jurisdiction of Jersey."

The preparation and release of the Edwards report takes place in the context of the OECD Report on Harmful Tax Competition and the EU initiative towards tax harmonization and imposing minimum withholding tax, reporting requirements for the payment of interest to residents of other EU countries earned on bank deposits in the other host country, or both. In fact, the United Kingdom's membership in the European Union has been a contributing element in its own initiatives to strengthen international financial supervision in its dependent and overseas territories.

The Edwards report takes a balanced approach of acknowledging and applauding the comparatively favourable financial supervisory standards in the three islands, considering the dependence of each of the islands on international financial business. The recommendations recognize the need to help the international financial services sector evolve rather than trying to destroy them. The pragmatic approach to improving financial supervisory standards is prudent, especially given the positive attitude of the three jurisdictions to cooperate in the implementation of the recommendations. Regulators and professionals in jurisdictions in which international financial services are an important part of the economy will recognize that many recommendations of the Edwards report will be adopted by international organizations active in the relevant subject matter areas.

The Proposed U.S. Know-Your-Customer Rule Will Formalize Internal Control Procedures:

The Proposed Regulations: The proposed know-your-customer regulation contained in the Board of Governors of the Federal Reserve System's memorandum dated September 28, 1998, requires banks to develop for the first time their know-your-customer programme, and continues to generate discussion. The proposed rule will also apply eventually to non-bank financial institutions and will have broad implications for private banking, offshore accounts, and the imposition of responsibility on covered persons to design, implement, and regularly update and adjust their know-your-customer internal control systems.

The proposed regulation will require institutions supervised by the Federal Reserve Board to develop and implement a know-your-customer programme. According to the proposal, the establishment of a know-your-customer programme is designed to protect the reputation of the bank; facilitate the bank's compliance with all applicable statutes and regulations (including the Bank Secrecy Act and the Board's suspicious activity reporting regulations) and with safe and sound banking practices; and protect the bank from becoming a vehicle for or a victim of illegal activities perpetrated by its customers.

Because the Board recognized that banks vary considerably in the way in which they conduct their business, the proposal permits each bank to develop its own know-your-customer programme as a system designed to meet the goals of the proposal. The proposed Federal Register notice will require banks to develop a know-your-customer programme that at least will provide a system for handling the following tasks:

1. Determining the true identities of the bank's customers;
2. Determining the customer's sources of funds for transactions involving the bank, including the types of instruments used and the sources from which the funds were derived or generated;
3. Determining the specific customer's normal and expected transactions involving the bank;
4. Monitoring customer transactions to ascertain if such transactions are consistent with normal and expected transactions for that particular customer or for customers in the same or similar categories or classes, as established by the bank;
5. Identifying customer transactions that do not appear to be consistent with "normal and expected transactions for that specific customer or for customers in the same or similar categories or classes, as established by the bank"; and
6. Ascertaining if a transaction is unusual or suspicious, in accordance with the Board's suspicious activity reporting regulations, and reporting it accordingly.

The proposal permits each bank to decide how best, consistent with its own business practices, it can identify its customers, understand the normal and expected transactions of its customers, and then monitor on an ongoing basis the transactions of its customers. Under the proposal, a bank must decide the know-your-customer programme suited to its specific needs, delineate the programme in writing, and demonstrate that it is complying with the programme. The proposal will require banks to understand to whom they are providing their services at the start of the relationship, to develop an understanding of the transactions the customers will be conducting, and then to monitor the transactions of those customers.

Some banks, especially those offering private banking services, have raised concerns about identifying their clients, especially since a main tenet of such services is the confidentiality offered and demanded by these customers through the use of intermediary entities, such as private investment companies, trusts, private mutual funds, or investment advisory accounts, and since these entities are often based at offshore locations. The Federal Reserve is convinced that the beneficial owner's identity is usually well known to bank personnel or that banks can obtain waivers from their customers for any perceived restriction of the release of beneficial owner information. In this regard, the Federal Deposit Insurance Corporation (FDIC) seeks comments on whether any actual or perceived invasion of personal privacy interest is outweighed by the compliance benefit.

While the proposal's requirement of identifying the true beneficial owner of each account of the bank is not intended to force a bank to disclose information in violation of foreign law, allowing any bank to avoid identification of beneficial ownership of any account would defeat the main purpose of the proposed rule—to ensure that each bank knows to whom it is offering its service. In this connection, the proposed rule responds to the criticism of a recent General Accounting Office (GAO) report that U.S. banks lacked sufficient documentation regarding the beneficial owners of offshore entities that maintained accounts in the United States.

In response to concerns raised by several banks as to the severe hardship and cost of the new monitoring requirements, the Board of Governors has emphasized that the regulation will offer flexibility and require banks to develop and implement effective monitoring systems, commensurate with the risks presented by the types of accounts maintained at the bank and the types of transactions conducted through those accounts. The effectiveness of the monitoring system of a bank's know-your-customer programme will be based on that particular bank's ability to monitor transactions consistent with the volume and types of transactions conducted at the bank. The FDIC is seeking comment on whether the benefits of implementing the know-your-customer requirements outweigh the costs involved and whether there should be a minimum account size threshold below which the requirements should be waived.

The design of a monitoring system should correspond to the risk associated with the types of accounts maintained and types of transactions conducted through those accounts. Hence, the design of such a system could involve the classification of accounts into various categories based on such factors as the type of account, the types of transactions conducted in the various types of accounts, the size of the account, the number and size of transactions conducted through the account, and the risk of illicit activity associated with the type of account and the transactions conducted through the account.

For certain categories of accounts, it may be sufficient for an effective monitoring system to establish parameters for which the transactions within these accounts will normally occur. Instead of monitoring each transaction, an effective monitoring system may involve monitoring only for those transactions that exceed the established parameters for that particular category of accounts. The proposed know-your-customer rule asks for the public to provide input on specific questions. The Federal Reserve wants comments to focus on the proposed definition of "customer" to ensure, at a minimum, that the definition is not overly broad and adequately covers "beneficial" ownership-related issues. Respondents are asked whether the proposal creates an uneven playing field for non-bank financial institutions, such as money transmitters and broker-dealers.

The proposed rule arises out of the Congressional hearings that have produced the enactment of the Money Laundering

Deterrence Act of 1998, which requires that the Secretary of the Treasury implement know-your-customer regulations within 120 days of passage of the legislation. Congressman Leach's staff informed the Federal Reserve that the primary reasons for the provision in the draft legislation is to ensure that legal enforceable regulations exist to require that financial institutions adopt know-your-customer procedures and that similar regulations are developed for the non-bank financial sector, including broker-dealers and money transmitters.

The Federal Reserve will continue to work with FinCEN and will start to coordinate with the staff of the SEC in helping programme such rules for non-bank financial institutions.

The Federal Reserve is awaiting feedback from other regulatory agencies, especially the Office of the Comptroller of the Currency (OCC) and the Office of the Thrift Supervision (OTS), before submitting the proposal to the Federal Register. It is also awaiting input from the Board of Directors of the FDIC on whether know-your-customer standards should be issued as regulations or guidelines.

The Federal Reserve believes that the proposed know-your-customer rule will enable financial institutions to obtain information from their customers regarding the identity, the types of transactions to be conducted, and the source of funds, among other things. Obtaining and reviewing such information will assist financial institutions in making a risk-based determination on various matters—including the extent of identifying necessary information and the amount of monitoring required—by permitting institutions to categorize their customers into different groups based on the types of services being requested and the magnitude and extent of the transactions being conducted. Effective know-your-customer programmes will require that banking organizations develop "customer profiles" to understand their customers' intended relationships with the institution and, thereafter, to determine realistically when customers conduct suspicious or potentially illegal transactions.

Legally, the Federal Reserve's proposal will revise 12 C.F.R. pts. 208, 211, and 225 by requiring state member banks, certain bank holding companies and their non-bank subsidiaries, U.S. branches and agencies and other offices of foreign banks, and Edge and Agreement corporations to develop and implement a know-your-customer programme within their institutions. The proposed rules define "customer" as "the person or entity who has an account involving the receipt or disbursal of funds at a bank and any other person or entity on behalf of whom such an account is maintained." The term encompasses direct and indirect beneficiaries of the account when the activity in the account involves the receipt or disbursal of funds.

"It also includes a person or entity who owns or is represented by the customer." Hence, a customer would include an account holder, a beneficial owner of an account, or a borrower. A customer could also include "the beneficiary of a trust, an investment fund, a pension fund or company whose assets are managed by an asset manager, a controlling shareholder of a closely held corporation or the grantor of a trust established in an offshore jurisdiction."

The proposed rule underscores the need to target private banking operations, since these customers utilize such account vehicles as personal investment companies (PICs), trusts, personal mutual investment funds, or are clients of financial advisors. Such accounts help protect the legitimate confidentiality and financial privacy of the customers that use such accounts. However, the need to identify properly the beneficial owners of such accounts, through an effective know-your-customer programme, is required to continue safe and sound operation of the bank. Hence, know-your-customer procedures for identifying the beneficial owners of private bank accounts should be no different than the procedures for identifying other customers of the bank. By developing special protections to limit access to information that would generally reveal the beneficial owners of these accounts, a private bank can address any needed confidentiality.

Once the proposed rule is published in the Federal Register, the public will have sixty days from that date to comment on the rule. The final rule may take effect at the start of the year 2000. Once the rule becomes final, the Federal Reserve will allow covered financial institutions a six-month grace period to fully implement know-your-customer programmes, after which time bank examiners may bring disciplinary action against institutions that violate the rules.

During the annual American Bankers Association/ American Bar Association conference on money laundering, Susan Tucillo, Vice-President and Senior Compliance Officer of Citibank, N.A., noted that the know-your-customer rules will generate a substantial amount of new employment because of the complexity of issues raised, thereby requiring "a fundamental retooling of the branch operation process." The proposed rules cover virtually every product line and will particularly cause problems for attorney trust accounts, escrow accounts, other high-turnover attorney accounts, letters of credit, and other banking and lending transactions.

The know-your-customer rule would require that banks ensure that all documentation on accounts domiciled in the United States. be made available to Federal Reserve examiners within forty-eight hours of a request. U.S. banks are concerned that these rules will limit their ability to do business in offshore jurisdictions where they compete with foreign banks from jurisdictions with less restrictive know-your-customer rules. An important issue raised is the definition of customer. The preamble explains that "customer" includes "direct and indirect beneficiaries" of the account, as well as "a person or entity who owns or is represented by the customer." The proposed regulation specifically the beneficial owners of PICs, trusts and "personal mutual investment funds," clients of financial advisors, and "borrowers." The Federal Reserve and FDIC maintain a customer also could include the beneficiary of an investment fund, a pension fund, a company whose assets are managed by an asset manager, or a controlling shareholder of a closely-held corporation.

The regulations and preambles are conspicuously silent on what a customer does not include, for example, shareholders of publicly-traded corporations or of widely-held non-publicly traded businesses. Further, the regulators state that in some cases persons with the know-your-customer obligation might need to obtain information about the controlling owners of a business or other legal entity. Hence, the definition of customer may have significant impact on many fiduciaries. In this connection, the Federal Reserve and FDIC are seeking comments on whether the proposed definition of "customer" is adequate to include all persons who "benefit from the transactions conducted at the bank, such as persons who establish off-shore shell companies... or otherwise conduct business through intermediaries." In addition, they seek comments on whether the proposed definition of customer is too wide and will unnecessarily include persons that pose minimal know-your-customer risk, that is, whether additional regulatory exceptions are appropriate.

At present, the proposed regulations do not have exceptions for foreign banks, foreign broker-dealers, or foreign investment advisors that are regulated in their home countries or in certain home countries that have sufficient anti-money laundering countries. Similarly, no exceptions exist for foreign open-ended collective investment funds such as mutual funds, which may have thousands of investors. However, the regulators would expect banks to identify the shareholders of a mutual fund established in an offshore jurisdiction that has a limited number of shareholders. In the case of accounts opened by mail or Internet, banks and other covered persons must give special attention to verifying addresses and telephone numbers, and to use commercially available data sources to verify the customer's date of birth and social security number.

The regulations require the bank to identify the beneficial owners of account holders that are offshore private investment companies, trusts, "private mutual funds," or investment advisors—in other words, high-risk customers—and to maintain data about the beneficial owner to the same extent as for U.S. persons. In the event that banks maintain the documentation about the identity of foreign beneficial owners, such as customers of a foreign investment advisor or the principal of a personal investment company outside the United States in a foreign branch or holding company, regulators would require that the bank furnish the documentation to a bank examiner in the United States within forty-eight hours of the examiner's request. No exceptions exist if bank secrecy or other law, such as the EU privacy directive, would preclude providing the documentation in the United States, especially with respect to existing customers.

Opposition from Private Sector and Congress: On February 3, 1999, a dozen members of Congress introduced four pieces of legislation:

1. *H.R. 220*—Freedom and Privacy Restoration Act of 1999 to prohibit the federal government from creating a national ID and medical ID by repealing sections of the laws passed in 1996 and would prohibit the use of social security numbers as an identifier.
2. *H.R. 516*—Know-Your-Customer Sunset Act of 1999 would bar agencies from following through on proposed Know-Your-Customer regulations.
3. *H.R. 518*—Bank Secrecy Sunset Act would repeal the law that gives federal bank regulators monitoring authority and devolves the power to the states unless Congress passes a better version of the law.
4. *HR 517*—FinCEN Public Accountability Act of 1999 would let bank customers check their own files and challenge information they believe to be false or inaccurate.

On March 4, 1999, Comptroller of the Currency John D. Hawke, Jr. testified that federal banking regulators' proposed know-your-customer rules should be withdrawn at the end of the public comment period. Hawke said any marginal advantages for law enforcement would be strongly outweighed by its potential for inflicting lasting damage on the banking system.

Christie Sciacca, associate director of FDIC's division of supervisor, also testified that his agency believes the "proposal cannot become final in its current form, if at all." Sciacca explained that most comments from the banking industry involved concerns about "the cost of compliance, customer privacy, and the competitive disadvantage if all financial institutions are not subject to the same requirements." At present, the status of the know-your-customer regulations are uncertain and controversial.

International Standards for Accounting in Anti-Money Laundering Campaigns

An important development is the establishment of international standards for accounting in anti-money laundering and financial crimes. The goals of accounting, as defined by the American Accounting Association, are to make decisions on the use of limited resources, including crucial decision areas, determine goals and objectives, direct and control effectively an organization's human and material resources, maintain and report on the custodianship of resources, and facilitate social functions and controls.

Auditing encompasses the following three major categories: (1) financial statement audit; (2) operational audit; and (3) compliance audit. In particular, a compliance audit has as its principal goal determining whether the entity under audit is following procedures or rules established by a higher authority.

Both accounting and auditing include within themselves certain fundamental notions on conformity with, and obedience to, applicable legal authority. These basic concepts involve the intersection of accounting and money laundering. In every jurisdiction, accountancy contains long-standing and deeply rooted requirements of impartiality, objectivity, and accuracy, using uniform standards and principles, and a code of mandatory professional ethics to support those obligations.

These obligations entrust accountants with the responsibility for determining whether financial statements are free from material misstatements, and for auditing internal controls and procedures relevant to the production of those internal controls. The "core competence" of accountancy in the area of internal controls and the accountant's obligations for impartiality, objectivity, and accuracy have led many countries to rely on accountancy in detecting and preventing money laundering and financial crimes such as fraud.

Training provides accountants with the requisite professional tools and expertise to enable them to compare different entities within a single industry and thereby detect certain anomalies. Accountancy emphasizes operational knowledge of industries audited and appropriate internal controls, applied to a particular industry. A growing requirement in accounting jurisdictions to combat financial crimes requires accountants to report discoveries of serious abnormalities to higher authorities in appropriate circumstances.

Worldwide accounting organizations have begun to give guidance to their accounting professionals concerning money laundering issues.

However, little or no international coordination has occurred, despite accountancy's overall global harmonization and increasing emphasis on international accounting standards. The Basle Committee on Banking Supervision of the Bank for International Settlements has issued its Core Principles for Effective Banking Supervision. In particular, Principle 15 states that "banking supervisors must determine that banks have adequate policies, practices and procedures in place, including strict `know-your-customer' rules, that promote high ethical and professional standards in the financial sector and prevent the bank being used, intentionally or unintentionally, by criminal elements." In addition, Principle 14 provides that bank supervisors must ensure that banks employ "appropriate independent internal or external audit and compliance functions to test adherence to" policies, procedures, practices and legal requirements, which include know-your-customer and anti-money laundering rules.

In the United States, the Bank Secrecy Act Advisory Group has established a sub-group, in coordination with appropriate accounting organizations and headed by an industry expert, to explore appropriate guidelines within the United States concerning money laundering. The group will explore issues and develop guidelines or suggestions on how to effectively provide useful guidance to the U.S. accounting profession on money laundering.

Accounting bodies and researchers working on money laundering problems have concentrated on six important issues: (1) legal issues; (2) auditing issues; (3) internal controls; (4) reporting obligations; (5) effect on financial statement presentation; and (6) enforcement activity. With respect to legal issues, all jurisdictions whose accounting bodies have worked on accounting guidance concerning money laundering have provided an explanation in layman's terms of appropriate legal issues that an accounting professional is likely to encounter.

For auditing issues, many accounting jurisdictions have issued a checklist of significant indicators accounting professionals can apply to potential money laundering concerns. Such guidance assists accountants in effectively performing their duties. Clear, specific guidance on standards within an audit of potential money laundering are critical to the accounting profession. While the technical specifics of accounting standards may differ throughout the world, the indicators of potential money laundering often do not. Use of harmonized checklists and indicators are important since money laundering is often transnational; prevention and investigation thus may require cooperation between accounting professionals in various jurisdictions.

Comprehensive internal risk control assessment is critical to application of auditing standards. The Swiss and U.S. professionals have provided effective models for internal risk assessment with respect to money laundering. Various jurisdictions have provided guidance as to the obligations of an accounting profession when potential money laundering is discovered. The guidance is divided between legal requirements and ethical obligations to report. While accounting professionals have ethical obligations of confidentiality toward clients, exceptions apply with respect to reporting crimes, such as money laundering.

With respect to the effect on financial statement presentation, several jurisdictions have discussed such effect after discovery of potential money laundering. The questions concern whether, and to what extent, an accounting professional must report to the audited entity the discovery of potential money laundering in the financial statements. Conflicts may exist between ethical and legal obligations of accounting professionals to disclose fully and impartially all relevant or material information in a financial statement on the one hand, and legal restrictions on the notification to unauthorized personnel of potential money laundering on the other.

Enforcement of accounting standards in money laundering is largely self-regulatory and authorizes a self-regulatory body to impose sanctions. One accounting jurisdiction has already imposed sanctions on a member based on money laundering and in the absence of any legal sanctions against that member. The accounting professional can play a critical role in preventing money laundering, especially in the development and application of internal controls and the assessment of risks. International cooperation is critical to effectively combating money laundering.

Case Law and Developments

In many countries around the world, major litigation is raging over the implementation of national anti-money laundering laws, often continuing for five years or more. For instance, the anti-money laundering litigation in the early 1990s in Luxembourg over assets of the Cali cartel in Luxembourg generated simultaneous litigation in Panama and

New York, and subsequently resulted in criminal proceedings against one of the U.S.-based attorneys for the Cali cartel over his conduct in handling the case. The broad nature of money laundering laws means that it can, and often is, added by U.S. prosecutors as a charge whenever a crime has been committed involving the transfer of money, property or both. Moreover, the technical distinctions in money laundering statutes sometimes can be important internationally.

A. Antigua Government Announces the Failure of a Russian-Owned Bank

During the first week of August 1997, the Government of Antigua and Barbuda announced the failure of the European Union Bank (EUB) – a fraud warning – and appointed Coopers & Lybrand as the receiver of a Russian-owned bank. The Antiguan Government further announced that it was pursuing Serbeveo Ushakov of Texas and Vitali Papsouev of Ontario, Canada, two Russian nationals who founded EUB and are believed to have fled. According to a media report, Evan Hermiston, resident manager in Antigua of Coopers & Lybrand's Caribbean branch, said the Antiguan Government had asked his firm to start investigating the bank during mid-July. Hermiston delivered a report during the first week of August.

The webpage established by EUB on the World Wide Web invited depositors to take advantage of "excellent interest rates, offered in a stable, tax-free environment, with utmost privacy, confidentiality and security." In October 1996, both the Bank of England and the U.S. Comptroller of the Currency issued warnings on EUB's operations.

Two Russians, Aleksandr P. Konanikhin and Mikhail B. Khodorovsky, founded EUB in June 1994. They described themselves as "brokers of oil, metals, and construction supplies and officers of the Menatep Bank of Moscow." U.S. and British officials allege the bank is linked to Russian organized crime. According to U.S. officials, Konanikhin was arrested in the United States on visa violation charges and is accused of embezzling more than $8 million from a Moscow bank. Both Konanikhin and Khodorovsky have since severed their formal connections with the EUB.

Two other Russians, Ushakov and Papsouev, who have disappeared, were listed as the bank's directors when it collapsed. As part of EUB's marketing on its now dormant Internet webpage, the bank stressed the benefits of the lax regulatory climate. The webpage announced that "since there are no government withholding or reporting requirements on accounts, the burdensome and expensive accounting requirements are reduced for you." EUB's Internet webpage allowed clients anywhere in the world to open accounts, transfer money, write checks by computer, and obtain credit cards twenty-four hours a day.

Although the Antiguan Government is claiming confidentiality laws and has declined to provide information regarding the number of depositors at EUB or the amount of money it had reported in accounts, bank records show the bank violated the rules almost from the start. Indeed, in October 1995, an official letter from the Ministry of Finance noted that the bank had failed to file an audited financial statement for 1994. In May 1997, the Idaho Department of Finance "declared the bank to be operating illegally" and ordered it to "stop soliciting deposits from Idaho residents over the Internet."

As a result of international pressure—that is, the warnings issued by the Bank of England, the OCC, and the U.S. State Department—the Antiguan Government closed another five Russian banks established in Antigua and issued new anti-money laundering regulations.

The combination of the U.K. and U.S. warnings and the latest problems experienced by EUB clearly hurts the reputation of Antigua and Barbuda as stable and secure environment. Indeed, over reliance on secrecy and insufficient regulatory frameworks and supervision can undermine stability. Ironically, secrecy and lack of regulation also focus the attention of foreign regulators and international financial organizations on financial institutions in such jurisdictions.

Nevertheless, since the British Government has closed many of the offshore banks and financial institutions in the Caribbean Dependent Territories, and since more traditional jurisdictions such as Panama and the Bahamas have tightened their own vetting and regulatory processes, unsavory characters and organized crime have targeted countries whose frameworks and vetting processes are comparatively liberal. John E. St. Luce, the Antiguan Finance Minister, has claimed that his government has passed strong legislation on anti-money laundering and has a committee reviewing these developments.(384) Earlier statements from the Antiguan Government stating that it had remedied the problems of offshore banks, however, have proven to be mere rhetoric and little substance. On May 6, 1998, the U.S. Attorney filed an indictment in the U.S. District Court for the Northern District of Florida charging "the Caribbean American Bank of Antigua and eight individuals with a loan scam that allegedly bilked more than $60 million from hundreds of people in ten countries and with related money laundering." The indictment seeks as one remedy the forfeiture of all the bank's funds and assets.

B. Canadian Supreme Court Orders Extradition for U.S. Money Laundering Sting

On July 26, 1997, the Canadian Supreme Court reversed the Ontario provincial appeals court and held that a Canadian citizen should be extradited to the United States. On a dual criminality issue, the Court concluded that the failed sting constituted the offenses of attempt and conspiracy in Canada. Arye Dynar, a Canadian citizen, was the subject of a U.S. money laundering investigation during the 1980s. In 1990, the FBI in Nevada began recording telephone conversations between Dynar in Canada and a cooperating informant in the United States known as "Anthony." According to the Court, "Mr. Dynar agreed with alacrity to launder money for Anthony."

Moreover, these conversations indicated that the money to be laundered was drug money. However, as it was a government sting, no real drug money existed. Dynar refused to travel to the United States. Instead, it was determined that Dynar's associate, another Canadian citizen named Maurice Cohen, would meet with Anthony's associate in Buffalo, New York, collect the money, and return it to Dynar in Toronto where it would be laundered. Cohen would return the laundered money less, of course, Dynar's commission. Cohen entered the United States and met with undercover U.S. law enforcement agents. No money was transferred, and the FBI aborted the operation by pretending to arrest one of the undercover officers.

Subsequently, the United States sought the extradition of Dynar on a two-count indictment returned in Las Vegas, Nevada. The indictment charged Dynar and Cohen with violations of U.S. money laundering laws of under the sting provisions of the U.S. Code. The first count of the indictment accused "both Dynar and Cohen of attempting to conduct a financial transaction involving property represented by a law enforcement officer to be the proceeds of drug dealing and the second count accused the two of conspiring to do so."

The United States requested the extradition of Dynar from Canada in 1992. Following an extradition hearing, Dynar was ordered committed for extradition. Dynar appealed to the Ontario Court of Appeal. The Ontario Court of Appeal reversed and set aside the extradition on the basis that there was a lack of dual criminality under Canadian law. According to the provincial appeals court, Dynar did not commit a crime under Canadian law because at the time of the activity no sting provision existed. As such, the money must in fact be derived from the commission of a crime. The Crown appealed to the Supreme Court of Canada.

The Supreme Court framed the issue before it in this way: The issue in this appeal is whether the respondent's conduct in the United States would constitute a crime if carried out in this country, thereby meeting the requirement of "double criminality" which is the precondition for the surrender of a Canadian fugitive for trial in a foreign jurisdiction. This issue requires the Court to consider the scope of the liability for attempted offenses and conspiracy under Canadian criminal law, specifically, whether impossibility constitutes a defence to a charge of attempt or conspiracy in Canada.

A majority of the Court ruled that "Dynar's conduct would have amounted to a criminal attempt and a criminal conspiracy under Canadian law." Even though Dynar's plan, if successful, would not have constituted a violation of the substantive criminal law in Canada at that time, the Court found that "the steps that Mr. Dynar took towards the realization of his plan to launder money would have amounted to a criminal attempt and a criminal conspiracy under Canadian law." As a consequence, the Court ruled that the trial court was correct in holding Dynar extraditable on both the charge of attempt to launder money and conspiracy to launder. The extradition order was reinstated.

United States and Mexico Duel over Money Laundering Case

A case that illustrates the tension over international money laundering and corruption between the United States and Mexico is a case resulting from a sting operation conducted by U.S. authorities primarily against Mexican banks. On May 18, 1998, a federal grand jury in Los Angeles charged three Mexican banks and twenty-six Mexican bankers with laundering millions of dollars in drug profits. According to an announcement by Treasury Secretary Robert Rubin and Attorney General Janet Reno, the charges represent the first time that Mexican banks and bank officials were directly linked to laundering U.S. drug proceeds for the Cali cartel of Colombia and the Juarez cartel of Mexico.

The indictment was the culmination of "Operation Casablanca," a three-year undercover sting operation led by the U.S. Customs Service that resulted in the arrests of twenty-two bankers from twelve of Mexico's nineteen largest banking institutions. The indictment indicated gaping loopholes in U.S. and Mexican laws that permit traffickers to move their proceeds relatively easily in spite of various anti-money laundering and reporting laws and regulations in both countries. The loopholes have been widely reported by law enforcement authorities. This section outlines some of the highlights of the investigation, the indictment, responses by the Mexican Government, and its consequences for U.S.-Mexican law enforcement cooperation.

Indictment

The three Mexican banks charged were Bancomer and Banca Serfin—Mexico's second- and third-largest banks, respectively—as well as Banca Confia, a smaller institution recently bought by Citibank. On May 18, 1998, the Federal Reserve Board announced it was filing civil actions against five banks with branches in the United States. Shortly after the indictment, Banca Serfin announced it would plead not guilty and asked William Isaac, former Chairman of the FDIC, to conduct an independent investigation of the accusations.

In a statement announcing the indictment, Secretary Rubin said that "by infiltrating the highest levels of the international drug trafficking financial infrastructure, [U.S. Customers officials were] able to crack the elaborate financial schemes the drug traffickers developed to launder the tremendous volumes of cash acquired as proceeds from their deadly trade." Attorney General Reno said that "the arrests and seizures disrupted a major money laundering operation that had served as an engine of the international drug trafficking trade."

Since its start in November 1995, the undercover sting was kept secret from the Mexican Government. On May 18, 1998, Mexican officials first learned of the investigation when Reno notified Mexican Attorney General Jorge Madrazo Cuellar by phone. Secretary Rubin also alerted his counterpart, Jose Angel Gurria Trevino, Secretary of Finance and Public Credit in Mexico.

U.S. authorities said that they discovered nearly 100 bank accounts in the United States had been used by drug traffickers to deposit laundered funds. On May 18, 1998, investigators seized those accounts that they estimated to hold approximately $122 million. The investigation began after the U.S. Customs Office in Los Angeles discovered that drug cartel members had laundered proceeds from U.S. drug sales in branches of Mexican banks near the border. The investigation grew to include the financial infrastructure of the Ciudad Juarez cartel. During the investigation, Customs Service undercover agents established a front company, the Emerald Empire Corp., with offices in the Los Angeles suburb of Santa Fe Springs, and posed as middlemen between the cartel financial directors and the Mexican bankers (mostly mid-level executives), who agreed, for a fee of four or five percent, to launder funds. The bankers had established phony accounts and used bank drafts to evade money laundering regulations.

The indictment indicated gaping loopholes in U.S. and Mexican laws that permit traffickers to move their proceeds relatively easily in spite of various anti-money laundering and reporting laws and regulations in both countries. The loopholes have been widely reported by law enforcement authorities.

According to the indictment, between February 1997 and May 1998, Confia branch lawyer Miguel Barba Martin and employee Jorge Milton Diaz managed to direct $11 million in drug money deposits into false accounts and transfer the funds into easily cashed bank drafts and other instruments. At one time, Reyes Ortega warned Victor Manuel Alcala, alias Dr. Navarro, an alleged capo for the Juarez cocaine cartel, that the new Mexican banking rules would make it more difficult to launder money in Mexico.

Hence, in late 1996, $650,000 from one deposit turned up belatedly in a phony business account established in the Cayman Islands as part of the scheme. "New accounts in false names were regularly opened and closed in various offshore locales to avoid detection." For instance, Alcala is alleged to have established "a textile company as a front in Tepatitlan, which opened accounts at Banoro, where the branch manager also proved helpful."

On May 18, 1998, the Federal Reserve issued "`cease and desist' orders against five foreign banks, including two of those under indictment, for failing to address serious deficiencies in their anti-money laundering programmes." The banks are Banca Serfin, Bancomer, Banamex and Bital of Mexico and Banco Santander of Spain, each of which operates offices in the United States. The Federal Reserve order requires the banks to implement new anti-money laundering procedures.

Mexico Will Prosecute U.S. Agents Who Operated Sting

Attorney General Madrazo Cuellar accused the United States of deceiving Mexico by making officials there believe that the entire three-year undercover operation had been conducted inside the United States. President Ernesto Zedillo ordered his diplomats to deliver the protest after he determined that conducting a hidden operation on Mexican soil violated the terms of several agreements between the two countries as well as the spirit of the close bilateral relationship.

On May 21, 1998, the Mexican Permanent Commission, which represents Mexico's Congress when it is not in session, voted unanimously to demand an investigation into "Operation Casablanca" and criticized possible intervention by U.S. agents. On June 3, 1998, the Mexican Government advised the United States that it would prosecute U.S. Customs agents and informers who executed an undercover money laundering operation in Mexican territory and would seek the agents' extradition in connection with the charges. At a meeting on June 1, 1998 in Caracas, Venezuela, Foreign Secretary Rosario Green of Mexico handed to U.S. Secretary of State Madeleine K. Albright a list of Mexican laws that the Customs agents violated according to preliminary results of Mexican investigations. In news interviews, Secretary Green reported that "Mexico is preparing to accuse the agents of entrapment, engaging in money-laundering, and usurping the authority of Mexican law enforcement." Meanwhile, Secretary

Albright acknowledged that ties with Mexico had been damaged at a meeting of the Organization of American States in Caracas.

In the aftermath of the indictments against Mexican banks and bankers resulting from "Operation Casablanca," Secretary Green has stated that Mexico now has evidence that U.S. agents broke Mexican laws during their investigations. The inducement of illegal acts, apparently conducted during the three-year money laundering sting when U.S. agents posing as drug traffickers persuaded Mexican bankers to launder alleged drug profits, violates Mexican law. As a result of the U.S. handling of the investigation, the whole structure of U.S.-Mexican antidrug cooperation will be reassessed in future meetings with U.S. officials.

Mexican officials are angry that indictments were issued only against Mexican banks and bankers, while U.S. banks named in the investigation went unindicted. The indictments "also reinforced perceptions of corruption in Mexican law-enforcement institutions and undermined efforts by the Zedillo government" to strengthen Mexican agencies responsible for monitoring and combating money laundering.

U.S. Response on its Lack of Notification to Mexico

In January 1996, U.S. officials informed Rafael Estrada Samano about the operation and asked for his help. Separately, however, U.S. officials gave a less detailed presentation to a deputy finance minister, Ismael Gomez Gordillo. Although U.S. officials asked Estrada to conduct a joint investigation, he did not respond and the United States abandoned the idea. Attorney General Madrazo Cuellar has said that the United States was vague about the operation and asked Gordillo only for information on some Mexican bank accounts, which he provided. Yet, U.S. customs officials grew suspicious about the lack of response they received from Mexican officials.

Julie Shemitz, an Assistant U.S. Attorney in Los Angeles, stated that U.S. officials did not share any information about the operation with Mexico while it was under way out of fear for the safety of the undercover agents. Shemitz said "[i]t's not that we don't trust Mexicans. We just didn't tell anyone. This kind of operation is so dangerous, and you can't play games with the lives of the officers."

As a result of the indictment, hopes of obtaining diplomatic protection for U.S. law enforcement agents have been discarded. Similarly, thoughts of following up on the investigation are fading.

Tax Developments

Professionals involved in international wealth transfer techniques must be aware of developments in international tax enforcement. Moreover, practitioners working in international tax enforcement must be aware of several important trends.

Recently concluded and ratified tax treaties indicate the trend toward more active enforcement and cooperation within such treaties and increased merging of provisions from treaties of mutual assistance in criminal matters with traditional tax treaty provisions. The United States has concluded several treaties with key countries used in international tax and estate planning, such as Switzerland, Austria, Luxembourg, and Ireland. These treaties contain active enforcement cooperation provisions.

The trend toward increased unilateral assistance in tax enforcement affects clients and practitioners in sometimes unexpected ways. While U.S. tax authorities have been in the forefront, many other countries, sometimes under pressure from multilateral development banks in the context of structural readjustment programmes, are conditioning loans on better tax administration and more active enforcement. Multilateral development banks are also making effective tax administration part of their good governance programmes. In recent years, the unilateral extraterritorial tax enforcement has manifested itself in draconian reporting requirements for foreign persons, foreign trusts, and persons who expatriate, such as surrendering their citizenship.

A growth area in international tax enforcement concerns pre- and post-judgment attachment, seizure, and freezing of assets. Increasingly, tax officials recognize that in an interconnected world at the end of a controversial tax dispute the ability to move funds instantly may make for a hollow victory unless tax authorities have the means to seize the funds in dispute or obtain sufficient security in lieu of the funds. Increasingly, the tax and non-tax enforcement areas are interacting. In this regard, tax enforcement officials and law enforcement officials are cooperating in an effort to combat the threats from transnational crime, especially transnational organized crime. An engine of increased international tax enforcement is multilateral tax cooperation. International organizations, such as the OECD, economic integration groups, and ad hoc groups are developing novel enforcement cooperation approaches and a more institutionalized approach. In particular, the OECD Harmful Tax Competition report has significant implications for fiduciaries operating internationally.

Asset forfeiture

From the beginning, one goal in anti-money laundering and other anti-crime initiatives has been to immobilize criminals and their assets by identifying, freezing, tracing, seizing, confiscating, and forfeiting the instrumentalities and proceeds of the crimes. Some countries, such as the United States, have active criminal, administrative, and civil asset forfeiture programmes. Some prosecutors prioritize asset forfeiture over criminal prosecution of defendants, especially in cases in which prosecution of defendants may not be possible.

Two Swiss cases discussed below indicate the increasing cooperation by the Swiss Government in assisting foreign governments prosecute corruption cases against former high level officials. The discussion below of the Mexican Government's seizure of accounts illustrates how many governments that traditionally have not had active anti-money laundering programmes are now implementing new programmes.

A. Swiss Freeze $13 Million of Bhutto Accounts

On October 15, 1997, the Swiss police announced that it identified SFr20 million (U.S. $13.6 million) in frozen bank accounts belonging to the family of former Pakistani Prime Minister Benazir Bhutto, in connection with corruption inquiries.(441) During the weekend of October 10-11, 1997, Bhutto denied for the first time that the Swiss accounts belonged either to her or to her relatives. Bhutto had been fired as Prime Minister in November 1996 on charges of corruption and misrule. As a result of the freeze order that followed the provisional blocking of the assets – a preventive measure taken the month preceding the freeze – the assets will remain frozen until the end of the investigation.

The Swiss authorities responded to a formal request for judicial assistance from the Pakistani Government. Pakistani investigators claim that the Bhuttos have deposited between $50-80 million in Swiss bank accounts. According to Falco Galli, Swiss federal police spokesman, the Swiss police "have not excluded the possibility of freezing more accounts."

According to Galli, the Swiss police froze seven accounts in seven different Geneva-based banks in three stages – on September 8, September 17, and October 8, 1997. The owners of the frozen accounts are Bhutto, her husband, Asif Ali Zardari, and her mother, Nusrat Bhutto. Senator Saifur Rehman, who heads a Pakistani government corruption commission investigating the affair, said that he would visit Switzerland to give evidence to Swiss authorities and request the freezing of more accounts.

The freeze orders and provisional blocking of funds, along with the Swiss actions in the Mobutu case and the overriding of bank secrecy in dealing with the accounts related to the Holocaust, indicate a new environment of Swiss cooperation with respect to foreign asset forfeiture cases. Nevertheless, the Swiss will act only in response to an actual criminal investigation and a request for judicial assistance, mutual assistance, or both, in connection therewith.

The Swiss action indicates the increased cooperation by governments when they are requested to provide assistance in corruption cases. Until the mid-1990s, governments and courts were reluctant to act in corruption cases, especially when they concerned former high level officials or political leaders.

B. Swiss Supreme Court Forfeits Portion of Marcos Money

On December 10, 1997, the Swiss Supreme Court, in a landmark decision after eleven years of litigation, ruled that $100 million of assets belonging to the late dictator Ferdinand Marcos must be returned to the Philippines Government, provided certain conditions are met. The decision applies to $100 million of the $500 million frozen in Swiss bank accounts since Marcos' abdication in 1986. According to Peter Cosandey, the Zurich District Attorney, a decision on the disposition of the remaining funds would be forthcoming.

The court ordered that the money be placed in an escrow account at the Philippine National Bank, which is partly owned by the Philippine Government. Provided certain conditions are met, the court has ordered that the funds held by Swiss Bank Corporation must be transferred to the Philippine courts, which will decide how to distribute them. The same decision will apply as well to the funds held by Credit Suisse, which are subject to the jurisdiction of another Swiss canton.

The order reverses prior rulings that the disputed assets could not be released until Imelda Marcos, who also claims the money, was convicted by a Philippine court. While she has been convicted and sentenced to a total of forty-two years for corruption, Marcos has not served time in prison. Instead, she is an active member of Congress. To ensure the transfer of the money, the Philippine Government must demonstrate and guarantee that the money "will be distributed by a court complying with the United Nations standards of legal process." The order also requests information "about deliberations on the award of the money and measures being taken to compensate victims of human fights abuses under the Marcos regime."

The ruling represented a setback for approximately 9,500 victims of international human right violations during the Marcos regime who have already obtained a judgment but are trying to levy against many of the same assets that the Philippine Government is seeking. Approximately one week before the order, a U.S. federal appeals court dismissed a lawsuit by Philippine human rights victims who had also made claims upon the money in the Swiss banks. The court ruled that the Swiss decision to block the Marcos accounts forestalled any action on the matter by U.S. courts.

In 1994, a U.S. federal jury in Hawaii found the Marcos Administration guilty of murder, torture, and violations of the provisions of international human rights conventions.(455) It awarded the plaintiffs $1.2 billion in damages. But the pendency of the court actions by the Philippine Government left Swiss courts and banks in a quandary. While they feared having to pay twice, they wanted to demonstrate that they would not protect a corrupt government that had stolen so much money over a long period of time.

Activity is underway in Manila to resolve the dispute between the Philippine Government and the Marcos family. The initiative is led by Magtanggol Guunigundo, chairman of the Philippines Presidential Commission on Good Government, which was established by former President Corazon Achino in 1986 to recover assets fraudulently amassed under Marcos and the Marcos family. Now, both the government and the Marcos family have said they want a final settlement. However, differences regarding the amount of Marcos assets still outstanding complicate such a settlement.

The decision represents a victory for those wanting to pursue civil prosecution against corrupt politicians, even when the assets are moved to foreign jurisdictions in which strong secrecy laws predominate. The effort to forfeit the Swiss assets of Marcos was especially difficult because the environment to penetrate and forfeit assets of government corruption was much less developed in the late 1980s than today. The case is also a precursor to future efforts to pursue the assets of corrupt leaders.

C. Mexican Seizure of Gaxiola Bank Account Signals New Cooperation and Tension in Anti-Money Laundering Enforcement Cooperation

Testimony by U.S. Deputy Treasury Secretary Lawrence H. Summers before the Senate Foreign Relations Committee on March 12, 1997, as well as other reports, indicate that the Mexican and U.S. Governments are actively cooperating in freezing and seizing assets, and on prosecuting money laundering, although tension exists over the effectiveness of the cooperation.

On January 8, 1997, the United States requested that the Mexican Government freeze assets belonging to a drug-trafficking suspect, Rigoberto Gaxiola Medina. The United States believes that substantial amounts of money may have flowed out of the account after the freeze request was made, perhaps because of corruption and a tip-off. Rather than seizing $183 million, only $16.7 million was frozen and seized.

According to a media report, two confidential chronologies of the case produced by U.S. officials show that agents of Mexico's National Institute for Combating Drugs did not act on the January 8, 1997 order until January 20. Another problem was that the Mexican official in charge of executing the order was Colonel Jose Felix Name, the Institute's chief of investigations. Name has been under suspicion since he was arrested and charged with allowing Humberto Garcia Abrego, a man accused of being one of Mexico's most important money launderers, to escape from custody.

When Mexican authorities reported to the U.S. Customs Service on the Gaxiola case, they reported that the accounts in question were depleted and only about $16.7 million remained. Mexican officials argued that the $183 million requested seizure did not take account of the frequent withdrawals Gaxiola had made over a thirty month period.

According to media reports, on March 11, 1997, at a meeting of law enforcement officials of the two countries in Mexico City, Assistant U.S. Attorney General Mary Lee Warren protested the apparent disappearance of the money. However, a senior Mexican Justice official who was present said "in no way" did the United States complain about the matter.

Mexican officials have stated that Gaxiola's accounts contained only $393,000 on December 31, 1996. On January 10, 1997, just before the Mexican Government moved to seize the accounts, the accounts contained $1.47 million. After the money was frozen on January 23, 1997, the combined balance was up to $16.7 million. These new deposits seem to rebut allegations of a tip-off.

The case indicates that, despite the tension between the two governments, progress is occurring in establishing legal and law enforcement framework to freeze assets in Mexico. The next push will come in the effort to enforce Mexico's anti-money laundering laws.

Mutual Cooperation Mechanisms

Increasingly, practitioners must be aware of an ever-growing web of bilateral and multilateral treaties, executive agreements, and memoranda of understanding that enable governments and law enforcement officials to obtain information on various crimes. Sometimes tax crimes are covered. For instance, all the modern U.S. mutual assistance in criminal matters treaties cover tax. On October 21, 1998, the U.S. Senate voted to approve for ratification thirty-nine treaties providing for international criminal cooperation, including nineteen mutual assistance in criminal matters treaties, eighteen extradition treaties, and one prisoner transfer treaty.

The evidence law enforcement officials need to prosecute tax crimes is often the same evidence that is required to show wrongdoing with respect to securities or commodities futures trading, drug trafficking, or transnational bribery. For instance, the OECD Convention on Combating Bribery of Foreign Public Officials in International Business Transactions, which took effect on February 15, 1999, obligates signatory countries to provide evidence in connection with alleged bribes of foreign public officials and eventually will require all signatories to eliminate tax deductions for payments that are bribes.

Similarly, in the investigation and prosecution of transnational organized crime, many law enforcement officials can obtain evidence on a variety of economic matters. Many governments, such as the United States, target alleged transnational organized crime members for tax crimes, as the United States did successfully with Al Capone.

Proactive policing vis-a-vis transnational organized crime has produced transformations in international criminal cooperation law in the United States and throughout the world, especially in the development of a financial enforcement regime. Antimoney laundering and immobilization of the assets and profits of criminals play an important role in these efforts. Globalization ensures that the number of transnational criminal investigations and prosecutions involving the United States will increase. Undoubtedly, an increasing number of cases will bring into play the potential applicability of the various rights guaranteed by the U.S. Bill of Rights or applicable provisions of international human rights conventions, such as the International Civil and Political Covenant. "The tension between the need for the United States to cooperate more with national governments and international tribunals and the concern for the fulfillment of constitutional and international human rights standards is likely to continue to grow."

Counsel representing investors, business entities, and fiduciaries can increasingly resort to international human rights provisions—in national judicial fora, international tribunals, or both—to adjudicate conflicts between new intrusive law enforcement techniques and substantive laws and international human rights and constitutional rights. These conflicts often result in intrusive search and seizure cases, enforcement of new due diligence requirements for businesses and individuals, asset forfeiture cases, restraint of individuals at borders, and so forth. The discussion of the restrictive provisions in U.S. mutual legal assistance treaties (MLATs) and the efforts to conduct intrusive search and seizure and evidence gathering without proper safeguards illustrate the types of defenses that persons implicated by these provisions can raise.

A. U.S. MLATs Restrict Their Use to Governments

Recent U.S. MLATs in criminal matters that grant the government compulsory process rights, as delimited by the respective treaties, expressly state that the treaties do not create the right for a private person to obtain evidence. The purpose is to prevent the use of its MLATs for suppressing or excluding evidence or for impeding its investigations.

Hence, if an adversely affected person wants to prevent the execution of a request that he believes was made in violation of the treaty, his only recourse under the treaty is to the executive authority of the requested country, not to its courts. Similarly, if he wants to contest that the requested country violated the terms of the treaty in executing a request, he may do so only to the executive authorities of the respective countries.

The treaty provisions do not prevent a person adversely affected by a request or its execution from asserting whatever rights he has under the laws of the appropriate country in its courts. For instance, a person whose home or place of business was searched and whose property was seized under a search warrant issued pursuant to a treaty request may assert whatever rights he has under the laws of the requested country to prevent that property from being turned over to the requesting country.

Similarly, a person whose records have been subpoenaed pursuant to a treaty request may assert whatever rights he has under the laws of the requested country, to prevent the production of those records, their transmittal to the requesting country, or both. An affected person would also presumably be able to seek to enjoin the requested country from taking an action not authorized by the treaty or its laws. In at least one case in which a defendant sought to use a U.S. MLAT to obtain evidence from a treaty partner pursuant to a treaty that was silent with respect to a defendant's right to seek evidence under it, "the trial court directed the Department of Justice to make a treaty request on behalf of the defendant."

The U.S. Government has agreed to provisions in its MLATs that accommodate concerns of its treaty partners about safeguarding provisions on international human rights. For instance, in the MLAT between the United States and Australia signed on April 30, 1997, the term "essential interests" that may be invoked to deny assistance to a requesting state includes a discretionary limitation on providing assistance in death penalty cases.

Potential remedies for rectifying apparent violations of binding provisions of international human rights include the following: to urge governments and international organizations to condition applicable MLATs, extradition treaties, and other international criminal cooperation agreements to comply with such provisions; to urge judicial tribunals through amicae briefs to condition criminal cooperation agreements on international human rights obligations; and, where appropriate, to help aggrieved persons initiate and prosecute actions in international human rights fora in order to reflect equitably their respective contributions.

B. The Fourth Amendment Right Against Unlawful Search and Seizure

"All searches and seizures in the U.S. must fulfill the requirements of the Fourth Amendment." Hence, a search warrant issued pursuant to a treaty request must fulfill U.S. constitutional requirements regarding probable cause, specification of the place to be searched, and specification of the things to be seized.

The majority of U.S. mutual legal assistance treaties in criminal matters specifically provide authority to U.S. courts to issue search warrants in execution of requests for assistance under such treaties. While some of treaties do not expressly confer such authority on U.S. courts, they still require the United States to conduct searches and seizures at the request of its treaty partners if the request contains information justifying such action under U.S. laws. "The absence in some cases of specific statutory authorization raises the issue as to whether those treaties sufficiently authorize the courts to issue such warrants."

In a decision that has potentially important implications for international criminal cooperation, the U.S. District Court for the Central District of California held that a freeze of a target's bank account of a U.S. securities enforcement investigation is unconstitutional as violative of the Fifth Amendment right to due process and the Fourth Amendment right to be protected from unreasonable seizures. The case began as a derivative action of an Securities and Exchange Commission (SEC) enforcement action. The SEC sued one of the plaintiffs, Michael Colello, for his role in a pyramid scheme. Colello asserted his Fifth Amendment right against self-incrimination during the investigative stage and has continued to maintain his silence.

The day before the Commission filed the enforcement action against Colello and the other defendants, the SEC sought the freeze Colello's Swiss bank accounts. The U.S. Department of Justice transmitted a request under the U.S.-Swiss Mutual Legal Assistance in Criminal Matters Treaty and Swiss authorities complied. Simultaneously with the SEC enforcement action, the court issued a temporary restraining order in the enforcement action, freezing all the defendants' assets located in the United States, including Colello's. The court, in a decision by U.S. District Judge Richard A. Paez, refused to grant the SEC's motion for a preliminary injunction against Colello, and the domestic asset freeze dissolved along with the temporary restraining order.

Colello and plaintiff Robert Romano—who was not a defendant in the enforcement action—filed a separate case on September 2, 1994 to challenge the constitutionality of the Swiss asset freeze, Colello and Romano named as defendants, among others, the SEC, its lawyers, and the Director of the Department of Justice Criminal Division's Office of International Affairs. The SEC had commenced its investigation in October 1993 against Cross Financial Services, Inc. (CFS) after discovering through a newspaper article that CFS promised very high rates of return to investors in a "government receivables" investment programme. On December 3, 1993, the SEC issued a formal order of investigation.

In April 1994, the SEC subpoenaed records and testimony from Michael Colello in connection with the investigation of CFS. During his testimony, when SEC lawyers questioned Colello about Carroll Siemens, letters of credit, European and American banks, and his bank accounts, he asserted his Fifth Amendment right against self-incrimination and refused to answer. On June 13, 1994, the Department of Justice sent a request under the U.S.-Swiss treaty for assistance from the Swiss Government, "seeking documents and testimony from banks in Switzerland to establish whether CFS made false statements about its investment scheme to induce people to invest and, thereafter, misappropriated investors' funds in violation of U.S. federal securities laws." In addition, the SEC requested that any funds "traceable to the subject matter of the request be frozen so that the funds later may be returned to the U.S. to compensate the victims of the fraud."

On June 15, 1995, the Swiss Federal Supreme Court rejected plaintiffs' contention that the asset freeze was improper. It explained, "In matters of judicial assistance, the Federal Supreme Court examines an administrative court complaint only to determine whether the preconditions for the provisions of judicial assistance have been fulfilled." If the judicial assistance is requested by the United States, the request cannot be denied merely on the basis of deficiencies in the U.S.

proceedings, because the treaty does not contain any corresponding provision.

Meanwhile, in ruling that the freeze was an unconstitutional seizure in violation of the Fourth Amendment to the Constitution, the Colello court rejected the government's contention that plaintiffs "assumed the risk" of depositing their money in a foreign country. The court stated that U.S. citizens are protected by the Bill of Rights from incursions by the U.S. Government on them or their property, regardless of its location. Similarly, the court found no authority for the government's notion that it "can circumscribe or limit the entitlement of citizens to constitutional rights via a treaty."

The court was troubled that freezing is permitted under the treaty based on "reasonable suspicion," whereas the Fourth Amendment requires showing "probable cause."

The court appeared troubled by the failure to implement legislation and regulations, although legislation was initially contemplated. The court also noted that, while the Department of Justice manual governs the conduct of the SEC and the Department of Justice, it does not require them to notify "the subject of a Treaty request or to provide a hearing before or after making the request." Additionally, the court noted that the manual contains no standards and includes a disclaimer stating that the manual provides only internal Department of Justice guidance and "is not intended to, does not, and may not be relied on to create any rights, substantive or procedural, enforceable by law by any party in any matter civil or criminal."

Finally, the manual states that no limitations are placed "on otherwise lawful prerogatives of the Department of Justice." The absence of U.S. statutory and regulatory provisions contrasts with Switzerland's approach. Switzerland has enacted law and guidelines under the treaty. The Federal Law on the Treaty with the U.S. on Mutual Legal Assistance in Criminal Matters of October 3, 1975 provides for certain "precautionary measures" to guarantee due process through requiring notice to the affected parties. In addition, the Federal

Office for Police Matters (FOPM) has also issued guidelines to inform interested authorities and citizens on what is meant and encompassed by international mutual assistance in criminal matters.

The decision may presage trouble on other criminal mutual assistance agreements when the U.S. Government tries to enforce them in courts. Indeed, although the American Bar Association and other interested bar groups testified previously against excluding from such treaties due process protections for defendants and third parties, the U.S. Government vehemently opposed such arguments. The decision seems to indicate that at least the court believes that a better balance is constitutionally required.

A similar difficulty may arise in the tax information exchange and cooperation area. There, in order to secure support for ratification of the Council of Europe and OECD Treaty on Mutual Administrative Assistance in Tax Matters, the U.S. Department of Treasury promised to issue regulations and stated that it would consider extending such regulations across the board to all tax information exchange agreements. Indeed, such due process seems compelled. However, many months after the Convention has taken effect, Treasury officials claim that their workload does not permit time for such a project. It appears that the role of courts can be important in developing incentives for officials to prioritize due process rights. The absence of adequate rights within enforcement cooperation treaties, together with aggressive enforcement actions and the inevitable cases where rights of individuals have been abused, may jeopardize the potential for success in enforcement actions.

International anti-money laundering efforts will increase as transnational crime and especially transnational organized crime continue to spread. The efforts of the United Nations and the G-7 Economic Summit Group to develop a convention and other mechanisms to tackle transnational crime illustrate the political consensus behind the new efforts. Some of the prospects for international anti-money laundering efforts can be viewed in the March 1997 release of the International Narcotics Control Strategy Report (INCSR), which contains a large section on anti-money laundering. It is worthwhile to summarize some of the discussions in order to identify trends, as well as develop and improve due diligence.

In October 1995, the United States initiated Presidential Decision Directive 42, which freezes assets and imposes economic sanctions against certain persons designated as narcotics traffickers affiliated with the Cali cartel. U.S. agencies in 1996 assessed which money laundering and financial crime situations affected U.S. national security interests, including drug trafficking, contraband smuggling, arms sales, terrorist financing, sanctions violations, and sales of weapons of mass destruction. In some cases, teams of U.S. officials visited governments to secure agreements on actions needed.

FATF achieved progress through starting the second round of mutual evaluations of each of its twenty-six members. FATF also warned its own members of shortcomings, especially Turkey and Greece. FATF approved proposals to update its universally-accepted Forty Recommendations to reflect new typologies and methodologies. Additionally, the Caribbean FATF started evaluations on its members. In Asia, an outreach programme was initiated.

Finally, a common forum for major international bankers and government policy makers was organized. In 1997, FATF's high-impact initiative external relations programme that began in 1992 and 1993 succeeded in establishing agreements with the Council of Europe, the Offshore Group of Banking Supervisors, and the CFATF. These agreements are intended to secure evaluation by outside experts to determine whether the majority of financial centre countries were properly implementing the minimal global standards on anti-money laundering.

During 1996, increased cooperation with foreign governments on major money laundering cases occurred. Asset sharing cooperation increased, as did the amount of U.S.

mutual assistance treaties in criminal matters, all with important anti-money laundering and asset forfeiture-sharing provisions. Adverse developments identified by the INCSR include the further penetration of financial systems by organized crime groups.

Transnational crime groups increasingly have used "new drug transit routes across ever more remote countries, most of which have no or few anti-money laundering laws." The result is the ability to move crime proceeds to the countries and systems whose financial standards are vulnerable and easily manipulated. Transnational crime groups can more easily identify and exploit "the differential between the levels of compliance with international anti-money standards," especially in Asia and Latin America.

New Laundering Modes

One development is that as new drug trafficking routes are spawned in Africa and the lower regions of the old Soviet regime, the list of countries more vulnerable to money laundering widens.

Perhaps more dangerous is the absence of implementation of anti-money laws or even ratification of the 1988 Vienna-U.N. Drug Convention. The INCSR lists Aruba, Colombia, Mexico, the Netherlands Antilles, Nigeria, Singapore, Turkey and Venezuela. Just as important, the anti-money laundering laws that governments enacted in the early 1990s are now no longer sufficient, especially given the increase in non-drug crimes, the use of new technologies, and more sophisticated ways to move money.

The proliferation of financial crimes include the more common types of financial frauds and new variations, especially the use of prime bank guarantees, phony or fictitious letters of credit, counterfeit or stolen bonds, and other monetary instruments offered as surety for loans, and other scares. Some of the new methods include the use of secret telex codes for bank-to-bank transactions in order to move $42 million in cash from the Hong Kong and Shanghai Bank in

Jakarta. The use of fake certificates of deposit drawn on other branches of an international bank that can range from $10 million to $25 million recently occurred. "`Fraudsters' will also use counterfeit letters of agreement, drawn on bank letterheads, seemingly vouching for a client from another branch of that bank," or confirming the approval of a bogus deal.

The INCSR reports on the ways in which money is laundered. Professional money launderers differ little in their money management than corporate money managers. Money brokers and transnational criminals collaborate to minimize their risk, partly through diversification of the means to transport, convert cash, or both, as well as to layer and integrate the laundered funds.

Challenges to Anti-Laundering Enforcement

Several aspects of contemporary banking make counter-money laundering initiatives difficult.

1. *Correspondent Banking:* Banking is increasingly global, inter-connected, and operates twenty-four hours. Large multinational banks have global branch and subsidiary networks as well as correspondent relationships.

   Correspondent banking enables launderers to initiate transactions through the weakest link in the bank. Once launderers start a bank relationship, they can quickly move money globally within the bank.

2. *Offshore Banking:* At the June 1996 International Conference of Banking Supervisors, banking supervisors from 140 countries agreed to adhere to twenty-nine recommendations "designed to strengthen the effectiveness of supervision by both home and host-country authorities of banks that operate outside their national boundaries." The recommendations were incorporated into a report by the Basle Committee on Banking Supervision, issued in October 1996.

Home supervisors must be able to assess "all significant aspects of their banks' operations, using whatever supervisory techniques are needed, including on-site inspections." Means to overcome impediments to effective consolidated supervision are suggested. The Basle report sets forth "guidelines for determining the effectiveness of home country supervision, for monitoring supervisory standards in host countries, and for dealing with corporate structures which create potential supervisory gaps." Additional guidelines are provided for host country supervision.

When the recommendations conflict with bank secrecy or similar legislation in certain countries, supervisors have agreed to use best efforts to amend the secrecy legislation. Countries with further recommendations were reviewed prior to the international meeting scheduled for October 1998.

3. *The Offshore Group of Banking Supervisors:* The Offshore Group of Banking Supervisors (OGBS) has concluded "an agreement with FATF on a protocol for evaluating the effectiveness of the money laundering laws and policies of its members." However, OGBS includes only about half of the known offshore banking centres among its members.

   A concern exists those different kinds of charters for financial facilities can be obtained for non-bank institutions—such as international business companies (IBCs)—that can conduct some of the same activities as banks and do not undergo the same regulatory oversight. This is a particular problem in the Caribbean.

4. *Private Banking:* Much competition exists globally to attract high net-worth individuals and companies as private banking clients. The transactions of these clients are treated confidentially. Such customers are treated with more deference and receive various

types of personal services. A concern exists that, in the competition to attract and maintain these clients, financial institutions or their officials may suspend or not implement anti-money laundering and other due diligence procedures.

5. *Cybercurrency:* The use of microchip-based electronic money for financial transactions, via smart cards and the Internet, has the potential to revolutionize the means for laundering money. Some new cyberpayments systems are engineered to be an electronic emulation of paper currency. Cybercurrency has the attributes of conventional currency: a store of value; a medium of exchange; a numeraire; potential anonymity; and convenience. Other features include transfer velocity—an almost instant electronic transfer from point to point—and substitution of electrons for paper currency and other physical means of payment. Cyberpayments also include other payment components, such as cyberchecks, cybercredit, cyberdebit, and so forth. This development requires close attention because the use of microchip and telecommunications technologies adds some significant new dimensions for law enforcement.

   Cyberpayments also include other payment components, such as cyberchecks, which emulate paper checks, cybercredit, cyberdebit, etc. Cyberpayments raise the issue of whether such payments can be made subject to monetary reporting and supervision measures. Law enforcement issues that will arise include fraud, counterfeiting, and computer hacking. High-speed, worldwide transfers add complexity to law enforcement's ability to trace criminal activity and recover illicit proceeds.

6. *Other Challenges:* Other challenges to anti-money laundering enforcement include the counterfeiting of currencies and other monetary instruments,

especially bonds, the rise in contraband smuggling, the acquisition of banks and other financial institutions by suspected criminal groups, and the resort by criminals to the use of smaller, pass-through banking, and electronic cash systems. As a result of the occurrence of financial crimes and money laundering with varying degrees of regularity in more than 125 jurisdictions, a continuing concern exists that some governments still have not criminalized all forms of money laundering.

Continuing Concerns

One major remaining problem is the inconsistent enforcement of anti-money laundering provisions. Sixteen of the sixty-four eligible governments ranked as high, medium-high or medium priority money laundering concerns by the U.S. Government in 1997 have not ratified the 1988 U.N. Convention. Hence, one-fourth of the world's important financial centre countries had not ratified this universal accord six years after its entry into force.

Many governments "have not criminalized all forms of money laundering and financial crime, nor given sufficient authority to banking regulatory bodies." Too many governments still limit money laundering countermeasures, "particularly the requirement that the offense of money laundering must be predicated on conviction for a drug trafficking offense." An equally distressing number of governments "still refuse to share information about financial transactions with other governments to facilitate multinational money laundering investigations."

In addition, a need exists for "enhanced bilateral and multinational communications to inform governments and financial systems in some systematic and ongoing way about the methods and typologies of drug and non-drug related money laundering and financial crimes." Concerns exist as well about "the concentration of economic power in drug cartels and other criminal organizations, and its potential translation into political power," especially in the Caribbean, Europe, the Middle East, and Asia, as well as the Americas.

The growth of free trade agreements and regional integration increases the opportunities to launder money. Finally, countries that cooperate on money laundering investigations and prosecutions need to share forfeited proceeds.

Enforcement Agenda

A broad enforcement agenda is suggested. Among the recommendations are the creation of international standards, agreements to exchange information, the establishment of linkages for cooperative investigations, and methods to supersede political resistance in various key countries to ensure such cooperation. Among the nationa]l laws required are those that establish corporate criminal liability for bank and non-bank financial institutions, apply to all types of financial transactions not limited to cash at the teller's window, apply reporting and anti-money laundering laws to a long list of predicate offenses not limited to drug trafficking, criminalize investments in legitimate industry if the proceeds were derived from illegal acts, and facilitate the sharing of financial and corporate ownership information with law enforcement agencies and judicial authorities.

The INCSR Report proposed the following sixteen action items:

1. Constant monitoring of money laundering patterns, trends, and apologies;
2. Improving analysis of money management practices;
3. Analyzing of non-drug-related money laundering and other financial crimes;
4. Equating economic power with political clout;
5. Eliminating systemic weaknesses;
6. Assessing the trafficker as entrepreneur;
7. Analyzing the impact of money laundering on national governments and economies;

8. Regulating exchange houses and remittance systems;
9. Concentrating efforts for maximum effectiveness;
10. Pursuing a continuously evolving strategy;
11. Intensifying the UNDCP programme to ensure that all significant financial centre countries implement fully the anti-money laundering and asset forfeiture provisions of the 1988 U.N. Convention;
12. Continuing the FATF focus, along with the Offshore Group of Banking Supervisors and other relevant organizations, on offshore banking;
13. Adopting of information standards by governments;
14. Increasing diligence by governments and banking systems alike;
15. Exerting greater efforts by governments and banking systems to identify and prevent a wide range of financial crimes; and
16. Consolidating supervision of the international banking system.

The report indicates that the anti-money laundering regime is in full-swing globally. It will continue to deepen as an area where international law, policymakers, scholars, practitioners, and criminals and their advisers will occupy themselves for the indefinite future with its developments.

In the short- and medium-term future, key national governments and international organizations will increase their financial enforcement efforts. These endeavors will include privatization of the law enforcement efforts, which in turn will saddle the private sector with additional responsibilities and more potential sanctions for non-compliance. The private sector will need to monitor carefully these developments and participate in the legislative and executive decision-making and in the work of international organizations. If abuses occur and are imminent, private individuals may want to consider judicial or other challenges. In many cases, better networking is required within the private sector to participate effectively in the shaping and implementation of new policies and law, as well as the manner in which they are implemented.

Private Sector Role

Globalization means that in the next millennium practitioners and fiduciaries must constantly strengthen their due diligence against money laundering, fraud, and crime. The drawback is that it requires more attention, more work, and perhaps more selectivity vis-a-vis new clients. Globalization also means that the costs of international wealth transfer will rise, provided clients can pay the load. Counseling transnational clients in international wealth matters may be unduly risky for professionals who do not exercise care and apply modern due diligence. Professionals must stay abreast of a wide variety of national, foreign, and international law developments. These developments mean that the millennium indeed will be a brave new world.

Index

A

AAA 48, 49
Accounts 4, 6, 8, 34, 35, 73, 87, 148, 158, 198, 201, 216, 225, 230, 231, 233, 236, 239, 242, 244, 245, 247, 248, 249, 256, 261, 262, 263, 266, 267, 268, 270, 274, 275
Adjustments 130, 131, 143
Administrative 1, 6, 7, 220, 265, 276
ADR 52, 54, 55
Advertising 24, 47, 57, 58
Airline industry 7, 61
Amenities 37, 38, 49, 50, 56, 64, 173
American Resorts Group 37
Amortization 81
Analysis 33, 208, 285
Announcement 259
Association 7, 48, 66, 218, 227, 233, 248, 251, 277
Astoria Hotel 36
Automated 8, 176
Availability 6, 22, 25, 28, 34, 198
Average room rate 53

B

Back office 26
Bank deposits 230, 241
Blocking 266, 267
Brand loyalty 57
Brand name 57
Branding 59, 71
Business affiliations 46, 57
Business travel 8, 54, 61, 71

C

Call accounting 41
Cancellations 13, 15, 22
Career development 49, 64, 68, 71
Cash 1, 21, 23, 41, 75, 173, 174, 175, 179, 181, 188, 190, 192, 194, 207, 220, 226, 229, 230, 260, 280, 283, 284
Catering 47, 48

Certified Hotel Administrator 66
Certified Rooms Division 66
Chain affiliations 57
Coaching 2
Commercial hotels 50, 56
Communications 34, 47, 185, 188, 191, 215, 284
Continental 38, 51, 56
Credit card 23, 192
Customers 3, 4, 6, 9, 10, 25, 30, 51, 55, 60, 61, 237, 242, 243, 244, 246, 247, 249, 250, 282

D

Dallas 27, 28, 35
Debit 22, 23
Debit cards 23
Demographic data 61
Department managers 68
Discounts 1, 144
Distance learning 66
Distribution 54, 61, 101
Diversification 280
Documentation 152, 244, 248, 250

E

Earnings 8, 43, 159, 160, 161, 162, 163
Educational 5, 9, 64, 65, 71
Electronic 9, 173, 174, 175, 176, 177, 183, 197, 198, 201, 208, 215, 216, 231, 282, 283
Elevator 41
Emergencies 178, 179, 191
Emergency 45, 124, 125, 176, 178, 179, 184, 185, 186, 188, 190, 191, 193
Employees 2, 3, 4, 5, 9, 26, 34, 46, 50, 51, 66, 67, 68, 99, 102, 108, 174, 175, 176, 177, 178, 179, 181, 182, 183, 184, 185, 186, 187, 188, 189, 190, 191, 192, 224, 238
Equipment 5, 25, 26, 57, 59, 66, 67, 140
Event 236
Executive 38, 50, 270, 272

F

Fairfield Inn 38, 48
Family 2, 9, 34, 37, 62, 63, 64, 71, 77, 90, 129, 266, 268
Feedback 197, 207, 208, 209, 246
Financial activities 223
Floor limit 13, 15, 17, 18
Founders 35, 70
Franchisee 57
Full service 55

G

Gift shop 60
Grand National Hotel 36
Gross income 53

Guest accounts 34
Guest checkout 40, 41

H

Hardware 30
Historical developments 71
Holiday Inn 2, 37, 38, 41, 51, 56
Hospitality 24, 25, 34, 35, 39, 43, 45, 46, 49, 51, 62, 63, 65, 67, 69, 70, 71
Hospitality industry 25, 62, 63, 67, 71

I

Income 25, 43, 53, 54, 61, 62, 63, 64, 71, 75, 84, 104, 155, 159, 160, 161, 162, 163, 201, 229
Independent 43, 57, 58, 59, 60, 71, 227, 228, 252, 260
Inquiries 1, 34, 142, 208, 266
International 28, 30, 34, 38, 56, 69, 70, 183, 184, 185, 187, 188, 189, 191, 192, 193, 194, 195, 196, 197, 198, 201, 202, 203, 204, 210, 211, 212, 213, 215, 216, 217, 219, 220, 221, 222, 224, 226, 228, 232, 233, 234, 237, 238, 239, 241, 242, 251, 252, 256, 257, 259, 260, 264, 265, 268, 271, 272, 273, 274, 277, 278, 279, 280, 281, 282, 284, 285
Internet 40, 41, 47, 51, 59, 67, 69, 187, 197, 198, 207, 213, 216, 217, 218, 249, 256, 282
ITT 38

J

Jefferson Hotel 48
Judgment 162, 265, 268

K

Keyboard 177
Knowledge 6, 46, 57, 64, 65, 68, 107, 236, 252

L

Language 5, 229
Laundry 3, 46, 47, 48, 50
Layout 65
Location 8, 28, 29, 46, 71, 175, 178, 182, 184, 185, 186, 215, 219, 276
Lodging 2, 5, 7, 37, 38, 43, 52, 54, 59, 60, 61, 68, 79

M

Maintenance 2, 3, 60, 74, 114, 140, 176
Management 2, 4, 7, 24, 25, 26, 29, 30, 35, 36, 37, 39, 40, 41, 42, 43, 45, 46, 49, 52, 57, 58, 60, 64, 65, 66, 67, 69, 70, 71, 153, 173, 174, 176, 177, 178, 179, 181, 182, 183, 191, 222, 228, 280, 285

Market orientation 46, 71
Market segments 38, 55
Marriott Hotels 37, 47, 56
Mass marketing 47
Meetings 208, 209, 211, 239, 263
Military 50
Motivation 6

N

National Restaurant Association 66

O

Occupancy 7, 44, 46, 52, 53, 54, 55, 69, 71, 72
Operational 57, 58, 66, 71, 179, 180, 224, 251, 252
Organization 6, 41, 46, 58, 67, 68, 70, 189, 196, 203, 213, 225, 238
Orientation 5, 46, 50, 71
Outsourcing 26

P

Package 23, 177, 211, 233
Personality 5
Personnel 1, 45, 175, 177, 179, 181, 184, 211, 221, 244, 254
Physical 127, 178, 282
Pleasure 38, 59, 61, 71
Policy 12, 15, 19, 20, 26, 149, 202, 207, 210, 222, 237, 278
Portman 39
PricewaterhouseCoopers 54, 55
Procedure 91, 93, 94, 99, 100, 101, 114, 116, 164, 167, 234, 235
Professional 5, 48, 52, 58, 60, 64, 65, 66, 67, 68, 69, 70, 71, 194, 252, 253, 254
Property 34, 35, 40, 42, 46, 47, 48, 58, 59, 60, 61, 64, 72, 80, 82, 88, 89, 116, 157, 159, 160, 161, 162, 163, 164, 165, 167, 169, 170, 171, 178, 179, 225, 230, 234, 235, 236, 255, 258, 272, 273, 276

Q

Quality 6, 13, 16, 28, 36, 38, 39, 40, 42, 55, 57, 58, 71, 127, 128

R

Recreation 1, 7, 62, 69
Referral system 57
Registration 3
Religious 171
Remote 29, 49, 182, 218, 279
Reservation 3, 5, 6, 7, 8, 11, 12, 13, 14, 15, 16, 22, 23, 37, 40, 41, 51, 52, 57, 58, 59, 187
Revenue 53, 54, 97, 229, 230

S

Safety 6, 26, 45, 46, 61, 64, 178, 186, 264
Sales indicators 46, 71
Security 9, 45, 46, 60, 76, 79, 80, 81, 82, 85, 86, 88, 90, 173, 174, 175, 176, 177, 178, 179, 181, 182, 183, 184, 185, 186, 187, 188, 189, 191, 192, 193, 249, 250, 255, 265, 278
Services 2, 3, 5, 6, 8, 28, 31, 32, 34, 38, 39, 40, 42, 43, 44, 46, 47, 48, 50, 51, 52, 53, 54, 55, 56, 57, 58, 60, 62, 64, 70, 71, 75, 76, 83, 84, 134, 135, 173, 178, 189, 201, 226, 228, 238, 241, 242, 243, 244, 246, 282
Sheraton 38, 41, 48, 52, 57, 58
Software 30, 45, 175, 177, 219
Super 126

T

Tax Act 104, 169
Taxes 22, 132, 140, 146, 192
Telephone 3, 4, 5, 6, 13, 14, 15, 16, 20, 30, 41, 63, 186, 192, 249, 257
TQM 39, 42
Training 1, 2, 5, 6, 7, 30, 45, 46, 50, 65, 183, 202, 209, 210, 211, 217, 219, 220, 221, 222, 224, 227
Transfer 6, 7, 43, 79, 80, 82, 96, 97, 101, 139, 165, 193, 198, 199, 229, 232, 255, 256, 261, 264, 268, 271, 282

U

Universal 193, 283

V

Vending 47
Visit 49, 56, 70, 71, 72, 266
Visual 177, 179

W

Waldorf Hotel 36
Waldorf Towers 36
Waldorf-Astoria 36
Work experience 49, 67, 70, 71
Workload 277

Y

Yield 52, 53, 237
Yield percentage 52, 53

Z

Zones 32